Tradeoffs

Edward Wenk, Jr.

Tradeoffs

Imperatives of

Choice in a

High-Tech

World

The Johns Hopkins University Press
Baltimore and London

The Johns Hopkins University Press,
701 West 40th Street,
Baltimore, Maryland 21211
The Johns Hopkins Press Ltd., London

∞

The paper used in this publication meets the minimum requirements of American National Standard for Information Sciences—Permanence of Paper for Printed Library Materials, ANSI Z39.48-1984.

Library of Congress Cataloging-in-Publication Data

Wenk, E.
   Tradeoffs : imperatives of choice in a high-tech world.

   Bibliography: p.
   Includes index.
   1. Technology—Social aspects.   2. Technology and state.   I. Title.
T14.5.W46   1986   303.4'83   86-45441
ISBN 0-8018-3378-7 (alk. paper)

To the attentive citizen

Contents

Acknowledgments

All authors must take responsibility for their texts, but it is rare for the product to spring entirely from one source. *Tradeoffs* is no exception. Some basic ideas are original, but some were inspired by other people. In those cases, all that I can claim in originality is their selection, connection, interpretation, and style of expression. Indirectly, I had many coauthors.

Some were direct sources of formal instruction: Wilmer A. DeHuff, J. Trueman Thompson, Abel Wolman, William Hoppman III, and Walter Gropius. Others were bosses-cum-teachers: Lawrence A. Menefee, Wendell P. Roop, Earl H. Kennard, Harold Saunders, Martin Goland, Hugh Elsbree, Jerome Wiesner, Hubert H. Humphrey, Lyndon B. Johnson, and Charles Norris. From them I learned about science and technology, aesthetics and ethics, business management and the great game of politics.

Others deserve special mention for their vital influence on my understanding of ecology and human affairs, economics and sociology, history and philosophy, of how human systems work and how decisions are made, and of the crucial role of values in social process: Philip H. Abelson, David Beckler, Kenneth E. Boulding, Harvey Brooks, Detlev W. Bronk, Jacques-Yves Cousteau, Emilio Q. Daddario, A. Powell Davies, Karl Deutsch, John Kenneth Galbraith, George and Eilene Galloway, Ferdinand Hamburger, Jr., John F. Kennedy, Alton P. Lennon, Raphael H. Levine, Warren G. Magnuson, George Miller, Charles A. Mosher, Don K. Price, Theodore Schad, Dorothy Schaffter, Charles Sheldon III, Arthur Stromberg, Sir Geoffrey Vickers, Walter Wilcox, Glen Wilson, and Philip Yeager.

In fostering a capacity to feel as well as think, I must acknowledge members of my family, especially my partner for over four decades, Carolyn L. Wenk, as well as many students who dramatized the future and underscored its importance in the calculus of technological choice.

Then there are those who read and criticized part or all of the manuscript: Dorothy Bates, Dorothy Bestor, Florence Broussard, William D. Carey, Jacques-Yves Cousteau, Edward E. David, Jr., Ernest F. Hollings, Thomas J. Laetz, Harold Linstone, Naomi Pascal, Nelson Polsby, Heidi Schmidt, Glenn Seaborg, Dael Wolfle, and an unknown referee for The Johns Hopkins University Press. For their kindness in providing careful and candid analysis, I am deeply grateful.

Finally, I want to pay tribute to two others: J. G. Goellner, director of The Johns Hopkins University Press, who personally reviewed the manuscript, then shepherded it through vital stages of publishing; and Carolyn I. Moser, whose sensitive editing helped give wings to the intricate arguments linking technology, politics, and people.

Tradeoffs

Introduction

here is a worrisome and discordant note in contemporary society between the tangible fruits of science and technology as the source of progress and their inadvertent role as a threat to life, liberty, and the pursuit of happiness. Indeed, this polarity has led to a deep emotional response, with widespread feelings of alienation, vulnerability, and impotence.

It is not just that science and technology appear, and are, complex and difficult to understand. It is not just that some events seem to operate through a kind of technological determinism. Rather, frustration and anger develop because the economic and political institutions of our society which convoy technology seem paradoxically to neglect vital social impacts on the very people who are supposed to be the ultimate beneficiaries.

Our society appreciates how much science and technology contribute to the quality of life: new freedoms, fresh opportunities, and material benefits. Indeed, they have seemed to offer a ticket to paradise. But humankind has also come face to face with the ominous side—the threat of nuclear war, of climate modification, of unwanted genetic transformations, and of loss of freedom, along with heightened risks and ethical dilemmas. Some of these effects imperil survival, survival to be both alive and free. To these overarching dangers are added robot-induced unemployment, the escalating costs of health care, famine in Africa, chemical and oil spills, computer fraud, and the problems of nuclear waste disposal. While these events are themselves disturbing, they are all the more alarming because control to head off unwanted side effects, even calamity, seems inaccessible.

Yet, even if it is true that all technology carries a hidden burden of untoward consequences, society is not likely to turn off the entire machine. We rejected the prescriptions of the 1960s counterculture because society simply did not want to return to candle and cave. Rather, people want a handle on the decision apparatus, to have a say in those technological choices which so profoundly affect their lives—decisions on the goals to which science and technology are directed, on the balance of benefits and costs, on the selection of winners and losers.

In essence, people want to head off unpleasant surprises, especially of the scale of the Bhopal and Chernobyl disasters. If there are repercussions that are hidden initially but may pop up in other remote districts or may burden our progeny, people want to know about such consequences so that they can determine whether the game is worth the candle. The attentive public wants to know what is at stake in technological choice.

By attentive public, I mean those members of our society who are concerned, who try to inform themselves on the issues of the day, and who take seriously their obligations as citizens to participate in governance and in setting a course for the future. Included are those who care about insults to the environment, the dilemmas of artificial life support, the power of television as an instrument of propaganda, and the possibility of nuclear calamity. Also in the population of attentive citizens are those in engineering, public administration, medicine, and law. By definition, these individuals are engaged not in vocations but in professions which, by their direct involvement with the public, carry a noblesse oblige of social responsibility. Such persons critically need a breadth of perspective on how the social context affects their practice, and vice versa.

The problem is that many who want to influence technological choice do not know how. If I have any single purpose in this book, it is to provide such insights. And if there is any single point of view here, it stems from a maxim that, just as war is too important to be left to the generals, technology is too important to be left only to the political, commercial, and scientific elite.

People in democratic societies have influenced other critical choices of public policy dealing with social equity, justice, harmony with nature, employment and retirement, peace. There is no reason why they cannot similarly influence the outcomes of technological choice.

Individuals do not need a background in science to understand how it affects their lives. Few presidents and few congressmen ever had specialized technical training, yet all are responsible for the most crucial decisions not only on contemporary affairs, but on survival itself. If citizens lack what today has been called scientific literacy, that is not a sufficient reason to abdicate their sovereignty as voters, as investors, or even as commercial customers. There is no evidence that technical knowledge freely translates into social wisdom. In the interest of protecting the most fundamental values of the American creed, there is no basis for accepting decisions made by a technological priesthood simply because the members of that priesthood possess specialized information or the power it confers.

This is not to deny that technical knowledge begets power. The challenge is how, in American society, to make that power accountable.

What I hope to do as author is to help people cope with the dilemmas arising from life in a technological world and prepare them to participate in the art of technological choice. Not only can this be a psychological therapy for overcoming gloom; with better understanding of how science and technology are mediated by familiar activities, people can exert more control over their technological future and that of their children.

Toward that end, we map a vast and highly convoluted territory which spans technology, culture, science, economics, and politics. We then examine powerful interdependencies between technology, the pulses of change it injects in our culture, and the social fabric in which it is embedded. The basic premise for this discussion is that technology is more than technique, more than hardware. It is itself a social system driven by specialized knowledge and involving all the institutions of our society and their communication linkages. As a social process, technology deals with people, with their values, with political choice in democratic governance, and with connections between all three.

Other arguments follow: every technology entails important side effects, some benign and some dangerous. Thus, the social management of technology requires close attention to uncertainties, to risks, to impacts external to the technological transaction or experienced in the longer term, and thus to the distribution of benefits and costs. Then we discover that it is essential not only to consider *what* we as a society decide, but also *how*.

What we are really talking about are the key decisions involving technology—what may be called the grand issues. Of crucial importance to the argument is a reality that these choices are made by public policy rather than in the marketplace. While most of these grand issues have attracted high-level political attention and extensive legislation, longer-term consequences have too often been neglected. It is almost as if the policy apparatus were deaf to signals about the future, or as if it chose pathways of least short-term resistance.

Next, we focus on the private industrial sector that produces and delivers goods and services, and on the private-public partnership that has been present from the founding of our nation. The connections of technology with science as a vital knowledge generator are then examined, along with the effects of creating an information-rich society.

The inquiry moves on to fundamentals of decision making, including the roles and behavior of politicians, lobbyists, the media, and citizens.

Here we attack the question of strategies for collision avoidance, of an imperative to look ahead. There will be things we see that we want; there will be things we see that we do not want; and there will be things we do not see. The very act of looking before we leap, however, of asking of technology not only "how" but also "ought we," gives us a chance to achieve higher levels of social satisfaction without the exorbitant costs of error, political conflict, or ecologically irreversible catastrophe.

There are two final premises. The first is that every choice involves tradeoffs. It would thus be a course of wisdom to illuminate these in advance so as to help balance the long- and short-term consequences, or the investments for accident prevention versus those for damage repair. The second premise is that the best final judgment in the long run rests with the people. Science and its numbers cannot be expected to provide all the answers to questions that are by their nature ambiguous, that must be tested against value preferences, and that entail winners and losers, many as innocent bystanders. Technical virtuosity does not bequeath broad understanding of our situation or answers to our ethical dilemmas.

The last chapter deals with technology and the future. Notwithstanding the promise of science and technology as a cornucopia of the good life for all peoples, within the foreseeable future at least, resources for that achievement are tragically inadequate. What is at stake, therefore, are tradeoffs—not only of costs and benefits on a project level but, at the most abstract and overarching level, of sacrifice.

Here, the reader is offered a set of principles to help in analyzing technological initiatives, not so much as criteria as to what is good or bad, but as a guide on how to think about the most salient question, "What might happen, if?" "to whom?" and "when?" The concluding section outlines ten specific proposals that could nourish initiatives by the next cycle of political leadership as well as furnish encouragement to the attentive public.

To communicate in a few pages a sense of how the entire technological system works is an ambitious task. From direct experience as a practicing engineer and in the policy trenches as counselor and scout, I have tried to comb out the essentials for a pragmatic understanding of technology, society, and politics. They are cast, however, within an ecumenical framework drawing on numerous academic disciplines and the intellects of a wide range of authorities. Indeed, readers should be aware from their own life experiences that no problem of our society can be understood exclusively from any single discipline. No area of specialization is adequate for comprehension of modern life, and even the sum of these sophisticated but narrow grooves does not add up to the whole of human society.

People learn to navigate on automobile freeways—crowded, sometimes slippery, always dangerously populated with irresponsible drivers. One crucial element of safety is a clean windshield, so that one is able to see the dangers ahead and thus maneuver to mitigate risk. So it is in the modern world. Reserves to correct mistakes have evaporated. Maneuvering room has shrunk. Survival depends metaphorically on learning how to maintain a clear windshield, to use whatever information is accessible about the way ahead, and to drive defensively. With such attitudes and aptitudes, everyone can be better prepared to cope in a technological world. For if we can be reassured that the future *is* malleable, and that technological choice is not just or primarily a technical affair, we should be able to create the futures we want and avoid those we do not.

1 / Technology and Culture

Living with Technology and Liking It, But . . .

hange is one of the most compelling truths of living. Some changes reflect the inescapable and irrevocable stages of natural law. Biological aging is inevitable. Continental drift is uncontrollable. But some elements of change derive from calculated human endeavor. Fundamental and dramatic shifts in individual and social behavior have occurred with charismatic leadership, some of it religious, some ideological, some purely exploitive of the human condition.

In contemporary society, the most powerful engines of change are human invention, innovation, and applications of scientific knowledge. Collectively, we call these functions "technology."

Technology has always been a source of cultural transformation. The artifacts left by our predecessors have become treasures of insight as to how people coped with their strenuous, hostile, and capricious natural environment. Indeed, we define these cultures by their tools and their material achievements. Technology was the springboard for change, from hunting and gathering to agriculture, from use of fire and the arrow to the intercontinental, nuclear-tipped missile. Once, the wheel was high-tech. Interactions between culture and technology are so powerful that we are spontaneously but wrongly inclined to equate technology with civilization.

In the modern world, we continue to employ these instruments of human processing to gain control over our environment—to such a degree that we not only live *with* technology; we *live* technology. Indeed, technology has demonstrated a fabulous capacity to generate new wealth even faster than capital alone, with a conspicuous virtue of enhancing material standards of living. By both developed and developing nations, it is regarded as a crucible for economic growth. Partly, this arises because technology has proven to be a key to abundance. Partly, too, this admiration is accentuated because economic growth is itself heralded as desirable. The products of a technological society entice exuberant consumerism, further pumped by technological leverage in advertising. And when changes occur in our economic situation, changes also occur in the way we look at technology.

Technology has also functioned as a source of treasured freedoms: freedom from the back-breaking labor of chopping wood, pumping water, and carting ice, and from slavery in the mines; freedom from disease and disability; freedom from geographical and cultural isolation and social immobility; freedom to spend more adult years on education; freedom to plan families. Technology has given more people than ever before the freedom to choose; and it has provided more choices: how and where we live; what we work at; what we eat; how we vacation. In short, technology has vastly enhanced the quality of life.

That propinquity of technology and culture has led to our taking technology almost for granted. Consider a typical working day. We awake to a radio alarm clock; switch off the electric blanket; dress in clothes of synthetic fiber; defrost orange juice and microwave our breakfast with electricity generated by nuclear power; commute to the office in a high-powered car listening to a forty-watt hi-fi stereo; travel up by elevator in time to receive a telephone call relayed by satellite from ten time zones away. These are machines for living. Their impacts do not stop at the end of the day. At night, it's the contraceptive and sleeping pills. Weekends, it's the high-tech sandbox: television; Atari games; helicopter ski lifts; power tools and power boats.

At a different scale, consider technology's impact on culture in reducing agricultural employment from 30 percent of the work force to 3; in facilitating both the congested, high-rise central business district and the traffic-strewn flight to the suburbs; in equipping a civilian population with more TV sets than toilets.

We began to glorify technology over a century ago, with its cascade of inventions: the steam engine, electric lights, farm machinery, the sewing machine, even running water. Then came the automobile, the telephone, radio, television, jet aircraft, modern medicine, and nuclear energy. Along with these inventions came a manufacturing and marketing infrastructure, soft technology to foster penetration into all of society.

In World War II, technology became the great equalizer, helping purchase victory with a minimum loss of life by superiority in industrial production and sophisticated weapons. That heyday of science as an endless frontier was further excited by the 1957 Soviet space surprise. We entered the competition with gusto. We adopted technology as our chosen vehicle to global superiority in the race for people's minds, as well as to domestic social progress.

Today we are hooked on technology. It underpins every aspect of life: national security; the energy supply; industrial productivity; food production; health care delivery; urban habitation and infrastructure; education, entertainment, and telecommunications. We refer to ourselves as the information society, a condition made feasible only by new advances in computer virtuosity.

Yet, we are not comfortable with all the changes wrought by technology. Every technology introduced for its intended benefits carries inadvertent side effects, direct and indirect. The direct by-products may be benign, or they may be harmful; or they may be both, but to different people. They are all the more bewildering because they are usually hidden, and may hibernate only to burst on the scene unexpectedly, endangering life, health, property, or the environment. Pesticides to improve agricultural productivity are poisonous; nuclear plants generate both power and dangerous waste; swift jet aircraft create objectionable airport noise; computers invade privacy. The list of direct side effects is endless, literally endless, because *every* technology plays Jekyll and Hyde. To these chronic disabilities must be added the risk of catastrophic accident involving hazardous materials in routine transit, chemical plant leakage, or nuclear plant meltdown.

The indirect side effects may be more subtle but, in the long run, even more potent. Technology has profoundly altered human institutions, life-styles, and basic values; witness the impact of the automobile and the pill on sexual mores. Because the pace of technology evolves more swiftly than social institutions that husband it, it has sparked disharmony in purpose and economic and social instability. Look at what has happened to the family farmer, selling out to the agrobusinesses. Indeed, technology has promoted the growth and power of industrial enterprises. Then, it has forced growth in government to regulate private initiatives so as to mitigate hazardous impacts. It has tended to nurture social as well as technical complexity so as to hinder public understanding, then to engender deep feelings of anxiety. In trying to cope, some people have turned to spiritual inspiration in a quest for a more comprehensible world, some to cults for the comfort of simplistic explanations.

Like any love affair, ours with technology has been carried on with euphoric highs, periodically tempered by cycles of reality testing. While achievements of ingenuity constitute an expression of our most treasured creative instincts, they also pose challenges in the management of technological change so as to extract its blessings without sacrificing our cultural ideals.

Toward a Social Management of Technology

Given our complex and confusing society, we need to have someone demystify technology. I don't mean trying to explain how complex machines work. We can leave understanding the insides of TV and the laser, the nuclear reactor and the CAT scanner, to scientists and engineers. What we need to know more transparently is how these discoveries influence our lives and the lives of our children. In other words, we need to be able to test the optimistic claims of technology's advocates that novelty and change always nurture progress, to understand whether the promised benefits are imperceptively accompanied by new or higher risks.

Healthy skepticism doesn't mean rejecting technology. New scientific discoveries are exciting. The human psyche seems tickled by unmasking nature's secrets. It's like solving a puzzle or deciphering a code. Applying that new knowledge to everyday dilemmas stirs the blood. We tend to love innovation, sometimes for its own sake. And furthermore, we get addicted because human experience has confirmed that technology contributes substantially to the American dream.

A search is then necessary to match the satisfaction of our needs and wants with the most appropriate technological means. Technology should be an instrument to achieve social ends, and not an end in itself. So we must inquire as to how we prioritize goals, set criteria for choosing means, and illuminate tradeoffs, say between solar and nuclear energy, between energy extraction and conservation, or between a new weapon system in space and arms control.

As I have said, *all* technologies can breed trouble. They carry a hidden load of unintended surprises. These side effects may be social, economic, cultural, or environmental. Some may turn out to be benign, a form of serendipity; yet others may be inimical to human life and the human spirit. To add to the few examples previously cited, the automobile, intended to provide swift and economical personal transport, entails a huge bill for premature death, disability, and urban air pollution, and an appetite for unlimited supplies of petroleum. Medical apparatus to increase the power of diagnosis and treatment is so expensive that bills for the nation's health care now exceed 10 percent of our GNP and lower-income citizens are excluded from a quality system.

In the 1960s, partly because of Rachel Carson's shocker, *Silent Spring,* about how pesticides were wiping out birds, we discovered that technologically induced risks to the natural environment had been quietly increasing. Here was the first cycle of reality testing in this technological century. To be sure, there had been a nagging anxiety about machines replacing jobs, and indeed, about the bomb opening a lethal Pandora's box. But because the political behavior of a society reflects the prevailing cultural focus, these concerns had to await the arrival in the 1960s of the countercultural revolution.

Some called technology a new social disease, so potent in its adverse effects that there were impetuous cries to turn it off. But technology was too tightly interwoven with our culture, indeed with almost every function in our society. We were not about to cut off our noses to spite our faces and abandon technological pursuits. Society thus had to deal with the adverse side effects by *social* innovation. In a primitive and innocent way, we instituted a doctrine of anticipation. By law, we required environmental impact analysis of all new projects *before* they were put in place. Later, we demanded total impact analysis. We used the legislative process to help us look before we leap, to seek answers to the simple question, "What might happen, if?"

In a remarkably short time, that love affair with the machine that had been going on for a hundred years in adolescent attitudes of unquestioning esteem suddenly matured to a more balanced perception: with the potential of technology to enrich people's lives come uncertainties and dangers. Society discovered that we had to do more than cope by the skin of our teeth; we had to exercise critical judgment.

For decades, we had been asking only, "Can we do it?" In the 1960s, we began asking, "Ought we to do it?" That deeper perception, however, is still accompanied neither by credible methodology nor by a durable commitment to harmony between, say, economy and ecology.

Consequently, in the 1980s, we wrestle with a different challenge concerning technology: "Can we manage it?" What we mean is the social management of technology. Since that phrase may be unfamiliar, we must draw on the analogy with "industrial management." That interdisciplinary body of knowledge is concerned with decision making, largely within the industrial firm, regarding how to achieve intended production of goods and services with optimum economy and efficiency. The social management of technology is also concerned with decision making and with the outcomes of technological initiatives. But unlike industrial management, it focuses on the broader consequences of technology and on the broader participation of society as a whole in the acts of management.

We thus develop an argument for the sharpening of civic competence to manage technology more adroitly. Otherwise, we may breed serious inequities as to benefits and beneficiaries, or inadvertently squander our natural legacy. Even worse, in being deaf to signals about the future, we may unwittingly disregard emerging threats to human society.

Beyond Technique: Technology as Social Process

People have two fundamental misconceptions about technology. In the first place, many think that technology is hardware—ubiquitous automobiles, 747s, telephones, Polaroid cameras, VCRs, and home refrigerators. These are devices we can see, touch, hear, and experience. We forget that technology is also software, or perhaps squishyware; people and their institutions must furnish instructions as to its use. So, at its root, technology is more than technique. This concept is consistent with Webster's definition as "the totality of specialized knowledge and means to provide goods and services necessary for human sustenance and comfort." Technology is thus a process, a social process of generating and utilizing knowledge so deeply engraved in our culture that everyone is now profoundly affected.

The second misconception arises because we forget that everyone is also directly involved in technology. That's obvious for the mechanic, the industrial manager, the scientist, or the engineer. All have a hands-on affiliation. But we neglect the bankers who decide on investment capital for plant expansion, or policy officials who make choices and allocate resources for weapon systems and for urban mass transit, or who set standards for water quality. And we disregard just plain citizens. They are involved in four different ways: as consumers of technological products, as voters on referenda for nuclear power, as investors in fledgling high-tech enterprises, and as unknowing victims of unfavorable impacts. Technology is not a spectator sport.

Almost all contemporary organizations, both public and corporate, are engaged in technology. GM produces cars; Exxon sells gasoline; RCA makes radios and television sets; AT&T and many other firms market communication services. Most government agencies also deal with technology: with armaments, nuclear power development, medical research, food production, water supply, toxic waste disposal, transportation safety, purity of food, effectiveness of pharmaceuticals, census information, and production incentives. Virtually all agencies created since World War II are rooted in some aspect of technology.

In advancing beyond notions of hardware, we discover technology's full significance in human affairs. Technology has altered risks to individuals and to society as a whole. For example, it has reduced infant mortality and infectious disease. Indeed, immunization and sanitary engineering to purify water and dispose of human waste have reduced premature deaths worldwide more than have any other medical achievements. But because of side effects, technology also has generated a new portfolio of risks such as those outlined previously.

There are other overarching repercussions. First, with swift transportation and instant communication, nations are now locked together as one world, technologically, if not politically. Events anywhere have effects everywhere. Second, technology increasingly intermingles people and nature, exposing the natural environment to human insults, accelerating uncritical consumption of nonrenewable resources and increasing the risk of a change in climate.

Next, through technology, cultures that were previously isolated by geography have been brought into contact and into conflict; remember the enigma of Americans held hostage in Iran. Within cultures, generations are being split by the pulse of change because some thrive on it and others are inordinately stressed. Severe collisions erupt between humanists and those enchanted by technologically pulsed materialism and indifferent to technology's social impacts. Tensions may be further aggravated by scientific contributions to longevity that increase the proportion of elderly.

In addition, at the institutional scale, technology acts as a mobilizing agent to concentrate wealth and power. It then plays a political role in every society, developed and developing, capitalist and socialist. It starkly accentuates distinctions between who wins and who loses, and how much. Indeed, technology tends to discriminate against the unrepresented and the disadvantaged, and to support the elitist establishment. Technology, at least in its impacts, is not neutral. Then, because of the choices involved regarding beneficiaries, technology has become more political. Conversely, through TV campaigning and computerized voter lists, politics have become more technological.

Next, we find that the grand decisions on technology are no longer made in the marketplace. They are made by public policy. Choosing those goals to which a technology is directed, creating an atmosphere for industrial innovation, setting priorities for research, making tradeoffs between employment and environmental protection, committing funds for massive civil projects or expensive weapon systems—these are today's salient choices. And the major actors in this process are not scientists and engineers. They are politicians, the people you and I elect.

These characteristic linkages with society are generic, applicable to almost every technology, whether television or nuclear weapons. The existence of such encompassing patterns may seem remarkable, but exceptions are rare.

Tomorrow, we should expect more technology, not less. To shape that future we need to acquire this sharper image of technology as more than technique or products. It entails a tangled skein of familiar social processes, communication networks, and institutions, along with natural processes and technical facilities, a blend of science and human values.

Amplifying Brawn, Brain, and Bureaucracy

To visualize its social, economic, and cultural impacts, consider technology as an amplifier. With lever and wheel and bomb, technology amplifies human muscle. With the computer, it amplifies the human mind and human memory. Indeed, in various ways technology amplifies human senses, enabling us to see invisible objects close by or enormous ones at great distances; to hear the inaudible; to measure infinitesimal moments of time. Almost all of the hardware that we deploy today amplifies something tangible.

Less apparent is the role of technology as *social amplifier*. It has spawned the population explosion, but it also magnifies the less tangible. Technology may either elevate or imperil the human spirit, facilitate or threaten freedom and self-esteem; it exalts the economic machine and expands material appetites and inequalities in their satisfaction; it stretches the boundaries of interpersonal transactions, the span, volume, and complexity of communication networks. It intensifies the potential for conflict. As technology increases demands on our social institutions, it exposes their weaknesses. Technology expands the number of options that confront our decision makers, increases risks to them, and heightens the cost from error. Not too surprisingly, technology amplifies the power of organizations and individuals who control it.

Inadvertently, technology increases the role of government. Indeed, technology and government have grown together and, given heavy government funding of research, somewhat because of each other. So technology amplifies brawn, brain, and bureaucracy.

The only feature of human experience not amplified by technology is time. With human affairs speeded up by technology, including change itself, and with our culture unwittingly applauding that achievement, we find a paradox. Technology furnishes more choices but less time to choose. With that situation comes stress, stress from the tyranny of the clock, stress from anxiety over the unexplored consequences of a hasty decision, and stress from fears that technology is out of control.

To avoid the penalties of impetuous decisions, we are obliged to ask how to steer technology to extract the most socially satisfactory outcomes. In building on the concept of collision avoidance, driving defensively means continuous anticipation. That is the basis of another fundamental connection of technology—beyond society and politics to its linkage with the future.

What's Playing Now at the Theater of the Mind?

To deal with the future, we must switch on the imagination. For it is here that we catch glimpses of what tomorrow may be like. Except for psychics, soothsayers, and prophets, who believe in external sources of their visions, the rest of us must admit that views of the future originate in our own minds.

Some features can be drawn quite rationally, based on projections of facts, statistical data, and trends. Some are based on religious beliefs, on connections between behavior today and rewards or punishment tomorrow, or on literal interpretations of the Bible, with its foreboding of Armageddon. Then there are those sketches of the future extracted from dreams of what we want the way ahead to be. The obverse images are nightmares of futures we do not want. Underlying our propitious dreams is the belief that the future is corrigible, that trends need not be destiny. Indeed, there is implicit in this approach a philosophy that destiny is a matter of choice, not chance, that it is within human power to create the future.

Creating the future. There's a challenge to kindle the hopes of almost everyone. Here is where one can turn on the theater of the mind. The question is how to write the script.

For almost a hundred years, that game has been played at every world's fair. It has been largely based on technology. The latest in science and engineering have been on display, accompanied by suitable hyperbole that turned each accomplishment into a circus sideshow. Thus were made public the first steam engines, electric lights, radio telegraphs, television, each with extravagant claims about what it would contribute to the good life. In addition, there have been exhibits predicting what the world would be like twenty, fifty, or one hundred years hence. Always, these represented more technology: prospects of individually owned helicopters filling the skies; of multistory expressways carrying streamlined autos with never a traffic jam; of houses entirely of plastic, self-cleaning like today's ovens, and equipped with robotic servants.

Yet almost all of these three-dimensional fantasies missed their mark. Indeed, so inaccurate were they that this fashion in world's fairs has almost disappeared in America if not abroad—to be replaced by Disney creations with greater emphasis on entertainment than on education. Nevertheless, those showmen were on the right track, for now it is technology far more than philosophy that has shaped the future. We need only recall the printing press, the clock, gunpowder, and metallurgy to recognize how different was the world after adoption of these innovations. Recent inventions such as the computer, cable television, and nuclear power will have similarly dramatic effects, well beyond immediate gratification by being user friendly. The impacts stretch far ahead, but they also extend laterally, indirectly affecting life today in many subtle and unexpected ways. Not anticipating some of these second-order consequences more warily may be largely a failure in imagination.

The crux of the matter is foresight. Shouldn't we be asking, "What might happen if?" For only by deliberately attempting to peer both ahead and sideways can we gain perspective on the various impacts technology may have on our lives. As we discover later, we must also ask, "To whom?" and "When?"

This appeal to foresight does not mean divination. Rather, it is a form of sagacity driven by an awareness that because the future is always uncertain, looking ahead is *not* primarily a matter of predicting the future. Rather, it is anticipating plausible future repercussions of today's decisions. As much as anything, it means anticipating the behavior of the deciders. John Naisbett in *Megatrends* said that the most reliable way to anticipate the future is to understand the present.

Two intertwined principles are worth remembering. Technology has a powerful influence on culture. But the reverse is also important. Our culture has had a major influence on technology: by defining social purposes to which it is directed; by delineating beneficiaries; by adopting tradeoffs; by mediating the ethics, for example, to limit damage to the natural world, to reduce risk and to show our concern for future generations. Our values may have more to do with technological choice than our technical precocity.

The technologically laden future isn't what it used to be. But human nature is. The balance between the bright and the dark side of the human personality has been made more poignant by the leverage of technology, by both its wholesome and its malignant potential. With a manifest cultural tilt of our society to the short run, we discover incongrously that both the will and the competence to look ahead seem lacking.

Everyone is concerned about the future because that is where we spend the rest of our lives. How we cope may depend on technological choices, not only those of inventors in the machine shop, of scientists in the laboratory, and of engineers in the manufacturing plant. Rather, the future depends most critically on choices made by citizens at the polling booth and on communications to their elected representatives.

Wiring the Planet

Today, technology has linked all nations together into one world. Whatever pure idealism is embedded in that statement, it would seem at first glance to fly in the face of some highly visible realities. Nationalism is still playing well on the stage of world politics. Appeals to patriotism prevail almost everywhere; indeed, such motivation conspicuously fuels unending warfare. The United Nations operates a daily forum for the purely rhetorical projection of hostile attitudes and narrow parochial interests.

At a more subtle level, children in their geography class first learn about the planet from maps that graphically dramatize territorial boundaries. History lessons are liberally spiked with dates of territorial disputes. Indeed, the territorial imperative seems alive and well.

That enduring notion opens up a perplexing contradiction, however, because in another representation of how the world works, boundaries are erased. Maps fail to expose the heavy traffic that crosses national limits. People travel. Fish freely migrate. Enormous tonnages of raw materials, commodities, manufactured goods—the merchandise of a modern civilization—pass over borders. So does waste, the garbage of industry carried haphazardly by air and by sea. Witness the planet-wide fallout from Chernobyl, the acid rain deposited in Eastern Canada that originates in the United States, and in Scandinavia, from the United Kingdom. And consider the nervousness of industrialized nations whose economic and military security were shaken by OPEC's 1973 moratorium and subsequent price increases, and who still depend on Mideast oil. These are the tangible displays of global flows, indeed, of interconnectedness.

The less visible commerce is just as significant. Capital that was once transported as precious metal, then as paper money, now moves imperceptibly by wire or radio. So do enormous volumes of data and information. No longer is it necessary to transport newspapers; type can be set remotely without any physical contact. Also crossing boundaries willy-nilly are ideas, the facts of science, the practice of medicine, the roots of culture, and culture itself. Designer jeans and Coca-Cola, not to mention the latest in jazz music and TV shows, are identical in downtown San Francisco and Western Samoa.

To underscore our planetary network, consider the impact of live television coverage from Vietnam or the media events of Iranian terrorists' dealing with our hostages. When President Reagan was shot in Washington, D.C., ripples were felt in the gold markets of Switzerland within minutes. No nation today, and few industrial firms, can develop their domestic policies, without recognizing the deep interdependence with foreign affairs. Japan markets electronic video recorders in the United States that are assembled in Malaysia, with silicon computer chips from Taiwan.

Global traffic in technological products is matched by a flow of technological know-how. The export of technical assistance—the core of what is often termed "technology transfer"—began after World War II with the U.S. Marshall plan. Much was aimed at rejuvenating war-torn Europe and Japan. But there was also a major thrust to help the Third World bootstrap out of starvation, poverty, and lack of prestige in an industrialized world. In the 1970s, many of these nations initiated a collective complaint in international forums that they were being denied fair access to know-how. Shortfall in their performance, however, has many sources. We have discovered that shipping tractors, the hardware, is simply not enough; a competent infrastructure in the recipient country is a necessary if not sufficient condition for effective transfer.

Institutionally, there is no world government. There may never be one. But the evolution of global affairs is reflected in the growth of inter-governmental unions, most with a technology-related agenda. The United Nations General Assembly, with 161 members, stands at the center of a constellation of treaty organizations: The U.N. Educational, Scientific, and Cultural Organization (from which the U.S. withdrew in 1984), the U.N. Economic and Social Council, the U.N. Development Program, and such specialized agencies as the World Health Organization, the World Meteorological Organization, and the International Telecommunication Union. To these can be added hundreds of bilateral accords.

Then there are nongovernmental organizations such as the International Council of Scientific Unions, and an incalculable number of interscientific, professional, and commercial linkages. Finally, there are an expanding number of multinational corporations. Whatever their virtues, their economic power, or their alleged menace, such operations are conducted with far more attention to transnational goals, functions, and computer networks than to cartography.

In short, swift transportation via jet aircraft, and instant communication via cable, radio, and television, have laced the planet with invisible networks that effectively surmount national borders, once conceived as fences. Moreover, it was a technological tour de force that afforded a historical view of interdependent life on spaceship Earth—the photo of the planet from a manned landing on the moon. We can literally see ourselves as a single, though not unified, human community.

There is yet another important technological connection. With the bomb comes the threat of a massive loss of life by nuclear antagonists and of possibly grave peril to innocent bystanders from a nuclear winter. Because of the potency of weapons technology, everyone on the planet shares a common fate; it is urgent that we recognize the need for a common agenda.

The paradox we discover is that this technological achievement has far outdistanced the political. Indeed, the medium *is* the message: with technology, we have wired the planet.

Ten Paradoxes of Paradise

While a strong case can be made for the role of technology in helping people realize their needs and wants, technology can create problems as well as promises. Indeed, the integration of technology with culture has created some perplexing situations.

First, we have more knowledge than ever before, yet less understanding. Scientific research is itself an enterprise of knowledge generation. What began with Sir Francis Bacon at the end of the sixteenth century as a way of systematically thinking about the world around us exploded in the nineteenth century into concerted efforts to observe natural phenomena and to establish laws of nature regarding causality. Accordingly, the number of scientists, of educational opportunities, of laboratories, of research products—publications of papers and books—has grown rapidly. So has the investment in research and development. Meanwhile, the appetite to apply this knowledge has also grown, as is apparent in the number of patents and quests for innovation and technology transfer. We have become an engineered society.

The trouble is that much of this new learning is compartmentalized. Largely, this is the nature of science, self-defining into narrower and narrower specialties. Each specialty advances along a cramped frontier and within strict boundaries. Each discipline develops its own jargon and its own intellectual turf represented by departmental structure within universities. Because the explosion of information within each field is so great, it becomes difficult for any specialist to explore beyond his chosen arena, even more difficult to communicate across these boundaries.

There is a similar gap between the knowledge possessed by specialists and its interpretation and communication to the great majority of clients of technological enterprise who are nonspecialists. People do not have a ready access to science because of its complexity. Conversely, understanding of the dynamic processes of society by technical personnel is at best spotty.

So chasms develop among scientists and between scientist and citizen. The information age in which we take such pride as a symbol of progress is undermined because that growing base of knowledge does not translate to understanding, especially of what science and technology do to our lives. Thus the paradox of more knowledge and less understanding.

A second paradox lies in the intended role of technology to reduce risk, for it is now also a source of risk. We are all aware of the dangers in nuclear weapons, world population outracing the food supply, inadvertent climate modification, urban chaos, resource depletion, institutional malfunctioning, global economic instabilities, even loss of freedom and pathological shifts in values from computer-assisted surveillance over human activity. Such new modes and scales of risk are unprecedented. All can be characterized as having conspicuous technological roots.

The technical aspects are not, however, the only source of risk. As our technologies become more complex, so do the social dimensions of delivery systems. Ironically, some of the risks may be rising because of this social complexity, which defies coherent internal management and public understanding as stubbornly as does the purely technical complexity.

So we encounter a third puzzle, that while technology can simplify and ease the tasks of living, it can also add complications. Such complexity adds to the predicaments in technological choice and also to the stress of decision making. The technological threats enumerated earlier are then more likely to occur, so that risks increase further because the quality of decisions declines.

A fourth paradox is that, in the interest of national defense, we have more arms and less security. Today, we have augmented weapon systems of unprecedented power, entirely as a product of a virile technology. But instead of their purchasing more protection against military adventures, they give us less. Indeed as the stockpile grows, and we talk of the "high frontier" for "Star Wars," we discover that unconditional viability has disappeared. The hair trigger of automatic "launch-on-warning" puts human fate in the hands of a computer chip. The temporary advantage ratcheted to our military by weapons development repeatedly disappears. Pure logic, much less a trenchant concern for survival, dictates that we must actively seek conflict management by nonviolent means.

A fifth contradiction lies in our having far better technical communications than formerly in terms of speed, range, and capacity but no greater sense of community. As was said before, wiring the planet has not diminished rampant nationalism. Enhanced communications have contributed little to neighborliness. The reverse may even be true. When people spend so many free hours watching television alone, or silently with others, they are deprived of opportunities for communication and sharing. Viewers witness more examples of violence than of compassion. In offices, the notion of electronic mail may have similar side effects of isolating individuals from each other. While the direct business at hand may be transacted more efficiently, there may be a serious loss in recognizing the human dimension and the rewards of collaborative effort. Computers may have brought premature death to body language.

Yet another paradox can be found in public attitudes toward government. People are demanding less government and lower taxes at the same time that they expect more protection from technology's risks. Notwithstanding the acceptance of many economic dicta of the Reagan administration, there has been public resistance to cancelling operations of the EPA.

A corollary of this enigma is that technology increases the need for astute and farsighted policy steering at the same time that confidence in government has generally declined. The need created by technology for more effective institutional functioning has not been accompanied by institutional wisdom. While technology has imparted greater momentum to what we call progress, it has failed to provide improved tools for social steering. The sophisticated information society may not have gained a corresponding measure of sagacity.

As we examine the social processes associated with technology, we discover three more paradoxes that are explored later in greater detail. We have more material benefits but no greater satisfactions. We have more choices but no more time to choose. And more years in school afforded by the economic surpluses conferred on our society by technology have produced neither more pronounced critical judgment nor a greater sense of the social contract.

2 / Technology & Social Systems

The Government-Technology Connection

The legends we live by include a common misconception about technology: that technological affairs are largely the province of the private sector. Now we find that venue shared by government, with some major implications.

First, a smidgeon of history. Modern capitalism grew out of the nineteenth-century industrial revolution. Owner-entrepreneurs first engaged newly discovered techniques to concentrate energy; that was the innovative core of the revolution. Then they concentrated venture capital, for to exploit that innovative capacity to meet human needs and wants, money was also required. With both financial and technical resources, firms could then operate the mines and the steel plants, build the railroads, manufacture automobiles, and, more recently, endow consumers with a supermarket of electronic toys.

What was true one hundred years ago—that private enterprise produced most of the hardware—is true today, at least, in capitalist nations. But there is a major new twist. Government is now in the technological act as a silent partner with industry. Moreover, a case can be argued that as technology became more intimately entwined with society, the most crucial decisions as to both technological ends and means shifted from the traditional marketplace to government.

Government is involved with technology in five different ways. First, private entrepreneurship and investment are directly assisted by a galaxy of land grants, subsidies, tax incentives, import quotas, and market guarantees. These inducements to stimulate technological activity go back almost to the nation's birth, so that over the intervening years, almost every sector has become a special pleader for handouts.

Second, the private sector is indirectly assisted by government funding of social overhead. Included in this notion are supports for higher education, specialized training, and research and development; fiscal aids such as the Export-Import Bank; such services as space shuttle launching of communication satellites; and assistance to companies seeking business overseas.

Third, by its deficit borrowing and its fiscal and tax policies, government heavily influences the capital market. Such manipulation impinges on interest rates, balance of payments, and inflation, and thus on venture capital for new industrial starts and on industry's ability to compete overseas.

Fourth, the government has been obliged to intervene through the regulatory process when technological activities of the private sector have been inimical to the public interest. Antitrust legislation and measures for railroad and steamboat safety, pure food, and abolition of child labor were put in place over a long period. Following World War II, when technological momentum increased sharply, government interceded in matters of air and water quality, occupational health, auto and aircraft safety, effectiveness of drugs, toxic waste disposal, and a myriad of other problems ignited by freewheeling industries mediating new and powerful technologies.

Finally in a fifth role, government is itself a major customer of technology. The Department of Defense purchases major weapons systems for national security, always government's first responsibility. Now, however, the techniques of warfare put a premium on quality and novelty of armaments, to the point that warfare has been revolutionized as a technological as well as an arms race. The nuclear-tipped missile has evolved with unprecedented lethality, greater range, higher accuracy, and faster delivery as a direct consequence of government-funded research and engineering. This technical cunning eventually percolates throughout the entire civilian market. In technical jargon it is referred to as spillover. But that government sponsorship has other repercussions: defense expenditures create deficits; defense industries compete for high talent and absorb much of the nation's best technical brains; research agendas in university laboratories are distorted by availability of defense funds.

All five of these activities reflect changes of a technological age. They are consistent with Constitutional law and custom, in that government is expected to make the most fundamental decisions—to build the common defense, to rank social priorities, to allocate resources, to organize economic, social and political activity, and to resolve conflicts among contending factions.

The vehicle for these decisions is public policy. Public policy defines both what governments do and what they may not do. With issues first dramatized so as to focus political energies on the choices ahead, the decision system affords citizens the rights of petition to explain how prospective action may affect them. No wonder the process seems to be primarily a grappling by special interests for influence. But what emerges in the way of policies constitutes the primary guidance signals by which separate parties in our pluralistic society can then steer collectively and coherently toward common goals. Public policies now set the course and the strategies for the most potent of our technologies. No small wonder we must be concerned with the art of technological choice.

What's So Special about Science Policy?

One particular class of public policies is different because these policies have a high content of science or technology, because they require different ingredients or processes of choice, and because of the type and scale of effects, both direct and indirect. Collectively, they have been termed "science policy."

Why are they so special? Distinctions first arise because of their essential factual content. Choices as to alternative technical means to achieve any social goal—uninterrupted, low-cost energy, for example—require an understanding of the scientific content of the technical means. Fact thus plays a crucial role that cannot be negotiated away by legislation. There is the apocryphal story of a state legislature a century ago that tried to assign to pi the value of 3.000 because it would be so much easier to remember and manipulate. In retrospect, such naivete may only tickle a laugh. The bald truth is that no amount of legal maneuvering or political bargaining can change natural laws, nor can idealistic hopes alter the principles of conservation of energy or preserve the health of an ecological community.

Further complications arise in this policy process because the facts change. New scientific discoveries have the unnerving ability to upset the status quo and thus undermine cherished ideas. Moreover, changes in scientific truths may occur faster than changes in public understanding or in the decision process.

To deal with this problem, science policy makers turn to experts. Some are primary, authentic sources of scientific knowledge. Some act as interpreters. Some are "hired guns," serving particular interest groups. Some are independent observers or critics. Arrayed on all sides of an issue, coveys of experts universally tend to overemphasize their own specialty. The sharper the expertise and the greater the involvement with purely technical details, the more isolated the individual becomes from understanding of the broader ramifications. Inadvertently, experts become swept along with institutional and political forces with which they are allied because they usually have a professional stake in the outcome. Objectivity becomes a very scarce commodity.

Another characteristic of technology-intensive policies is the increase in options. How should future urban congestion be met—by wider highways, or by buses, subways, or elevated tramcars, or by subsidized cablecommunication to decentralized, suburban offices?

A further distinction is that of cost, because almost all technology-intensive policies carry high price tags. Some are enormous: a billion for each Trident submarine, hundreds of billions for "Star Wars" weapons defense systems; huge investments for electrical power generation, subways, container ports. And associated with most of these fiscal underpinnings are the realities that once these investments hatch physical plant, they are here to stay. You can't move dams or subways. In effect, these science policies are irreversible. Even weapon systems lead a life of their own whereby the infrastructure and jobs built around their production and deployment makes it almost impossible to turn them off, even when found wanting in performance. Cancellation of the American SST in 1971 and of recent nuclear power plants constitute very rare exceptions. Technological momentum seems like technological determinism.

Here is another manifestation of the ubiquitous side effects of all technologies. They may be beneficial. But when they are harmful, we are dismayed that remedies may be economically intractable, politically infeasible, or ecologically impossible.

All of which underscores the conclusive impact of technology on the human and natural environment. That combination of potency, inevitability of unwanted consequences, and the cost of antidotes adds up to new orders of challenge in science-related policies to make error-free decisions.

Finally, for reasons explained earlier, science policies cannot be advocated solely on the basis of ideology, partisan political platforms, or response to single-issue advocates. Nor can conflict be readily eased by political tactics if the result flies in the face of sound technical foundations. Technology-intensive policy thus differs markedly from social or economic policy. This is not to say that science policies ever can or should be immune from normal politics. It is simply that they contain inherent constraints that must cool passionate, unrestrained, and sometimes irrational advocacy.

Although the quest for some overarching science policy is periodically attempted by scholars, and by policy makers frustrated by complexity, careful analysis should erase expectation of such a comprehensive envelope. Nevertheless, individual science policies may be conveniently packaged in two categories. These were first identified by Harvard professor Harvey Brooks as "policy in science" and "science in policy."

The first group encompasses decisions on the content and health of science and technology resources, the knowledge-facilitation function of government. Included, of course, are policies concerned with the size of funds devoted to research and development; their distribution by performing institution among industry, universities, and government; and priorities among different fields. Within this rubric also are policies concerned with support for laboratories and instrumentation, including "big science" facilities such as high-energy particle accelerators and orbiting telescopes; for higher education and for institution building; for processes of technology transfer; for enhancing capabilities for decision making in government at all levels; and finally, for communication networks to store and retrieve scientific information.

Conversely, "science in policy" decisions relate both to priorities among the entire range of social purposes which depend on utilizing science-based technological means, and to the tradeoffs among different goals—the costs, risks, benefits, and beneficiaries—and between the longer- and shorter-run consequences. Included are critical choices among alternative means, including options in delivery systems as well as hardware. Science in policy freely translates to decisions on technology, toward whose enhancement this book is directed.

Both concepts acquire clearer significance with examples, discussed in Chapter 3.

What You Can't Model You Can't Manage

Given technology's ubiquity and its power to affect human affairs everywhere on the planet, there is a strong incentive, even urgency, to attend to the steering of technology so as to obtain the most socially satisfactory outcomes. Also, given the role of public rather than private policies to execute that steering, we must examine what constitutes the social management of technology, and tools for its practice. Toward that end, we need a mental model of how the technology-enriched social system really works. For without a cognitive model to facilitate understanding of such an elaborate and labyrinthine enterprise, we have no hope of managing it in the sense of directing it toward the desired social performance.

There are two underlying premises. We have established that every institution and every individual is in some way a participant in technological enterprise. And we have established that technology is a social process that deals with knowledge. Now we consider how to integrate these factors, say in relation to a particular product or service. To map such an array of interacting elements, however, we must guard against such a narrowness of concept that different maps would be needed for each different output: for production of TV sets as compared to food; for autos as compared to health care. In other words, we need a generic schema that would apply to all specialized technological systems, each distinguished by the outputs selected to be delivered, but *not* by system structure or behavior.

The result can be portrayed in an abstraction that I have called a "technological delivery system," a TDS. Simply stated, it is a symbolic network that incorporates all essential organizational components, internally differentiated and hierarchically interrelated. One component may be devoted to knowledge generation through research or invention. Another may function as a management organization to mobilize knowledge along with natural resources, human resources, tools, and capital to produce the intended goods or services. This is what economist John Kenneth Galbraith called "technostructure." A third element represents national government, functioning in all five roles sketched previously. Then we need to portray people—individuals and interest group clusters—that define the body politic. In turn, they transmit signals of their needs, wants, and values and indicate acceptable tradeoffs. To complete this diagram, we add the judiciary, state or local government, other countries, and finally, the media.

Interconnecting these organizations is a lacework of communications. Through well-defined channels, information flows in all directions. It is the vital substance that animates all units to interact coherently and to collaborate in a common purpose, eventually to deliver the particular output which distinguishes that TDS. That interaction, incidentally, occurs through familiar social, economic, political, and legal processes.

This network, illustrated in Figure 2.1, is a "system" in that it incorporates inputs, outputs, components, and linkages that satisfy the rigorous technical definition of the term. Or "system" may be viewed simply as a metaphor signifying comprehensiveness, the syntax of technological enterprise. The inputs include specialized knowledge of scientific technique and of management, capital, natural resources including energy, human resources, and human values. The outputs include both the intended goods or services and the unintended ramifications—impacts on people, the natural environment, and the system itself. The organizational components include university research laboratories, private industrial firms, interest groups, government agencies, the president, the White House and Executive Office coterie, both houses of the Congress, the courts, and the press.

The linkages are simply lines of communication. Most of the traffic concerns substance. But that information *in* the system is not confined to formal channels. There are many back doors. Washington leaks like a sieve. Who talks to whom, and through what circuits, quite apart from

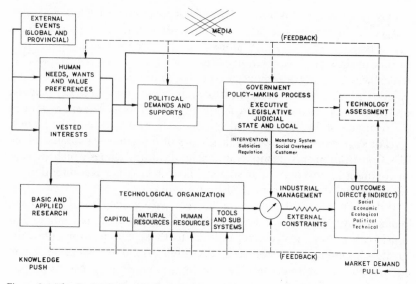

Figure 2.1 The Technological Delivery System

what is said, may furnish clues as to how the system works. That constitutes a second class of information—*about* the system: the lines of authority and responsibility, the power brokers, recent political battles, the status of action papers, the availability of resources, and the decision timetable. Such knowledge is especially valuable in exposing opportunities for access to the power structure, tips that are merchandized by Washington law firms, often of retired insiders who have copies of the "map" and maintain their membership in nonpartisan "old boys' clubs."

Superimposed on the network is another information environment operated by the media, significantly enriching all the formal linkages and providing the only mechanism whereby *all* participants can potentially share in knowing what is happening—and in time to react.

The route by which information is transferred from knowledge producer to knowledge consumer is confused, ambiguous, and subject to all kinds of damage. Messages may be delayed, distorted, impounded, fragmented, tainted, or lost. Those who control information in the system wield the greatest influence by deciding what is filtered or enhanced before release, and what is deliberately withheld. Much as presidents may detest leaks, they or their press officers deliberately act as anonymous sources to manipulate the press (by offering career-related goodies—tips—to tame reporters) and the electorate. Indeed, survival of democracy may depend on the transparency and integrity of that information process.

Having generated this universal model of technological delivery, we can test its validity in specific cases. Assuming that confirmation (and I have yet to discover exceptions in almost one hundred detailed studies that include the U.S. and other nations), a question arises as to how it is possible to deal with so many different species of hardware, such a range of shifting values, the vicissitudes of organizations, changes in the cast of key players, and the novelty introduced by technological innovation. The answers lie in the relative stability of the social system itself, of structure at the highest level of aggregation, and of the basic rules of the game—laws such as the U.S. Constitution and the most fundamental cultural values which are held in common in any particular society. That is how we accommodate to what author Alvin Toffler called future shock.

If the TDS is considered analogous to a wiring diagram of a hi-fi set, policies may be thought of as the music coming through. Listening to that music can be very instructive, both as to those compositions with the greatest harmony, and as to the capacity of the sound reproduction system to function as desired, here producing a concert of great brilliance, harmony, variety, and enjoyment, with the entire nation as audience.

Switching on the System

To understand the interaction of technology with people and politics, we have examined a conceptual model incorporating all of the key actors who play a role in making and carrying out the grand decisions. That TDS diagram of the policy process provides a purely static representation of system attributes and their connections. The process, however, is dynamic. Figuratively then, we can switch on the model by opening communication channels which link participating organizations, and then trace the subsequent animation.

There are two conspicuous triggers for action. The first is scientific discovery or invention. These knowledge producers "push" the technological delivery apparatus to adopt the innovation and translate knowledge to goods or services. Second, there may be crisis, market demand, or pressure from vested interests who perceive or represent a social need or want. These knowledge consumers impose a "pull." Management within the technostructure responds to both stimuli. Sensing either opportunities from discovery or unmet demands, industrial managers evaluate the situation, mobilize the resources, physical and human, reconnoiter impediments, then plan and act.

Such organizational initiative is not independent, however, because government is directly or indirectly involved in almost every transaction. Other signals are injected into the network by governmental apparatus fulfilling the five technological functions mentioned earlier. Public policy provides, therefore, powerful instructions and resources to techno-structure management. What then happens depends critically not only on the policy but on implementation. Returning to the metaphor of the hi-fi set: by listening to the sounds, we can judge both the quality of the musical composition and the quality of the instrument itself.

But by what objective standard can performance be evaluated? The initial proof of the pudding lies in the direct outcomes and whether they measured up to expectations. At one time that was the *only* question society addressed regarding technological innovation. Now, with politics focusing on side effects, there are many more questions. Confidence is still not very high, however, that the public decision system can cope with the fast pace and the kaleidescopic content of technological choice or with the agony of making tradeoffs. Interest always focuses on narrow goals. When policies wobble, there is usually a rush for a new but still circumscribed policy rather than a serious examination of the decision process itself. We don't check on whether shortfalls in performance form a pattern, as though some common disability were undermining *all* policies. Yet if one generic model at the highest level of abstraction can subsume all specific technologies, we should be able to discover generic criteria by which we can describe and judge system performance.

The most powerful evidence of how the system works, and how well it works, is found by observing the behavior of the system when it is under stress. The flash point of a decision is the starting point. From that instant, we can look in both directions. We can search backwards through the legislative history: the detection of a problem, publicity on the issue, advocacy and opposition, the role of facts, the surfacing of alternatives for action, analysis, debate, bargaining, compromise, and finally choice. We can also look beyond the decision, to describe its implementation and consequences. Did the policy achieve intended outputs and the intended distribution of benefits, risks, and costs? Was the implementation efficient? Did it inflame or deter conflict? Were resources for implementation ample? Was management competent to deal with complex and massive technology or, as investigation into the *Challenger* accident suggests, did it suffer from internal information blockages, turf disputes, political favoritism, or cover-up? And we can ask: Was the system itself protected so as to insure stability in social-cultural relationships, desirable power distributions, equitable access to power by all competing interests, and continued vitality of the decision authority to cope with future surprise? And how about the fidelity of information networks for decision making and implementation, monitoring, feedback and social accountability, versatility with internal arrangements and preservation of resources and flexibility to exercise future choices? Finally, we can inquire as to whether widely shared values and our most basic creed were preserved:

were side effects—benefits, costs, and risks—equitably distributed, including effects on future generations?

Day-to-day experience confirms another principle intimated before.
Not only does technology have significant impacts on society. The reverse
is also true: culture has a critical impact on technology. The metaphoric
ship of state may be heavily powered by technological engines, but
collective steering by public policy may be fundamentally driven by
prevailing value preferences. In the 1980s, there are noisy shouts from
militant, single-issue groups, with the loudest voices raised on incandescent moral/religious/ideological grounds and on tax reform, almost
drowning out voices from the 1960s protesting disservice, disenfranchisement, and disamenities and demanding consumer and environmental protection. Of equal potency but not so audible are the voices of
vested interests who espouse "getting government off our backs," a slogan
that may be rhetorical camouflage for vested interests to burrow in further
for special privilege.

The subtle impact of society on technology also results from the social
settings or context of the decision: the cast of characters, including specific
organizations and their most cherished values; their behavior and ethics to
maintain their power status; the constraints of past decisions and of
external events; and the repercussions from earlier and completely separate power struggles. These constitute a dramatic counterpoint to the
notion of "technological impact."

Observing TDS's after they are switched on reveals other general
attributes. Since discrete policy actions animate all participants in a TDS,
the behavior of individuals and institutions may serve as diagnostic tools
so as to reveal values, goals, expectations, capabilities, and relationships.
For example, because institutions are habitually committed to growth in
economic performance or political power, they tend to become self-
centered, coasting on a momentum of past successes and indifferent to
externalities, that is, to the adverse impacts on others.

Careful analysis of the public record shows it far richer in data regarding
TDS behavior than often believed. Among other things causality may be
inferred from a chronology of key events. Next, from the record, we find
that the organizational elements within the system do not maintain fixed
properties. After vigorous interaction with a neighbor or a traumatic
external event, each component is likely to undergo some transformation.
In this respect, social systems are unlike physical systems such as the hi-fi,
where each component is constant regardless of the system in which it is
wired. Also, some malleability occurs because TDS's do not operate in
isolation; all policies interact with others. Basically, therefore, organizations and individuals react in dialectical terms that constitute learning
exercises. Indeed, the failure of policy leadership to learn may reflect

debilitating rigidities in coping with changes wrought either by technology or by shifting popular tides.

In short, we arrive at a striking conclusion: technological delivery systems are not mechanisms. They are organisms!

Third, the loops of individuals and organizations responsible for making decisions may be vastly different from those responsible for implementation. Although separation of these loops is common, the absence of linkage may introduce major shortfalls in ultimate policy performance.

Fourth, vital information in the system is usually controlled by those wrestling for power and contaminated by bias and self-interest. That information in the system also includes feedback. Monitoring the execution of policy thus affords opportunities to take corrective action. Deficiencies are pronounced, however, in systematic data collection and in long time lags in sensing malperformance. Even more troublesome is the deliberate neglect or concealment of malfunctioning by those whose power and prestige may be threatened by change, but who control the information essential to accountability. Investigative reporters have compiled long lists of underperforming weapons systems, but such systems continue to be built and even deployed.

Finally there is the problem of complexity. For instance, historic structures and processes have been subject to disruptions and rapid change. Food production in the nineteenth century could have been represented in a TDS model by only two parties, the farmer/producer and the marketer/consumer. Now, separate entities are involved to provide hybrid seed, irrigation, fertilizer, pesticides, farm machinery, energy, transport, and packaging. And loans. Virtually all of these ostensibly private-sector functions have public-sector counterparts. Agencies to provide price supports, conduct research, construct water supplies, monitor food purity, and arrange for foreign sales make modern food production a galaxy of interrelated elements.

Given the fact that food production today is twenty times more efficient in use of human resources than a century ago, we must conclude that for several decades now we have mastered both the hardware of agriculture and the social management process. In the 1985 uproar over farms threatened by foreclosure simultaneously with cuts in subsidies, we are witnessing some painful withdrawal symptoms. The social process may need vital reform.

In general, a TDS analysis demonstrates that political boundaries no longer constrict traffic. Ecological effects drift willy-nilly. A tanker casualty may involve local environmentalists, state and national regulatory authorities, and claims against a ship owner of one nationality carrying cargo of another and violating rules of a third.

The number of interacting and interdependent elements may be increasing. Goaded and teased by pulses of technological change, these institutions also change. So do the legal ground rules. New communication linkages spring up across functional, national, and cultural boundaries, many fuzzy or hidden. The velocity of change may outpace the natural speed of human activity. Indeed, knowledge may be growing while ignorance is not diminishing; memory and human cognition may be outflanked by a torrent of specialized information.

In short, the problem of TDS operations is not simply one of growing technical complexity. We are concerned with a diversity of societal elements interlinked by complicated networks. They are subject to the jerk of events along with systematic and smoother accommodations to change. The challenge, therefore, is one of keeping the management of technology within bounds of human comprehension.

3 / A Sampling of Issues

Milestones of Technological Policy

or almost a century, the tapestry of technology-intensive public policy which we now live with has been woven one strand at a time. Now, the mesh of innumerable actions is so firm and the patterns so varied that a comprehensive treatment may be overwhelming; it is certainly beyond the scope of this book. Yet some policies, by their novelty, by their high social impact, or by their endurance, merit recognition as milestones. The synoptic catalog on the following page is not intended as an award of distinction, but rather, as an illustration of the range of subjects now encompassed by policy intervention and as a concrete base of examples by which we can test overarching and pervasive characteristics of the public decision process.

This panorama reveals not only the great variety of technologies that have been subject to policy intervention but other important features, such as the institutions affected or the specific functions to be performed. Some policies are intended to develop or stimulate a particular sector, such as for construction of highways or hospitals. Some are specifically to regulate processes, such as transportation or communications, or to protect lives, as with aviation safety and pesticide control. Some policies create new institutions to accommodate novel technologies, such as the AEC and NASA. Some are to provide advisory functions for the president or the Congress—OSTP and OTA, to be specific. Some deal with management of natural resources, such as fisheries and oil, or the entire natural environment. Some deal with weapons development or their control. All are subject to potential amendment or to deliberate suppression by an unsympathetic chief executive when accompanied by an indifferent or flaccid legislature.

1899	Rivers and Harbors Act, to maintain freedom of navigation	PL 55-425
1906	Pure Food Act, to assure safety	PL 59-384
1934	Communications Act, to foster and regulate telephone, radio, and television traffic	PL 73-416
1946	Atomic Energy Act, to create the civilian Atomic Energy Commission and foster peaceful uses of atomic energy	PL 79-585
1947	Insecticide, Fungicide and Rodenticide Act, to protect agricultural workers	PL 80-104
1948	Hospital Survey and Construction Act, to expand hospital facilities in rural areas and set the stage for rapid expansion of health-care delivery	PL 80-725
1950	National Science Foundation Act, to fund basic scientific research	PL 81-507
1954	Atomic Energy Liability Act, in event of an accident to limit liability of private firms in the nuclear industry	PL 83-703
1956	Air Pollution Control Act, to set standards to protect human health	PL 84-159
	Federal Aid to Highways Act, to fund state construction of a national highway network	PL 84-267
1958	National Aeronautics and Space Act, to create NASA and authorize a massive space initiative	PL 85-568
	Food Additives Act, to safeguard human health	PL 85-929
1960	Motor Vehicle Effects Act, to study sources of pollution	PL 86-493
1961	Arms Control and Disarmament Act, to create the Arms Control and Disarmament Agency	PL 87-297
1962	Authorization of research on the B-1 bomber	
1966	Heart Disease, Cancer and Stroke Amendments, to increase priority for research on these diseases	PL 89-239
	Air Pollution Standards Act, to reduce pollution from automobile exhaust	PL 89-272
	Marine Resources and Engineering Development Act, to establish an unprecedented national ocean policy and assign responsibility for policy generation to the president	PL 89-454

1970	National Environmental Policy Act, for the first time establishing guidelines and procedures for environmental protection; also to create the Council on Environmental Quality and the Environmental Protection Agency	PL 91-190
	Occupational Safety and Health Act, to provide for a broad policy and create a single agency for implementation	PL 91-596
	Clean Air Act, to strengthen existing legislation	PL 91-604
1972	Technology Assessment Act, to provide a new future-oriented Office of Technology Assessment (OTA) for Congress and to examine impacts of projected technological initiatives	PL 92-484
	Federal Water Pollution Control Amendments	PL 92-500
	Marine Mammal Protection Act	PL 92-522
	Consumer Product Safety Act, to create a regulatory commission	PL 92-573
	Noise Control Act	PL 92-574
	Coastal Zone Management Act, to encourage states to manage valuable shorelines, balancing preservation with development	PL 92-583
	Ratification of the SALT-1 treaty for arms control	
1973	Clean Air Act	PL 93-319
	National Health Planning and Resources Development Act, to encourage states to institute measures to upgrade quality and reduce duplication of health facilities	PL 93-641
1976	Fishery Conservation and Management Act, to assert national jurisdiction over resources out to 200 miles	PL 94-265
	National Science and Technology Policy Act, to establish a comprehensive policy for the first time and to provide the president with advisory machinery, the Office of Science and Technology Policy (OSTP)	PL 94-282
	Authorization of development of cruise missiles	
	Toxic Substances Control Act	PL 94-469
	Resource Conservation and Recovery Act, to identify the source, transit, and disposal of hazardous waste	PL 94-580
1977	Earthquake Hazard Reduction Act, to foster research on prediction	PL 95-124
	Department of Energy Organization Act, to concentrate all energy development functions in one cabinet-level department	PL 95-91
1978	National Climate Program Act, to initiate	

	research on long-range trends inimical to public welfare	PL 95-367
	Outer Continental Shelf Lands Act Amendments, to alter arrangements by which the public trust of seabed resources is leased for private development	PL 95-372
	Airline Deregulation Act	PL 95-504
1980	Acid Precipitation Act, to study sources and effects of acid rain	PL 96-294
	Fire Prevention and Control Act, to improve research and training capabilities	PL 96-472
	Pacific Northwest Electric Power Planning and Conservation Act, to establish guidelines and an advisory commission to balance development and conservation	PL 96-501
	Nuclear Safety Research, Development, and Demonstration Act	PL 96-567
1981	Product Liability Risk Retention Act, for consumer protection	PL 97-45
1982	Nuclear Waste Policy Act, to establish for the first time a procedure and timetable for the safe disposal of radioactive waste from civilian power plants	PL 97-425
1983	Authorization of construction of the B-1 bomber	PL 98-212

Even this brief inventory of technology-intensive public policies dramatizes how pervasive technology is in our culture, how significant is government policy in its steering, and how great will be the demands on future policy as technology increasingly dominates the culture.

Case Study: How America Killed Its Railroads

Policies represent decisions. At the federal level, they are celebrated by passage of identical bills in both houses of Congress, and signing by the president. These highly visible events are both an end and a beginning. Enactment represents the end of a long history of gestation—from issue identification, advocacy, policy design, debate, and generation of consensus. And it represents the beginning of an open-ended saga of implementation. Each of these two stages raises major generic questions that deserve analysis.

In the first stage, what happens during policy germination such that an issue is given priority over other contenders? Considering the noise level in a vigorous, changing, pluralistic, and cantankerous society, can we characterize which topics win?

Generally, such an issue has five attributes. It is an unsettled question of vital concern, so salient that it has attracted special recognition. Next, it can be phrased with sufficient clarity that it is susceptible to solution. Third, issues almost always open up conflicts among affected parties; indeed, controversy may be the primary evidence that an issue exists. Only when these signals become sufficiently intense is there a concerted effort to formulate solutions, including the drafting of alternatives. Then it is possible to sort out the last key attributes of an issue: that it has ramifications for both advocates and opponents that can be settled only on the political stage, and that both action and inaction have widespread repercussions, lateral and ahead.

Consider, for example, the Highway Trust Fund policy enacted in 1956, Public Law 84-267, which made possible a continental network of first-class roads. The concept of a nationwide system of highways was conceived in 1923 as a result of studies by General Pershing. Those primitive concepts were further advanced during the Depression, and some were implemented as a source of jobs. But serious policy initiatives had to wait until after the dust of World War II had settled. By the early 1950s, there was roaring advocacy. What was first rationalized on grounds of national defense and full employment of returning servicemen soon erupted into a parade of all those drivers having a love affair with the auto, who wanted a system of roads to travel coast-to-coast without a traffic light.

America got its wish. Legislative action was slowed down only by a debate on how to pay. In 1985, the system of roughly 50,000 miles was essentially complete. But implementation, the second stage, has had grave repercussions.

This is how America killed its railroads.

As intercity travel grew by air, but especially by car, railway passenger traffic declined. Railroad management abetted that trend by failing to replace rolling stock worn out through heavy wartime use, and by cutting costs on cleanliness, comfort, and convenience. Because passenger service was never as profitable as freight, the industry accepted a decline in passenger traffic with equanimity, even with quiet pleasure. Overlooked in this entire calculus was how riders felt about the truncated service, when, for example, the number of scheduled trains that in 1920 approached 20,000 dropped by 1980 to about 250. And no one considered what the impact might be if an oil moratorium or an increase in world oil prices led to fuel rationing and crippled private use of automobiles.

Belatedly, the railroads also discovered that their freight service was jeopardized by competition from truckers. Unit trains could still carry loads of such bulk commodities as coal and wheat cheaper than could trucks. But the vast quantity of break-bulk cargo was moving intercity by truck, including overseas shipments that were arriving in containers as readily dispatched from ship to truck and trailer as to a rail car.

The financial crisis of the railroads attracted national attention, necessitating eventually both a public bailout and a subsidy. The Conrail enterprise was invented as a management device to keep the railroads of the Northeast operating, eventually at a profit. And Amtrak was introduced to insure continuation, albeit limited, of intercity passenger service. Meanwhile, commuter lines were being subsidized by state and local government. By 1985, the effectiveness of even these lifesaving measures was uncertain.

Curiously enough, with highway transportation even more competitive because the public would be underwriting the roadbed, the railroads did not lobby in sufficient time with sufficient vigor to challenge highway policy. For one thing, they were the captives of an obsolete notion, dating to the 1920s, that roads built with federal subsidies "to get the farmer out of the mud" would help the railroads because these arteries primarily connected the outlying farms to their depots. Only after the momentum for superhighways was unstoppable did the railroads raise alarms on the degree to which trucking should be taxed to cover the added costs of pavement to sustain loads from trucks as well as private cars. But it was too late.

Even though the political process usually depends for some of its wisdom on cries of distress from interests adversely affected by a technological initiative, hindsight reveals that if broader transportation needs of the country had been treated comprehensively rather than mode by mode, there would have been early warning of the risk of killing the railroads. In the face of the popular will to concrete the countryside, supported in 1952 by both presidential candidates, it is very doubtful that the highway program would have been arrested. Indeed, there is very little reason, in retrospect, to feel that insofar as highways alone are concerned, the policy is anything but a huge success. With foresight, however, mitigating measures could have been introduced sooner to head off the costs in taxes for railroad resuscitation and the loss in service that, as compared to superlative passenger trains abroad, may prove even more tragic in the future.

The point of this anecdote is not so much to pinpoint rail transportation as it is to highlight a general problem. The more massive a technology, the greater seems to be the political momentum for implementation and the greater the difficulty in identifying the tradeoffs occasioned by its accomplishment. This is especially true when government itself promotes a technology, develops a comfortable relationship with private interests, and then loses both objectivity and vision in representing the public interest. Perhaps in 1985, the Strategic Defense Initiative is following a similar course.

In the past, when the realities of the tradeoffs demanded correction, the nation was relatively rich enough and resilient enough that it could institute remedies without too much pain. There was wealth, and there was political maneuvering room. Now there is a haunting question as to whether the reserves of purse and of national purpose have dwindled to such an extent that we cannot pay the bills for neutralizing unwanted side effects, outcomes which could have been anticipated but were not.

No Sick Leave for Robots

The art of social forecasting is frequently disparaged as pure guesswork at best and chicanery at worst. Nevertheless, it has been practiced for decades and has a better track record than often credited. In the commercial world, it wears the label of market research, the attempt to determine the potential of future sales of a particular product or service. This means sampling public needs and wants, attitudes and tastes, affluence and disposable income; and it entails the monitoring of trends. Also researched are demographic forecasts as to market size—for example, the number of teenagers buying phonograph records, the shift in population over age sixty-five, the number of single-parent families, the extent of migration to the Sunbelt. Finally, estimates are made of the competition and its tactics.

Most industrial enterprises employ this management tool to stay in business. Looking ahead successfully affords lead time for planning, mustering resources, retooling production equipment, and establishing distribution networks. Similarly, firms try to predict the future costs and reliability of supply for critical materials, the availability and cost of skilled labor, and the amount of capital needed for plant expansion.

While specialists peer ahead at the market potential, there is a corresponding effort to forecast progress in science and engineering around which a new product or service may be woven. Are breakthroughs likely that would provide a competitive edge, at least for a while? Can invention be protected by a watertight patent? Can innovation be artificially stimulated? What fields of science are going through stages of rapid discovery that promise commercial application and warrant accelerated engineering development (and advertising) and transfer to the production line?

One technology late in the 1970s that was subject to such research and led to swift diffusion is robotics. The industrial robot is a machine that has the mechanical dexterity to perform tasks usually performed by skilled humans. Whatever operations and sequences are desired can be programmed into the control apparatus. Or the robot can be equipped with sensors so as to distinguish assorted conditions in its external environment and respond according to instructions to accommodate variability. While the robot is dumb and performs best with repeated operations on long production runs, it can be guided with sophisticated computer programs to custom-produce even small batches.

When perfected, the robot offers innumerable advantages over its human model. It can repeat operations at higher speed, and with conspicuously higher precision. That capacity affords reliable control of quality. Unlike its human counterpart, the robot never tires. There are no unions that require bargaining over wages, vacations, or health benefits. In short, the robot is fully subject to management control. Given these advantages, the robot's industrial proliferation is not surprising. This explosion first occurred in Japan, but the United States is swiftly catching up.

To be sure, some costs are higher because this evolution transforms a function from one that was labor-intensive to one that is capital-intensive. Higher skills must be expected of the remaining human workers, and there must be changes in management style to prevent anomie. The firm is thus obliged to investigate which short- and long-term direct costs must and can be internalized. Into this calculation must also be factored enhancement of product attractiveness, especially in terms of higher uniformity, quality, reliability, and of course, lower sales price.

There are, however, significant external costs, economic and social. While some assembly-line workers can be retrained, many cannot and lose their jobs. This imposes a painful burden on them and their families in loss of stability, earning power, and self-esteem. Then come the interventions by a compassionate society: unemployment benefits, food stamps, Medicaid, subsidized housing, and other elements of a safety net. Immediately, we can see the connections of robot technology with public policy.

In 1946, the federal government took a serious look at the prospect of future unemployment, legislating a Full Employment Act. In 1978, through the Full Employment and Balanced Growth Act, the threshhold of unemployment considered socially unacceptable enough to trigger alarm and intervention was set at 4 percent of the work force. Memories of suffering during the Depression were still sharp, and there was a collective public concern that this not happen again.

By the 1980s it was clear that the full employment policy was being largely ignored; then it was disowned. In 1985, unemployment had dropped from highs of 13 percent three years earlier to about 7 percent, but there was little prospect that it would be shrunk further, and government policy was directed more toward questions of deficit reduction, improved trade balances, and income tax reform. Indeed, the government sought continuously to paint a rosy economic picture in which unemployment was drowned out by other economic indicators. Yet this prospect of long-term unemployment translates to about ten million families. The rush to robotics in the United States insinuates an even heavier loss in jobs, but failure to respond to the threats of foreign competition which benefit from robotics poses a different risk. This enigma is typical of the emerging predicaments of a technological society and demonstrates the unlikelihood of facile solutions.

History teaches, incidentally, that there have been repeated cycles of technology-induced displacements of the work force, at one time firing up the so-called Luddite revolution, which sought to turn back the clock by smashing factory equipment. But it also teaches that over the long haul technology is durably embraced as a midwife of social progress, that painful transitions can be expected, but that solutions must usually be sought in social rather than technical innovation. Past dislocations have been eventually absorbed, but always as new markets opened up domestically and internationally. Today, that quest may require the United States to adopt a completely different strategy, to match the alacrity of other nations that have found a key to public-private partnerships.

The anomaly is that, while the industrial sector is so aggressive in its search for opportunities and in its tactics to avoid impediments to growth, *a similar practice of foresight is absent in the public arena.* Repeatedly, unpalatable social implications of technological innovation have surfaced, attracting public, even political, attention. Yet the policy apparatus acts with great viscosity, if at all, in the presence of early warning. In Chapter 5 we decipher why.

The robotics revolution seems unaccompanied by a determined and focused examination of broader cultural ramifications. In that regard, the case of robotics is not unique. It might therefore be illuminating to survey a selection of other technology-related issues which earned newspaper headlines between 1970 and 1978 but which, unlike the instances yielding explicit technological policy, had not been politically resolved by 1986:

1970   Automobile air bags were proposed as a safety measure; requirements were unresolved in 1985.

Steps were proposed to deregulate airlines so as to foster their economic viability; legislation was enacted in 1979, leading to many new commuter lines, but by 1986 bankruptcy or its threat occurred in several major airlines.

Amtrak was created to preserve limited passenger railroad service, yet many services were later cut; in 1984, there was discussion of further reducing subsidies, in 1985, of eliminating them altogether.

Health effects of cigarette smoking were confirmed, leading to warnings on labels and some restrictions in advertising; despite additional evidence of harm, in 1985 tobacco subsidies continued.

Costs of health care—then amounting to 6% of the GNP—were causing alarm, but major policy initiatives at cost containment were frustrated by the hospital and medical lobbies; health maintenance organizations were encouraged as a step toward reform but have not been subsequently fostered; by 1986, costs had escalated to 11% of the GNP, and no overarching policy was in sight.

The B-1 bomber was advanced as a follow-up of aging B-52s, but was declared obsolete and costly compared to airborne cruise missiles; in 1983, the issue was reexamined and B-1 production approved, even though production of cruise missiles was sharply expanded; by 1986, the B-1 decision was being reevaluated in light of imminent production of the "stealth" bomber.

Siting of nuclear power plants drew objections because of charges of unsafe locations or design; notwithstanding the energy crisis in the middle 1970s and the sharply increased prices, new plant orders terminated; by 1980, 15 plants under construction were aborted, some in the aftermath of the 1979 incident at Three Mile Island; by 1982, research on nuclear power was accelerated, while government funding of such alternative sources as solar energy was sharply curtailed.

Industrial chemicals, many of them known and others suspected to be hazardous, were increasing in number and application; despite new legislation in 1983 to authorize EPA to regulate such materials, information on health effects was known concerning only about 200 of the 20,000 or so materials in common use.

A breakthrough in weapons development led to policy approval of MIRV warheads, multiply targeted reentry vehicles; the Soviets emulated this innovation, and in 1984, studies revealed that the stability of arms control was jeopardized; consideration was being given to the policy of one warhead per vehicle.

The continued use of high-sulphur coal was questioned because of higher air pollution, yet its regulation was successfully fought by eastern coal producers, who had more support than western producers who were marketing low-sulphur fuel; in subsequent years, evidence was mounting that severe environmental damage was occurring in New England and Eastern Canada because of the acid rain from such combustion; attempts to step up research were thwarted until 1980 and regulation still opposed by the president in 1985.

1973   In light of the Arab oil embargo, attention turned to the potential of oil shale as a domestic source of petroleum, a step which U.S. energy companies had long pushed intensively, provided development was fostered by a federal subsidy; in 1978, they succeeded in having such legislation passed; by 1984, all but one of the pilot plants had been shut down because the prospects were poor for extraction at a cost that could compete with the world crude price at the time, a price which shrank even further in 1986.

1978 Fraud through the use of computers was increasing; financial institutions were reluctant to admit losses for fear of inciting further theft; subsequently, the number of break-ins to computer facilities and networks, including those of military installations, credit stystems, and personal records, increased even more because of inadequate or inept security precautions; questions arose as to whether existing laws were a satisfactory deterrent.

Technologies related to human reproduction—*in vitro* fertilization, surrogate mothering, and abortion—were apparently well developed; intense lobbying erupted on both sides as to legal constraints.

From these few examples, we discover that an issue often reached a high level of inflammation and public concern many years, even decades, before policy intervention. It is clear that the time had to be just right: the problem had to be highly visible, perhaps of crisis proportions; the political atmosphere had to be congenial to movement. This does not necessarily mean harmony among conflicting public views. Ideology if not idealism is still a viable political commodity. Yet the different vectors of pressure must have spawned a resultant such that the political judgment deemed action preferable to inaction. But look at all the unfinished business.

With impeccable hindsight, we also find many policies went awry. There have been serious gaps in action; sometimes zigs and zags of unproductive, myopic, even wrong-headed response. Or delay. Later, I will try to explain why.

In sins of either omission or commission, the portfolio of technologically loaded issues expands because the burden of unresolved dilemmas is compounded by the constant eruption of new dilemmas. As the backlog grows and as the pace of effective intervention lags, the agenda of unfinished business accumulates and tempts hasty action. More choices have to be made, but there is no more available time to choose.

Under that stress, anxiety rises, and the probability of impetuous choice multiplies, with all the penalties of poor judgment that we experience in moments of personal recklessness. *Every* decision becomes endangered. Thus appears a very high incentive for generic remedies to a common pathology.

4 / Technology and Risk

umankind has forever lived at risk. Throughout history, there have been risks of bodily harm from accidents, disease, wild animals, natural disasters, and extremes of weather. And there has been overhanging violence at the hands of other people. The reality of perils has been continuous and widespread. Even in the twentieth century, we wonder about progress in risk reduction beyond greater control of wild animals and disease.

Apart from bodily harm, risks may be psychological and emotional: the risks of coercion; of deprivation of basic human rights, freedom, and dignity; of deprivation of equitable access to resources; of opportunities for self-fulfillment. In the West, there has been demonstrable progress in these respects, but even so, personal security is not unconditionally guaranteed.

So we must live with the sober truth that there is no such thing as zero risk. This caveat, however, does not diminish two unheralded hallmarks of civilization: the eternal quest for greater safety, and its eternally uneven achievement, because new risks arise as their precursors are quelled.

Today, all of these concerns have become more poignant because of technology, its influence in human affairs, and its capacity for indirect and sometimes harmful impacts. What an irony, given that technologies have almost always been introduced to reduce risk. With the bomb, nuclear power plants, the proliferation of fossil fuels, information management, electronic surveillance, genetic manipulation, and toxic substances, completely new dangers have been generated, of greater scale, intensity, speed of injection, or ubiquity. Not only is the scope extended geographically. The risks can become a hidden endowment for our progeny. Hazards may or may not be worse for the individual than what has gone before, but they clearly pose a different challenge to the human species as a whole. Today the human race has an entirely new portfolio of risks.

Given the venerable craving for safety, under these threatening circumstances, how safe *is* safe? Agreeing that safety is the absence of risk but that risk cannot be abolished, what threshhold level is acceptable? Can that condition be derived by scientific theory?

The first thing we must recognize is that safety in terms of acceptable risk is a social judgment. No number expressing acceptable risk can be derived analytically. Investigating how safe is safe involves two considerations. The first is a technical matter of estimating the twin components of risk—the probabilities of occurrence and the severity of harm. These can be based on what we know. The second consideration is based on what we believe: the cultural and ethical factors that revolve around norms in valuation of a human life, or of property, or of the natural environment. At stake are tradeoffs, say, between life and the costs of measures for its protection and extension, or between one risk and another. Salient are perceptions as to whether those at risk are the source of risk or the unconsenting victims of initiatives by others, and whether these exposures are subject to human control.

This opens a question about disparities between perceived risk and actual risk. These do not arise from different technical approaches. Exaggerated perceptions stem from low public confidence in those institutions expected to manage risk because the institutions seem remote and their accountability diffused, or their bureaucracy's goals diverted from high performance. Witness the unfocused anxieties over nuclear power. Differences also arise from heightened expectations of safety in a more civilized society, from unbalanced media publicity, and from just plain confusion by those biased or uninformed. Or the reverse: the perceptions of smoking hazards, which are suppressed, distorted, or inhibited because the situational risk *is* completely under individual control.

In estimating the consequences of a threat and the probability of occurrence, we must distinguish between two classes of events. Some occur often enough to be statistically accountable, but with a range of consequences that are implicitly acceptable, or at least susceptible to control. In the second class are those rare events that are catastrophic in their effects and under no conditions acceptable. At one time, only these acute risks attracted public notice, as with heavy loss of life from a fire at sea on a passenger vessel. Since the 1960s, the less visible, chronic risks such as exposure to asbestos have captured attention, and then legislative action.

Dealing with cultural and ethical dimensions of the safety enigma, however, goes beyond statistics. Different cultures place different values on human life. And these standards change with time. Universally, there are subtle collective judgments, and practical limits as to how much trouble and expense a society will be willing to invest to reduce fatalities or extend life. There are collateral judgments on the acceptability of different kinds of risks and on questions of equity between whoever generates risks versus those who bear them.

For society to judge how safe is safe enough, there must first be simple awareness. Although the general public has always been an affected party in technological enterprise, it was often unaware of imminent decisions and possible hazards. Moreover, the general public was seldom represented in the bargaining by key parties at interest. Until activists such as Ralph Nader courageously publicized the fact that GM's Corvair was "unsafe at any speed," and until the subsequent formation of organizations representing consumer and environmental interests and the work of a few investigative reporters, most people even lacked access to information essential to realizing their exposure to risk and strategies for its mitigation. Those enterprises which generated risk never advertised the situation, and many sought to conceal it. Johns-Manville's knowledge of lethal asbestos hazards four decades before judicial intervention is a case in point. At least, that was the situation before the 1970 enactment of the National Environmental Policy Act and its requirement for impact analysis. Not that NEPA was the only legislative remedy, but it is symbolic of a cultural shift.

In effect, we had an age of technological innocence. To some extent, we still have one. Only after the Bhopal, India, chemical disaster in 1985 did residents of Institute, West Virginia, learn that they had been exposed to similar risks at the nearby Union Carbide plant, where safety reporting requirements had been violated.

Even today, few people understand the hardware, and they are not comforted by expert opinion, especially when it is mustered on all sides of an argument. For one thing, attitudes toward risk by the expert and by the nonexpert differ radically. The expert tends toward overconfidence in numerics and in the capacity to control risk, whereas most other people feel vulnerable to risks that they are politically impotent to control, no matter how sweet the assurances from technology's advocates. This anxiety is further inflamed because research has produced information on the nature of risk faster than mechanisms have been put in place to abate that risk. And all too often, technocrises are exploited by a headline-hunting media corps. No wonder there have been frantic searches for risk reduction without a recognition that in almost every case strenuous tradeoffs are involved.

The purpose of government regulation of technology is to protect the public from a wide range of technological hazards, in other words, to manage risk. Over the years, the government has mandated immunization to improve public health; antitrust measures to block monopoly pricing; food and drug standards to assure purity; surveillance of ships, planes, and railroads for enhanced passenger safety; and protection against polluted air and water or toxic substances. In broadest terms, these initiatives are intended to reduce uncertainty and surprise, to enhance the visibility of cause-effect relationships, to anticipate lateral and future impacts and counter deafness to early warning, to illuminate alternatives, especially those that spur prevention and exercise of responsibility by all parties, and to reconcile conflicts between and among public and private or other contending interests.

How the process achieves these goals is far more perplexing because of the need to scan for tradeoffs. In 1985, the President's Council on Environmental Quality called for intramural standards in methodology for risk analysis.

Paradoxically, there is the possibility that machinery and legislation put into place to reduce public risk may add so much to social complexity that it inadvertently increases risk. For beyond a certain critical size, government activity extracts such high transaction costs for internal communications and coordination, and breeds such social incoherence and inadvertent conflict, that the entire decision process may be disabled. Well-intentioned risk abatement may sometimes prove counterproductive.

Along with the executive and legislative branches of government, the judiciary branch is also in the risk management act. Courts adjudicate liabilities and award damages, but always after the fact. Seldom has the court system operated in an anticipatory mode. Now, however, they deal with litigation over whether risk management processes meet legislative intent, as when ruling on completeness but not content of environmental impact analyses. The courts have also established new principles in such matters as mandating that when parties, including the government, know they are a source of risk, they have a fiduciary responsibility to warn the public. In 1985, such bold concepts were being put to the test.

Later, we will explore the need to involve all stakeholders in the risk assessment process, early on. In this way, tradeoffs can be illuminated so as to foster informed judgment on equity and on ways to diminish conflict. Then society can choose how safe is safe enough.

When Voluntary Risk Becomes Involuntary

Exposure to risk can be voluntary or involuntary. Not only are there differences in the concurrence of the persons at risk; there are also markedly different attitudes in the levels of acceptability. That is to say, when people are unwilling or unwitting targets, when they feel they have no control, or when many lives are at stake, they demand greater protection from risks than when there are dangers having their knowledge and consent.

The field of transportation offers examples regarding both involuntary and voluntary risk. In these matters of public safety, government first intervened about 150 years ago because of the heavy loss of life from explosions of steamboat boilers. The public clamored for protection, and the government responded with study initiatives (the first research grant ever sponsored), design rules, and inspections. Not long after, government became involved with railroads because of head-on collisions and breaking rails. Then came safety regulation of passenger vessels to minimize threats of fire at sea and collision. More recently, the focus shifted to aircraft. As planes grew larger and lost more passengers in crashes, greater regulatory supervision was demanded. The public simply would not tolerate frequent events involving heavy loss of life, and as it has after each rash of calamities, it used the political process to make known its threshhold levels of risk. Flying in commercial airliners became considered "safe," both because safety regulation has fostered a low accident rate and because the public has confidence in the process whereby government oversees common carriers. The sharp increase in fatalities in 1985 has forced a new cycle of attention, however, because the open competition caused by deregulation has led to the founding of many new airlines and to tendencies to cut costs; because, in the aftermath of the air controllers' strike, the Federal Aviation Administration has cut the number of experienced air controllers; and because the FAA budget was cut further.

Passengers in all types of common carriers consider themselves at involuntary risk. When public transportation is chosen because of speed, convenience, or price, passengers forego options in comfort, privacy, schedules, routes, stops, and destinations. In a practical sense, they have lost control over their situation and expect a high degree of protection. As said before, so it is in commercial aviation.

On the other hand, passengers in small private planes, called general aviation, are considered to have chosen that mode of transportation voluntarily, with the presumed advantage of maintaining options. While such aircraft are subject to safety inspection and while flight operations are subject to some air lane rules, the required level of safety is significantly lower than for commercial systems. With the latter, the number of passenger-miles per fatality is perhaps a hundred times greater than in general aviation. Thus with private aircraft, passengers are assumed to have made a conscious choice in trading off risk for freedom from constraints of commercial travel.

Another example lies in skiing. Cable lifts that carry skiers to the top of the run are regulated by local authorities as common carriers because the participants are regarded as not having a choice in means for reaching the top. And once on, they have no choice as to when they get off. They are at involuntary risk. The lift is consequently subject to close safety regulation. Coming down, however, the skiers are on their own, at voluntary risk so to speak. If the number of accidents going up were as numerous as those coming down, there would be hell to pay by public outcry, and insurance rates would be prohibitive.

Safety on the highways has received attention because of the high fatality rate and the continuous exposure of innocent victims. Drivers are subject to tests and licensing. Vehicles are subject to safety requirements in manufacture, and in many states to annual inspection. To be eligible for federal subsidy, state roads must avoid dangerous curves and reduced visibility on hills. Local jurisdictions have a plethora of rules for safe driving, police surveillance, and penalties for infractions. All of these regulatory constraints have been generated by public demand. Now that the public realizes that a very high fraction of fatalities is associated with drunken driving, it has pressured the political apparatus for more severe penalties. All because of the involuntary risks to even safe drivers.

This question of voluntary versus involuntary risk has been somewhat blurred in matters of consumer protection in that the public has increasingly demanded safer products for which they have clear purchase options. Product liability has become a pronounced field of jurisprudence. But the fuzziness continues, much of it prompted by politics tilted under imbalanced pressures of vested interests. Smoking is well documented as injurious to health, the source of premature death, and, according to OTA, the source of enormous economic as well as social cost. But it is considered a voluntary risk. Politically imposed regulation has gone only so far as to require labelling or separation of smokers in work or public spaces.

The degree to which governments may intervene in private voluntary risk is thus unsettled. The same cannot be said of technological enterprises affecting large numbers of people involuntarily, and it is those which characterize modern society.

Ignorance, Error, Blunder, Folly, and Mischief

Daily life is loaded with technologically induced frustrations: a car that won't start, a power outage from an unpredicted storm, or even a missing part in an assemblage for a Christmas-time mechanical toy. Frustration turns to shock and anger when a bridge fails, a plane falls out of the sky, a spacecraft shuttle explodes, a hospital patient unexpectedly dies, or a trainload of hazardous material is spilled.

Who or what is to blame? In a healthy search for villains, we can often pinpoint the cause and thus prevent repetition of the accident. Such a quest for safety is driven by a single principle, our value on human life. We are unwilling to accept unnecessary deaths or injuries, especially to unsuspecting subjects of risk.

In much of the twentieth century, we have believed in machines with an abiding faith that ranged from blind adoration to authentic experience that some hardly ever fail. Witness the reliability of the modern refrigerator. We have believed that, with talented engineering, systematic proof testing, and service experience, every piece of hardware can be made equally perfect—if we are willing to pay the price, for economics plays a major role in the safety equation.

Fundamentally, decisions on acceptable risk involve tradeoffs. Where the consequences of premature failure do not entail serious loss in lives, wealth, or ecological integrity, people will accept a cheaper product of poorer quality or shorter durability. If only functional inconvenience is at stake, buyers are expected to beware and consult consumer research reports. But such tradeoffs are not socially acceptable if they endanger lives of consumers. That is why government agencies on auto safety insist on recalls.

Today, as technology grows more complex, any malfunctioning machine triggers study not only of individual products but also of complex technical systems. These systems involve people as well as machines, so that failures can be traced to human shortcomings as well as to mechanical. It is perhaps ironic that machines introduced to replace the less reliable human function are still vulnerable to human fallibility. Recall the nursery rhyme about a kingdom that was lost because a horse was lost, in turn from a shoe that was lost because a shoenail was lost: no one seemed interested in pinning down the fault as between a defective nail and sloppy blacksmithing. There was no National Transportation Safety Board to investigate.

Only after major loss of life on trains, ships, manned spacecraft and planes, and in buildings has attention converged on the human element. What investigators uncovered in these systems was that *people* were usually the major source of failure. Not only is there human error, as we define mistakes in judgment. Also triggering calamity are ignorance, blunder, folly, and mischief. Roughly 80 percent of maritime accidents, for example, stem from human factors: faulty determination of ship position, not maintaining a lookout, overloading, indifference to weather, violation of navigation rules, and problems with alcohol and drug abuse. Curiously enough, in the 1970s, as the Coast Guard required more technological aids for ship navigation, the number of accidents did not shrink. Indeed, there was the appearance of a syndrome called the "radar-assisted collision," a situation where overconfidence in the hardware went hand-in-hand with inadequate personnel training, faulty equipment calibration, muddled procedural rules, or inadequate emphasis on professional, human responsibility.

Given the inevitability of human imperfection, we try to make intricate and dangerous technological systems both foolproof and damnfoolproof. For otherwise, nature is sure to find the hidden flaw. Sometimes this is in operation of hardware, sometimes in management decisions. In the twenty-first century we will utilize technologies more, not less. And these are likely to be as complex as today's, and as potent in generating risk. Contrary to the myth of the intelligent machine, people will continue to be involved in design, manufacture, testing, operation, and servicing.

Nowhere is this challenge more sharply defined than in control of nuclear weapons. Already we have experienced false alarms when early warning apparatus failed or spurious warnings were generated through mistaken radar interpretations of Canada geese or a rising moon.

Apart from human inadvertence, we cannot ignore mischievous intent. Terrorism, for example, may erupt from pathological mixtures of zealous religiosity and a disdain for human life, now far more worrisome because of technological leverage.

How do we upgrade the competence of human decision making to match the demands of the hardware? Or could it be that by information overload and complexity, or by mechanical actions whose speed outpaces human response time, technologies are "stretching the mind beyond the end of its tether"? Clearly, higher skills are called for. But reducing the scope of human fallibility may demand more than simple technical skill. We must renew cultural values of personal and corporate responsibility and integrity, along with a heightened pride of craftsmanship. That is the only route, for example, to improve the performance of weapon systems that repeatedly fail quality inspections or performance requirements at enormous cost to taxpayers and higher risk to the nation's security.

Apart from systems failing because of human error in design or operation, they also fail for want of adequate maintenance. Indeed, in all technical systems, one reality is that after installation all require careful monitoring. But such checking is expensive. In the 1980s, when an epidemic of highway potholes and dangerously weakened bridges was reported and euphemistically called "problems of infrastructure," the trigger for surprise was never made clear. Because the federal government picked up 90 percent of the tab for *new* highways, states had opted for two decades to put up the remaining 10 percent for new construction by transferring funds from maintenance budgets. Is this a consequence of human error or blunder? Or does it fit the pattern of situations where lessons are ignored that contribute to what Barbara Tuchman eloquently called "the march of folly"?

With all technologies, safety is an issue, whether explicitly or implicitly.

Thus *every* technology-intensive policy incorporates a decision as to acceptable risk. The public is entitled to know not only what the overall degree of risk may be, but also what may be the special vulnerability to human error—thus not to be lulled into the fallacy that substitution of machines for humans guarantees reliability.

Engineering with Margins of Safety

Virtually all technological artifacts are engineered. That is to say, buildings, dams, automobiles, telephones, kitchen aids, and even some toys are deliberately proportioned and interconnected to perform a particular function through steps of requirements analysis, design, construction, and testing. Collectively, these processes make up the professional practice of engineering.

Until the last century, designs were based largely on trial and error. Artisans would build something—a Gothic cathedral for example—and if it collapsed, they would attempt to learn from that bitter experience and improve on the next version. Thus, empirical rules were adopted and standardized. A century and a half ago, engineering began to base design more systematically on fundamentals from natural science, especially from classical physics. The strength of structures and materials, the flow of fluids, the thermodynamic transfer of energy, the exploitation of electromagnetic phenomena—all were the subject of study in the laboratory. Engineering became technically far more precise. But rules from empirical experience could not be entirely discarded. Most significant among these rules was the adoption of arbitrary margins for safety.

In social terms, the safety margin is an act of professional responsibility to protect the general public and the user from bodily harm, economic loss, or functional inconvenience. It is a technique to reduce risk to socially acceptable levels. This very act is what distinguishes engineering as a profession rather than as simply a calling. It also reflects the distinction between scientists, endeavoring to understand nature, and engineers, who are called upon to control natural phenomena for human benefit.

In technical terms, in structural engineering the safety margin is usually an arbitrary addition to expected or specified loading. If its value is taken as four, then the structure or machine being designed should be able to sustain a load before failure of four times the expected, the excess quantity representing an overload that constitutes the safety or contingency margin. If the floor in a building must carry heavy filing cabinets that impose loads of 40 pounds per square foot, joists, beams, girders, and columns would be proportioned as though the loading were 160. By making the structure or machine several times larger than necessary to carry the specified loading, engineers reduce risks from uncertainties. Such uncertainties arise because many design factors are inexact, indeterminate, or not subject to control. Materials are not uniform in strength; they corrode or are weakened by fatigue with oscillating loads or by exposure to radiation. External forces may exceed design limits; surprise forces from earthquake or collisions may not have been anticipated. Quality control in fabrication may be clumsy, or maintenance may be lacking. Even the engineering principles have gaps, especially if the object has never been built before at that scale, and the designer's imagination may have been flaccid. Finally, there is the possibility of human abuse and the demons of error, idiocy, blunder, and mischief. From the point of view of risk reduction, high safety margins are indicated. But the extra material imposes extra cost or weight, leading to loss in functional performance. The most demanding skill in engineering design may thus be the *acute weighing of tradeoffs*.

The sheer beauty of precise design is suggested by Oliver Wendell Holmes' poem "The Deacon's Masterpiece." In that parable, the designer so carefully proportioned and crafted the "wonderful one-hoss shay" that when it expired, every element failed simultaneously. None was a whit too large or a whit too small. Now, however, engineers are inclined to use fail-safe criteria wherein an overload might permanently warp an aircraft wing, for instance, without its rupture.

Besides overload margins, another principle can be invoked to increase safety, or to reduce the consequence of failure. This is the notion of redundancy, of having alternative pathways to sustain satisfactory operation, or to limit damage, in event of casualty. But these fail-safe approaches also have costs.

A third approach to risk reduction is to proof-test exhaustively a prototype of the engineered product. Unknowns in design methods can be explored by this technique and then increasingly refined so as to lead to lower margins of risk.

Finally, safety margins can be increased by such steps as fine quality control in manufacture or fabrication, preventive maintenance, regular inspection for aging, and discipline over abuse.

Even with all these precautions, however, there have been failures. In 1940, the Tacoma Narrows suspension bridge in the state of Washington was set into self-excited vibration by high winds blowing on the delicate web of roadway and wires. It collapsed. The cause was the engineer's lack of imagination as to forces of wind-induced oscillations because no suspension bridge had ever before displayed this aerodynamic instability. In 1975, the Teton Dam in Idaho collapsed because geological weaknesses at its juncture with the canyon wall had been overlooked. In 1976, a major air collision resulted from human error in the control tower. In 1977, a large oil spill at the Bravo rig in the North Sea resulted from an error in the drilling procedure. As said before, human fallibility is often the cause of such accidents, and margins of safety cannot compensate for all such eventualities. Later, we consider *Challenger* and Chernobyl.

Good engineering also cannot forestall failures in technological functioning caused by political factors. In the 1980s for example, highway bridges have been collapsing with embarassing frequency. Most were old and corroded. The problem, however, was not only loss in load-carrying capacity due to age. Many failures could be attributed to increases permitted in truck weights, far beyond design specifications. Highway engineers knew and warned of this risk. But under intense pressure from the trucking lobbies, state legislatures and the federal government caved in and relaxed load limits. No matter how rational an analysis, it is impossible to anticipate the influence of politics on engineering. Could a coincidence of the *Challenger* launch on the morning of a State of the Union message have impaired the judgment of the managers?

A similar problem has been exposed with the malperformance of weapons systems. All too often, defense officials pressed the design beyond the state of the art. Requirements were continuously increased; modifications went untested. Then, for reasons of institutional momentum, safeguarding of contracts, or the prestige and career prospects of individual project leaders or policy officials, production was ordered before prototypes were debugged.

Incidentally, the concept of margins has very wide application. To protect health, permissible levels of toxic chemicals or radioactivity are established with arbitrary margins. So too when extrapolating results of potentially harmful drugs from tests of animals to human dosage.

To recapitulate, there are no absolute guarantees against failure, only probabilities. The generally high performance of engineered products confirms the effectiveness of the safety-margin concept in socioeconomic enterprise. However, engineers usually have only a single opportunity to reduce risk in the course of their design. Occasionally they can intervene in systems operation, especially as data unfold on close shaves, encounters that spotlight vulnerability and provide the opportunity for correctives; registering and analyzing patterns of near-misses have been effectively used by the Federal Aviation Administration to improve airline safety.

The importance of performance monitoring suggests that society usually has multiple opportunities to control risk, *provided* that information on dangers is present and that there is a political will to take prophylactic action. Nevertheless, it is ironic that as society is exposed to more technology-induced perils such as the prospects of "launch-on-warning" of nuclear-tipped missiles, we have not invested as much energy and imagination to reducing risk by mitigating the *need* for a hair trigger as we have to invent new species of defense hardware.

As noted above, the rational introduction of safety margins by technicians can be undermined by political considerations. Often, these tradeoffs
are made without the benefit of cool-headed analysis; instead, they are
nudged one way or another by political pressures, the emotional content of
the situation, and the weighing of political risks to the decider. This is why
the question of technology-induced risk goes beyond a narrow inquiry as
to reliability of the hardware. With technologically heightened exposure
to danger, we are additionally obliged to inquire as to the satisfactory
functioning of political institutions who manage the hardware. Do *they*
have fail-safe practices?

Grim Ferry Tales: A Case Study in the Politics of Risk

Puget Sound, in the northwest corner of the state of Washington, plays
host to an archipelago of rare beauty and charm. Its four major islands are
served by ferries, some large enough to carry 2,500 passengers and 200
vehicles. For several decades, that system has met needs of travelers and
has been distinguished by freedom from serious accidents. Still, ferry
docks have been bruised; vessels have been scarred and damaged; and
there have been numerous albeit undocumented close shaves. Both the
ferry management and the public felt that the system was safe. Then, in
October 1982, research was completed on marine traffic safety in Puget
Sound that raised vital questions on unnecessary risks. That study was
ignored until an accident involving the ferry *Elwha* occurred the following
September. Then the politics of risk followed the classical pattern: neglect
until some event dramatizes an old and hidden but significant danger.
Many lessons can be learned from this ferry tale.

While the study of marine traffic safety set forth ten major recommendations, one main concern was the virtual absence of lifeboats on the Puget
Sound ferries. The ferries did carry enough life jackets to service all
passengers in event of a serious casualty that required abandoning ship.
But there was no way to keep people out of the water. In warm climates,
that might not be too serious a problem. Puget Sound waters, however, run
about 48 degrees Fahrenheit, and the average person in flotation gear is
likely to succumb to hypothermia in less than an hour. Until questions
were raised by this study, both the state ferry management and the United
States Coast Guard, which has jurisdiction over marine safety, accepted
these risks to the ferry passengers. And if passengers were aware of
potential risks, they were lulled into complacency by their institutional
guardians.

When asked about the situation, the ferry managers contended that
ships carried no lifeboats because none were required by the Coast Guard.
Then too, lifeboats are costly, and the state ferry system had been in

continuous fiscal distress, so it was not about to move voluntarily. The Coast Guard contended that (1) casualty statistics confirmed that bad ferry accidents were rare; (2) should a vessel be sinking, rescue craft were not far away; and (3) in any event, it was safer for ferry passengers to remain on board, since even if the boat were cut in half, both halves would float. All three arguments proved untenable, but an inquiry into each and the eventual actions by safety authorities exposes some basic principles concerning risk and its (mis)management.

Dealing with these three in reverse order, the Coast Guard preference that passengers remain on board neglects the extra hazard of fire from gasoline in auto fuel tanks or of the boat's capsizing if rammed by a much larger vessel. And it ignores the fact that older ferries had little or no underwater compartmentation that would preserve buoyancy in case of hull rupture.

The assertion that rescue craft could be on the scene promptly is not borne out, since there was no credible contingency rescue plan, especially for the San Juan islands, where commercial traffic is sparse and unpredictable, and severe weather conditions add to the hazard. Moreover, rescue vessels would have a a difficult time in fog or at night, especially if people were in the water and being scattered by swift currents.

Lastly, in statistical analyses of accidents, a major distinction must be drawn between those of limited consequence that happen often, and those of catastrophic proportions that occur rarely. For the first group, probabilities of future accidents and their various causes can be extracted from past experience. Not so with the infrequent calamity. Even if it never has happened, there can be no assurance that it never will; and there is no way to determine from any data on minor accidents how close the system might be to the threshhold of intense danger.

The quest for risk reduction then requires other probes: fault tree analysis, casualty data assessment, generation of imaginary accident scenarios. To deal with the worst-case scenario, as it is called, requires detailed study of the anatomy of an accident. Whatever the cause, we find that virtually all operational failures follow a pattern: For a time, all is going well. Then circumstances unfold as a prelude to casualty. Signs of trouble may be present, and if so, may be detected by people (or machines) in control, followed by collision avoidance action. If successful, that sequence becomes a near-miss incident. On the other hand, if warning signs are absent, ambiguous, obscured, delayed, or wrong, or if the operator misinterprets them, or if he properly interprets them but fails to take fitting preventative measures, or if machinery fails, or if several things go wrong simultaneously, that incident becomes an accident. Consequences may then range from trivial to severe, from fender bender to catastrophic loss of life, depending largely on actions by the operator— along with just plain luck.

The decision process thus involves threat perception, situation analysis, and response by conscious choice, all depending on good information and on the alacrity, skill, training, and experience of the operator. The ferry study emphasized both the quality of available information and the competence of the user. Recommendations were made for better weather data, especially the possibility of sudden fog, and for clearer communications between ships and the existing traffic control center (analogous to ground control of aircraft) and between contiguous ships. Collateral proposals were made to stiffen qualifications for mariners, require retesting, and subject violators to more severe penalties.

After the safety report was issued, there was not simply benign neglect. Officials of both agencies levelled attacks on the research investigators, charging them with naivete. Then came the *Elwha* accident. On a routine ferry run, its skipper sailed off course for sightseeing in a narrow cove to aid viewing of a waterfront home belonging to a wheelhouse passenger. The *Elwha* hit a rock, tore open the bottom of the ship, sped out of the cove, and docked. Its skipper claimed that he would have made it without a casualty if the steering had not failed! (Subsequently, the Coast Guard dropped charges of negligence when the master resigned, but the ferry system went to court to try to collect damages.)

As expected, the event attracted a spotlight of media attention. And it was not long before both newspaper and TV commentators were asking why the research report was ignored. The authors of that report saw a golden opportunity to refocus attention on their neglected recommendations. In the aftermath of renewed initiatives by the research investigators, including appeals for congressional investigations, some recommendations were heeded. In 1984, the Washington State ferry management ordered life rafts. The Coast Guard began a study of the necessity of life rafts as the basis for future rule making, stiffened up personnel testing and ship inspections, and reexamined its contingency rescue plans. Traffic control radio procedure was changed; the possibility was investigated of using ships and planes that normally transit the area to supplement the few fixed weather stations in furnishing data on fog and local storms; and an experiment was begun to collect close-encounter data following the FAA model.

However, a major recommendation to limit ferry speed in fog was ignored. Then, in December 1985, a very close encounter occurred because of the speed factor, this time with a member of Congress on board. And early in 1986, the ferry *Hyak* went aground as a result of pilot error. Mandated life rafts were absent and the contingency rescue plan inoperative because ship and shore emergency radios were on different channels. Perhaps, some four years later, the safety study will be adopted by responsible authorities. Although there is no way of knowing how much these steps will reduce risk, all are certain to be positive.

This anecdote thus epitomizes how risk affects normal human pursuits and can be mitigated. Why the responsible authorities have not been diligent in implementing existing law is not so easily explained, especially when the remedies for alleviating unnecessary risk were so relatively inexpensive. In March 1986, the Coast Guard commander of the thirteenth district, which includes Puget Sound, retired to an appointment as manager of the ferry system. At the very least, the ferry tale illustrates how different parties have different perspectives, how the regulators and regulated often share similar views on maintaining the status quo, how they collaborate in fending off outside criticism, and how public safety is traded off with economics.

5 / Technology and Politics

Government: Power Broker or Steering System?

cholars of American government have consistently emphasized its flexibility. Notwithstanding a written Constitution which endows a stable framework, and a creed of government by law and not by men, the practice of government has been neither rigid nor unchanging. It has been pragmatic; it has oscillated under shifting public attitudes; and it has been engraved by leaders with different personalities, ambitions, character, style, and ideology. Salient changes in doctrine also flow from constitutional amendment and evolving interpretations by the Supreme Court, usually in tune with vital signs in our society. It is thus not easy to describe how the government operates, or to characterize a prevailing philosophy with such labels as conservative and liberal, Republican and Democrat.

Given that technology imposes special demands on governmental decisions, it is important to distinguish between government's functioning as a power broker and as a steering system. Before we do so, however, we need to examine the kinetics of the policy process.

Most issues seem propelled by either crisis or pressure. Legislative histories generally confirm this pattern, although there are exceptions. Some issues are also driven by a tidal wave of popular sentiment where people lead their leaders. A few issues are decided by rational problem definition, goal identification, and then a process of defining options, tracing their consequences, establishing criteria for choice, and formally choosing—what political scientists term legitimation. In most cases, however, initiatives do not even begin unless there is a palpable emergency—a response to our crisis culture—or unless a vested interest has the power and skill to maneuver the issue over the noise level threshhold of other contenders so that it captures attention on the legislative calendar. These vested interests are no longer purely those of commercial enterprises—farmers, auto manufacturers, bankers. The body politic is lumpy with so-called single-issue advocates who rally around such issues as nuclear power, abortion, pensions, and tax reform.

With crisis and pressure predominating, policies tend to be reactive rather than anticipatory. To some degree, this is in keeping with democratic principles of the founding fathers, who hoped to blunt excessive domination of the agenda by autocrats at the top. The president and congressional leaders seldom want to get too far out in front of the voters. Some wait for the crowd to march and then position themselves in front of popular causes, theatrically assuming the mantle of leadership. Occasionally, others sense that the direction is wrong and courageously function as teachers to argue a shift. History remembers as exceptions those great leaders who had both visions of the future and the political will to lead away from catastrophe or toward a higher ground of social achievement. The case of Woodrow Wilson and the League of Nations shows that not all succeeded.

It is this very notion of foresight that distinguishes governmental style as between that of a steering system and that of a power broker. Steering is a process that heavily seasons decisions with information about the way ahead: forks in the road, obstacles, dangers of hostile competitors, and opportunities for course correction. Also implied is the potential for the decision system to learn and for the leadership to teach, elements of effective political process distilled by former Congressman Charles A. Mosher from long experience at the firing line. By no means, however, does the metaphor of steering imply political control.

As a broker, government serves as umpire among contenders for power, for privilege, or for the public purse. The brokerage process revolves around political bargaining, with the relative influence of different parties often weighing as heavily as the merits of their case. But almost always, each group argues from its parochial *short-term* interests. In whatever compromises are negotiated, accommodations are usually made between different immediate benefits.

These pressures tilt the legislative process to favor what is urgent rather than what may be important. Because future effects are neglected and because there is seldom a viable constituency for the future, tradeoffs between the short- and the long-term consequences are not considered.

Nominally overlooked, therefore, is the reality that today's decisions cast a long shadow ahead. For one thing, it takes years for an issue to mature from problem discovery and exposure through phases of legislative debate, decision, appropriation, and then implementation. By then, the social setting may have changed. So may the problem itself. So may the potency of the solution. The time horizon for policy design, implementation, and evaluation for possible twists and turns thus extends substantially ahead.

No wonder, then, that policy serves as a bridge between the present and the future.

Also buried in the virtues of foresight is detecting the capacity of technology to trigger unintended consequences. Most of these are manifested long after technological initiatives. Such unwanted effects cannot always be avoided or mitigated, but in the spirit of preventive medicine, there is potential benefit from adroit steering in all of its nuances. If anticipation fails, damage can be limited by careful monitoring, feedback, and agility in steering, by resiliency to shock and by swift repair.

The system operates in an atmosphere characterized by the cliche "Pay now or pay (more) later." When economic or social reserves are exhausted, however, the pain of operating on credit and the associated repercussions may be staggering. Deferred payments for the Vietnam conflict and the military buildup in the 1980s are cases in point. With the impacts of technological choice so portentous for modern society, it becomes imperative to enhance information and its sensitive, prudent use for political navigation, rather than primarily abiding by the outcome of a contest between muscular interests.

Steering versus brokering need not be a matter of the exclusion of one for the other. Franklin D. Roosevelt was a master at the combination. Presidents Truman and Kennedy leaned more than most to a steering mode. President Carter endeavored to use steering too, but the cultural environment was intensely hostile, tending more toward short-term gratification, and the political environment was veering toward satisfying self-interest. President Reagan read both of these trends and ran against steering. Whatever ideology he espoused has often been tempered under threat of defeat by quiet compromise.

One thing is certain: political steering of the disjointed sociotechnical system by public policy is becoming ever more demanding. And brokering with the tremendous influence of government may not meet the emerging needs of what Zbigniew Brzezinski in 1970 called "the technetronic era."

The conservative columnist George Will believes this may be a constitutional problem. Writing in *Statecraft as Soulcraft,* he contends that the founding fathers, in creating a system of checks and balances through separation of powers, counted on separate factions of a pluralistic society bent on the passions of self-interest to submerge those appetites in dedication to the commonweal. That Newtonian concept of social equilibrium has spawned a form of decision paralysis. Remedies can no longer be found in clever new institutional arrangements, nor in a clear appeal to fundamental creeds of justice, social equity, fairness, and compassion; unfortunately, technology has fuzzed up ethical principles. Yet, as a corporate enterprise government must stand for something. It cannot simply be a referee at a technological ball game. It must learn to steer by collective wishes of the polity. And it must have powerful information to steer by.

Indeed, the changing nature of the decision theater cries for analysis and political reform. If public preferences for relatively more steering versus brokering comes in cycles, it behooves the voters, as the twentieth century draws to an end, to take another look at the health of the entire governmental process instead of letting it churn out issue after issue, all of them hog-tied by high costs from failure to look ahead. The word *government*, incidentally, is derived from a Greek root meaning "art of the steersman." The social management of technology implies that technology requires more than scientific literacy. It requires a heightened civic competence in the practice of democracy.

The President as Systems Manager

Scholars periodically debate whether the presidency has lost or gained power, in absolute terms or relative to the other two branches of government. And they draft report cards on individual performance. Regardless of the prevailing academic view or a demonstration of the strength or weakness of a particular incumbent, there are certain constant realities. Modern presidents always play a vital role in the nation's technological affairs. If nothing else, the modern state defines the political space in which key technological acts now occur. Legislation is a chronicle of public policy, and every bill, with or without technological ingredients, requires the president's signature to become law.

In the context of technology-intensive policies and in contemporary jargon, the president is the nation's systems manager.

Put another way, the president occupies a central position of power to set national priorities of public purpose and public purse. He then has the salient duty to harness the energies of a variegated society and is expected to exercise a sensitive balance among different interest groups so that none can unduly dominate. Indeed, the American creed operates so that even a majority cannot extinguish the rights and opportunities of a minority. That exquisite balance, however, is not a matter of static equilibrium. It is constantly shifting, with events in the national economic and social situation, with changes in our culture as influenced by hidden springs of the counterculture, and with shocks from technologically-induced novelty. Early in America's youth, the French political analyst de Tocqueville characterized America as always in motion, so frenzied that there was little time for contemplation; he would be astonished at how fast these pulsations, lurches, ricochets, and reflexes may now occur.

As a result, the president is obliged to examine a constant parade of issues and their effects on the nation and on its future. It would be naive not to appreciate that the incumbent also weighs the impact of his decisions on his office, his party, and his place in history.

Notwithstanding the fact that few presidents have had backgrounds in science or engineering—Jefferson, Hoover, and Carter being the exceptions—all have been obliged to deal with the technology-loaded issues that have streamed across their desk. President Franklin D. Roosevelt, responding to Albert Einstein's disclosure, took the fateful step, without congressional knowledge, of developing the atomic bomb. President Truman chose to use it. He also promoted the Marshall Plan for foreign technical assistance, accepted proposals to create the National Science Foundation, and approved the establishment of a civilian-managed Atomic Energy Commission. Eisenhower is identified with the proposal Atoms for Peace; he responded to the 1957 Soviet space surprise by backing creation of NASA and was the first president to have a White House science advisor. Kennedy stepped up the space race to the moon, sharply expanded the portfolio of federal support for research and graduate education, boosted science at the centennial of the National Academy of Sciences, and initiated arms control through the nuclear test ban. Johnson created a Department of Transportation and implemented the first national policy to explore the oceans. Nixon jumped on the bandwagon of environmental policy and also proposed a policy for energy independence following the 1973 oil moratorium. Ford, Carter, and Reagan have all had responsibilities for development of new weapons systems—such as the B-1 bomber and the MX, cruise, and Pershing II missiles—and for renewing authorizations concerned with quality of water and air. Here lies the evidence that presidents are unrecognized managers of the nation's technological systems.

Their learning curve, incidentally, has had to be sharply compressed, because from 1961 to 1981, no president served two terms. This may be a clue that the successful exercise of political power had become so exacting as to defy the capacity of available leadership. In addition, consensus is harder to muster. One problem may be that, shoved by technologically induced change, social preferences are oscillating faster than the political apparatus can sense and respond. And there may be so little tranquility between pulses that citizens buffeted with chronic anxiety sought political respite in 1984 with an incumbent exuding confidence and promising "to stay the course" in resonance with their feelings.

More and more, presidents are confronted with extranational circumstances and surprises which are beyond control but which have enormous impact on domestic affairs. Most conspicuous are terrorist activities, or their threats. Then there is the unending confrontation with the Soviet Union and the contest in weapons technology, and the competition with Pacific Rim nations over high-tech merchandise. Less obvious but influential are the economic and political instabilities of the Third World, especially where American security interests, banking, and commerce are directly involved and, as has been true for almost a century, seek to influence foreign policy in their behalf. Presidents are thus the unwilling victims of the jerk of events.

Obviously, although presidents are at the helm, they need some aids to navigation.

Radar for the Ship of State

Every year the president's job gets tougher. More critical choices have to be made, often perplexing choices because they are laden with technology. The problem is not, however, aggravated by technological change itself. Activist presidents are committed to transformations. To help the United States compete in the world economic and political marketplace, for example, presidents have taken initiatives to explore outer space and to revitalize American technological enterprise; the Strategic Defense Initiative is dependent on ultra high technology. Rather, the problem lies in change over which presidents have no control. And it is here that they must confront technology head-on as a major root of the vexatious conflicts and shifting social agenda of the nation that accompany the issues and options unrolling on the president's desk. Just a few examples from current issues show the connection: reducing waste in developing and manufacturing weapon systems; diminishing unemployment and meeting competition from the foreign use of robotics; marketing America's agricultural bounty abroad and continuing that production without subsidy; mitigating acid rain; meeting the escalating cost of medical miracles; controlling information leaks and computer crime; limiting proliferation of nuclear materials and disposing of radioactive waste.

How can an incumbent without technical training handle such sophisticated questions? Should we expect leaders to be scientists or engineers, or to possess the newly minted notion of scientific literacy? Probably not, or at least not soon. For one thing, most scientists and engineers do not have the temperament for politics. They have trouble dealing with ambiguity; they are unused to settling questions by the adversarial process rather than by cold logic; they prefer to deal with machines rather than people, partly because machines are more susceptible to control. In career terms, few technologists have a political power base to compete, and they may not want to risk defeat because of the difficulty in restarting professional engines.

Not surprisingly, here as with other areas of intense complexity, presidents resort to advisors. History teaches that this process has been employed by all political leaders, from tribal chiefs to Roman emperors. Some counselors have been chosen for their wisdom and special knowledge; some for magical powers to prognosticate or to entertain; some because of their outreach to powerful constituencies that a leader might want to pacify.

To assist the president in spotting opportunities or in safe navigation in the area of science and technology, there is a fundamental requirement for staff expertise—in effect to function as radar for the ship of state. First and foremost, any such advisor must facilitate presidential goals by practices congenial to the presidential style of decision making. But to be fully effective, such counsel must be independent, as free as possible from strong personal bias or the influence of internal or external lobbies.

As the following historical review makes clear, all presidents within the last half century have increased the technical capacity of their office by creation, strengthening, or rearrangement of advisory apparatus.

1933 President Roosevelt requested that the National Academy of Sciences create a Science Advisory Board to help combat economic depression.

1941 President Roosevelt strengthened the National Defense Research Committee created in 1940 and established the Office of Scientific Research and Development in the Office of Emergency Management, Executive Office of the President (EOP), by Executive Order 8807, to enlist university-based science to the war effort.

1944 President Roosevelt commissioned a study by Vannevar Bush regarding postwar support of academic science.

1947 Responding to President Truman's request for a study of advisory machinery, Dr. John R. Steelman proposed creation of three science advisory units for the president. One, the Interdepartmental Committee on Scientific Research and Development (ICSRD), was established by Executive Order 9912. (The others were established by President Eisenhower.)

1950 President Truman accepted a study prepared by Vannevar Bush and established the National Science Foundation (NSF) by PL 81-507, with responsibilities to develop national policy for basic research and education in science.

1951 A Science Advisory Committee was created in the Office of

Defense Mobilization, EOP, especially concerning defense and intelligence matters.

1954   ICSRD was augmented by Executive Order 10521, with the NSF responsible for generating national science policy.

1957   In the aftermath of Sputnik, President Eisenhower established the Office of Special Assistant to the President for Science and Technology, in the White House—the post of science advisor.

The ODM Science Advisory Committee was moved from the EOP to the White House and designated the President's Science Advisory Committee (PSAC); it was intended to provide an external network involving top talent in the outside scientific community.

1959   A Federal Council for Science and Technology (FCST) was created by Executive Order 10807, upgrading ICSRD, and chaired by the president's science advisor, who then wore three hats; it was intended to provide an internal network of top talent within the federal establishment.

1961   The Senate Subcommittee on National Policy Machinery proposed the creation in the EOP of an Office of Science and Technology (OST).

1962   President Kennedy established the OST by Reorganization Plan No. 2 of 1962 through a transfer of unused functions of the NSF, with a director appointed by the president on advice and consent of the Senate. Three earlier advisory functions were retained.

1966   President Johnson activated a statutory National Council on Marine Resources and Engineering Development in the EOP by PL 89-454; it was chaired by the vice-president, with a presidentially appointed staff director.

1970   President Nixon approved creation of a Council on Environmental Quality in the EOP, authorized by PL 91-190.

1971   Marine Council authorization was permitted to expire.

1973   President Nixon disestablished the OST by Reorganization Plan No. 1 of 1973, with some functions transferred to the NSF; NSF's director was appointed as the president's science advisor.

1976   With congressional initiatives and pressure, the National Science and Technology Policy, Organization, and Priorities Act was signed into law by President Ford as PL 94-282. It created an Office of Science and Technology Policy (OSTP) in the EOP, along with an interim President's Committee on Science and Technology (PCST), a Federal Coordinating Committee on Science, Engineering, and Technology

(FCCSET) similar to FCST, and an Intergovernmental Science, Engineering, and Technology Advisory Panel (ISETAP) for communication with the states.

1977   By Reorganization Plan No. 1 of 1977, President Carter transferred some of the duties of the OSTP director to the president, along with functions from FCCSET, PCST and ISETAP, and abolished those three organs.

1978   Executive Order 12039 to implement Reorganization Plan No. 1 transferred responsibility for two reports required by PL 94-282 to the NSF and reestablished FCCSET at a lower level to serve the OSTP director rather than the president.

1985   A presidential commission proposed that President Reagan abolish the OSTP and consider creation of a cabinet-level Department of Science and Technology.

Of all these initiatives, those by President Roosevelt in 1941 and by President Eisenhower in 1957 were organizationally the most significant. By the highly visible creation of new agencies, they used the traditional structure of government to symbolize national purpose and priorities. The institutional medium was the message.

One key elaboration. Distinctions need to be carefully drawn between the president and the presidency, and between the White House and the Executive Office of the President. The presidency is a constitutionally created office of great power and dignity that symbolically and operationally demands universal respect. In their day-to-day agenda, incumbents may have parochial, even venal motives for their actions. But they have universally been aware of how their personal conduct reflects on the office. This partially explains why President Richard M. Nixon resigned rather than expose the office to the debilitating processes of impeachment. The point is that there are important differences between staff whose loyalty is to the individual president in the White House and staff in the EOP, who consider themselves as serving and preserving the presidency. In the aftermath of Sputnik, President Eisenhower created an advisory post in the White House, but for a variety of reasons, including the presidential practice of gagging all White House staff with executive privilege to prevent their testifying before Congress, pressures were put on President Kennedy to shift the science advisory function to the Executive Office of the President. With its director then subject to the advice and consent of the Senate, Congress would have legal access to that expertise. Also, by having a stronger legislative underpinning, the operation should be less vulnerable to the whims of the chief executive.

A number of additional inferences can be extracted from this chronology. Most actions were taken in response to external events: the Depression, World War II, the Soviet space surprise associated with the cold war, congressional pressure to strengthen advisory apparatus, and most recently, foreign commercial competition. Most presidents tailored the functions, structure, and size of advisory units to their personal taste, notwithstanding creation of all units since 1962 by legislation. In 1973, Nixon killed the science advisory office, probably out of pique because his science advisor, Edward E. David, Jr., refused to become a political operative and campaign for the SST, which internal studies showed conclusively to be unpromising. With advocacy by the American Society for Public Administration and by the elite of the scientific community, individual members of Congress pressed to resurrect the advisory function. In 1976, President Ford responded to this initiative and reframed the Office of Science and Technology Policy out of the ashes of the OST. In 1985, the science advisory function was again being threatened with extinction, although seasoned observers wouldn't bet on its demise. Nevertheless, the style had changed from that of presidential counselor to presidential advocate.

Paradoxically, Congress has shown little inclination to examine the effectiveness of these units, partly because they are reticent about meddling in what they consider the president's family business, and partly because there is little political hay to be reaped in such arcane issues. In 1985, however, the House Science and Technology Committee opened a study to update Vannevar Bush's treatise *Science—The Endless Frontier,* which rationalized government support of science. Coincidentally, this committee and the Senate Commerce Committee may decide to examine the performance of the Office of Science and Technology Policy.

Whatever the vicissitudes of these advisory units, all have engaged in nine functions:

1. Personal, confidential advice and counsel to the president
2. Policy planning and priority setting through the budget process (with an unstated expectation by scientists that the office will protect funding for university-conducted basic research)
3. Coordination of certain transagency functions within the bureaucracy
4. Reciprocal communication with the scientific and, recently, the industrial community
5. Reporting to the Congress (since 1962)
6. Reporting sporadically to the public
7. Communication with state governments (mainly 1976–80)
8. Nomination of scientific "goodies" that can be employed as bargaining chips in foreign policy negotiations, or as "sparkles" in presidential political initiatives

9. Symbolizing the importance of science and technology on the presidential agenda, thus providing continuity between such special science messages to Congress as Kennedy's in 1963, Nixon's in 1972, and Carter's in 1979

The scope of issues tackled by these advisory units is essentially as broad as those coming before the president. During the 1957–62 interval, however, most attention was devoted to weapons analysis, with the advisor often put in the position of devil's advocate to question the technical feasibility of an endless stream of proposals from the Pentagon. Interestingly enough, many challenges proved successful. Early in the Kennedy administration, the science advisory apparatus concentrated on arms control, albeit with emphasis on purely technical rather than political factors so as to enhance saleability to the defense community. Later, however, emphasis began to shift to the civilian sector, partly because of assurances by Secretary of Defense McNamara that his own staff would keep the military brass in check. By late in the Johnson era, science advisors were cut out of weapons reviews, partly because of the tension between the scientific community represented by the Office of Science and Technology and President Johnson over Vietnam. In the Reagan administration, the OSTP has become a public advocate for presidential initiatives, especially for high technology related to defense and for assistance to industry.

Despite the presence of science and technology in an enormous range of separate policies, the 1976 science policy act was the first official recognition of the "profound impact of science and technology on society." It asserted the nation's overarching commitment to apply science and technology vigorously to promotion of such national goals as the "general welfare, security, economic health, conservation and efficient utilization of natural and human resources, and the effective functioning of government and society." The act emphasized coherent and long-range policy planning and technology assessment for wise choice and anticipation of future concerns. It also focused on effective utilization of manpower, consideration of research and development as an investment in the future, perceptive review of policies and programs to assure effective implementation, and regular publication of reports on the status of science and technology, and on the outlook ahead for the next five years.

The performance of these advisory units has been graded periodically by neutral observers and by the Congress. Marks have not been uniformly high. Most often, the shortfalls of the office have been regarded as owing to indifference on the part of the president, personality clashes between individuals, or loss in influence in power struggles among presidential staff. But the advisors have stumbled when dealing with the economic, social, and political ingredients of civilian technology. Also, except for the 1961–66 interval, the coordination function has been given short shrift. Partly, this is because of the difficulty of gaining coherence within the bureaucracy and the energy and time entailed in persuasion. Partly, it results from advisors' having little skill or appetite to engage in group problem-solving.

Since passage of the 1976 science policy act, there has been another conspicuous failing. Virtually no staff have been assigned in the advisory office to deal with impact analysis or to develop future perspectives. Yet one of the most unusual features of the legislation was the sprinkling throughout of provisions emphasizing consideration of the future in technological choice. That neglect is largely explained by the husbanding of the small staff to work on immediate issues, in the crisis-management atmosphere of the presidential office. Unless there are rewards to advisors for taking a long view, by presidential instruction, the legislative intent will continue to be a hollow promise.

Which leads us back to the notion of advice represented by the metaphor of radar: a looking ahead for storms and shoals and salient opportunities to apply today's technology to tomorrow's problems. Only by such navigation can a course be run with minimum risk of mistakes by omission and by commission.

Congress: The Other End of the Seesaw

In the same way that the president engages technology-laden policy and appropriation questions, so does Congress at the other end of the Washington seesaw. The founding fathers intended Congress to carry out three functions: to set the nation's course and to limit executive authority through legislated policy; to raise money and appropriate funds for implementation; then to monitor the executive branch and verify its effective management and consistency with congressional intent. By practice, a fourth function has evolved, that of educating the electorate through published records and special research reports and through hearings and floor debates, which are now telecast.

Unlike the executive branch, where power is concentrated in the office of the president and the processes for managing the bureaucracy are rather clear-cut, Congress represents a diffused and ragged source of power, and its workings, through the legislative process, are far more complex, arcane, and viscous. One hundred senators (101 if the vice-president is included) and 435 congressmen and congresswomen often charge off in separate directions, each one believing he or she has faithfully served a local constituency. At one time, party loyalty engraved some discipline on the legislative process, but it now wobbles with uncertainty. Responsibilities are fragmented among dozens of independent subcommittees whose proliferation is arrested only about once every ten Congresses. So chairmen of committees and subcommittees act as sovereign monarchs of independent fiefdoms. Additional disjunction stems from the fact that one committee in each house controls authorization, the thrust and limits of purpose, while another controls appropriation purse strings. When consensus has finally been achieved on a major issue, members often hang onto it unrelated but unpopular bills like Christmas tree ornaments to assure passage of contentious and doubtful offerings. As a result, the legislative process suffers outrageously from incoherence.

Some reforms occurred in 1974 when the Congressional Budget Office was created to generate a unified budget representing Congress-wide priorities rather than a patchwork of unrelated parts. Nevertheless, Congress often displays a randomness evoked by short-term expediency, with preferences steered by powerful committee chairmen and goaded by aggressive lobbyists who watchdog amendments that might chamfer their preferences. Thus, Congress plays many games. Some are set by the rules of each house, called into play during Indian wrestling over highly charged issues. Witness the Senate's permissible filibuster. Other maneuvering stems from internal rivalry between individual members and among committees. Here, major ploys are driven by anxieties over committee jurisdictions, each carrying the aura of influence that could satisfy certain vested interests and then redound to individual power and prestige, campaign financing, and enhanced reelection prospects.

This imperative for reelection kindles other behavior patterns. The most pronounced is a bias toward short-term expediency at the expense of the long view. In the quest for voter esteem, it is tempting for legislators to advocate measures that are on their constituency's front burner. Notwithstanding the political rhetoric of commitment to future generations in the preambles of new legislation, the defense of future interests is scattered. In legislative bargaining such considerations are usually neglected.

With all these idiosyncrasies of democratic government, it must be said that members of Congress work grueling schedules, endeavor to fulfill their kaleidoscope of responsibilities, walk continuous tightropes between national and provincial interests, and with conspicuously few exceptions, keep their integrity intact. The pressures are excruciating because all that sits between them and the steady flow of angry constituents and zealous lobbyists is a secretary in an outer office.

Since so many contemporary issues have technological content, every technology-related policy initiative carries a congressional brand, confirming both the executive-legislative partnership in the sharing of power and the legislature's crucial involvement in all technological delivery systems. Nevertheless, with a few exceptions after World War II, Congress did not become self-consciously involved with science policy until after the Soviets launched Sputnik in 1957. In the late 1940s, there had been incandescent debate over putting the field of atomic energy under civilian rather than military managers; simultaneously with creation of the AEC, the Congress established a Joint Committee on Atomic Energy that in its heyday became a powerhouse of advocacy and kibitzing. Congress also got into such defense issues as backing nuclear power for submarines and accelerating missile development.

The 1957 Soviet space shot, however, generated a form of national hysteria over competition with the Soviets, in which the relative status of all science and technology was inferred from space accomplishments and then used as an index of comparative military strength. This in turn was translated into a measure of capacity to wage foreign policy.

Because of the political energy ignited by the space issue, the Congress responded with unusual alacrity. Extensive hearings convened under Senator Lyndon B. Johnson led to passage of the 1958 Space Act and the creation of the National Aeronautics and Space Administration (NASA). Simultaneously, the Congress created a new committee in each house with unprecedented jurisdiction over space affairs. These concoctions were not symmetrical, however. The House Science and Astronautics Committee (later renamed the Science and Technology Committee) had a far wider jurisdiction, as the title suggests, than the Senate counterpart, the Aeronautical and Space Sciences Committee (which was disestablished twenty years later and its jurisdictions over science affairs assigned mainly to the Commerce Committee).

In further reaction to that external stimulus, the Congress in 1959 began to strengthen its own science advisory function in the Legislative Reference Service (now called Congressional Research Service). By having its own resident expert, the legislature hoped to overcome being outgunned by the Executive Branch, not only in access to expertise, but in being vulnerable to self-serving bureaucratic testimony presenting only those facts that supported the administration's position. That miniscule capacity of only one person, the author, was expanded in 1964 to the LRS Science Policy Research Division (with the author returning as its first director). Then in 1972, Congress further reinforced this research capability in science policy by spawning an Office of Technology Assessment. Meanwhile, its old reliable staff arm, the General Accounting Office, expanded its scope from fiscal to program review and, under a visionary comptroller-general, buttressed its science policy capabilities.

While these three units differ markedly in size, intellectual horsepower, style, and public image, collectively they represent a powerful source of information and analysis for their clients. All have been distinguished by their integrity, loyalty to professional standards, and independence from partisanship or special-interest perspectives. As a result, apart from serving the Congress, these research units serve the general public. Their reports provide a wealth of information to citizens and nongovernmental organizations that can facilitate the citizenry's understanding and taking a position on pending bills. When these reports are added to the hearing transcripts and committee reports pouring out of Congress, it is easy to confirm the role of the legislature in public education, although a good argument can be made that this bountiful resource of independent policy analysis is so neglected as to represent a colossal unused library.

Case Study: A Policy for Neptune

While there is no simple route to understanding how the technological delivery system works, case studies help. They are especially valuable if documentation is supplemented by eyewitness accounts and if the case is not so idiosyncratic as to mask general principles. The one sketched here concerns the design of a first policy to relate the oceans to U.S. national interests. That concept of policy design closely follows that in engineering—the analysis of requirements to solve the problems, a nomination of components to achieve the desired function, and a strenuous trading off of optimum properties of each to achieve a harmonious ensemble.

It is ironic that a nation founded by sea, depending on fishing, whaling, and mercantile trade for economic development in its infancy, and afforded freedom from hostile attack by two salt-water moats, should have waited almost two hundred years to adopt a comprehensive national policy for the oceans. But such are the lessons, and the enigmas, of history. Only in 1966 did the Congress pass and President Johnson sign the Marine Resources and Engineering Development Act into law, signalling unprecedented recognition of the U.S. stake in the whole gamut of marine affairs.

Public Law 89-454 was remarkable in other ways. Unlike most legislation prompted by crisis or pressure, this act emerged as almost a model of rational analysis; and unlike the case of space exploration, there were no conspicuous threats from a Soviet maritime competitor, nor any hysterical overreaction. No powerful lobby prowled congressional corridors clamoring for special privilege to coopt riches of the sea. Indeed, the realistic quip about political lethargy was, "The fish don't vote."

In short, the bill mandated five innovations. First, it established a national policy for the oceans, focused on a comprehensive, long-range, and coordinated program in marine sciences. Here, the term *marine science* was defined as shorthand for science and technology. That the bill was directed to more than support for science was emphasized in title and text; technology was to connect marine resources to human need, with engineering playing a role as mediator.

Second, the bill took note of the diffusion of ocean-related activities in some twenty-three agencies of the federal government. Since the president was the only officer in common charge, the bill placed on the incumbent a responsibility for leadership in carrying out the new policy. At first glance, this assignment seems natural. In legislative practice, however, new statutory functions are usually pinned on an operating agency or its most senior officer rather than on the president. But here, not only was this role as policy implementer almost unprecedented; the president was also required to submit an annual report to Congress cataloging marine activities government-wide and summarizing accomplishments toward legislative purpose.

Next, the bill provided machinery to advise and assist the president in fulfilling these tasks. Created was a cabinet-level council, with a full-time, presidentially appointed staff director, to develop two sets of proposals to the president. The first set was substantive. Its provisions would entail initiatives by which potential of the sea could be linked to problems of international maritime law, food shortages, increasing demand for fuel and minerals, disposal of urban and industrial waste, population pressures and conflicts in use of the coastal margin, and finally, gaps in scientific knowledge that needed to be filled if the promise of the sea were to be realized. The second set of proposals which the council was expected to generate was administrative, especially to assure internal coordination of the numerous federal agencies sharing marine science responsibilities.

In its fourth major innovation, the law said that the vice-president should chair the council. Giving a vice-president *any* statutory duties was most unusual, since the constitutionally defined functions for that office were largely as a standby in the event of death or disability of the president. Now, however, the vice-president was expected to become, in effect, the nation's chief oceanographer.

Finally, the act created a presidentially appointed advisory commission of outsiders with numerous tasks, but primarily with the chore of recommending improved governmental organization for ocean-related activities. By such reform, marine activities spread so thinly among so many agencies would have a more visible and coherent focus, and could prosper in the rough-and-tumble competition for budgetary support with powerful, nonmarine agencies. Presumably, too, consolidation would lessen unnecessary duplication.

Given the extraordinary origins and content of this action, it is of interest to track the legislative history.

The federal government had established a long-standing interest in separate marine activities. Early on, it prepared navigation charts. It protected the merchant marine from piracy; then it subsidized ship construction and operation. The government assumed responsibility for constructing ports and harbors, dredging channels, and arresting beach erosion. It undertook to protect fishery stocks from foreign incursions. Finally, it was the federal government, through the Navy in World War II, that became the major source of funding for oceanographic research. Each of these functions was pursued parochially by separate authority with modest funding and at low rungs on the bureaucratic ladders in different agencies. Almost all these agencies, however, had their hand in research.

Taking note of the public indifference to ocean affairs, except in wartime, and of the weak scientific support underpinning their interests, several federal agencies having maritime missions requested in 1956 that the National Academy of Sciences (NAS) study needs and opportunities and recommend actions. The academy's report was delivered in 1959, at a time when reactions were still inflamed by the Soviet space surprise. The general atmosphere was thus far more hospitable than it might otherwise have been to NAS proposals for at least doubling federal funding for oceanographic research over the next ten years.

There was, however, a serious impediment to action. The lower-level bureaus sponsoring the study were politically too weak to solicit implementation. Moreover, both the White House and, in particular, the president's science advisor were unfriendly to the proposition, the latter reflecting a bias within the scientific community that regarded oceanography as being at the bottom of the scientific pecking order. With astute foresight as to this contingency, the members of the academy who had conducted the study began a campaign to enlist support of key members of Congress, especially chairmen of the House and Senate committees having jurisdiction.

At that time, science was almost automatically accorded special privilege by Congress. The leadership in both houses vied with initiatives to implement the academy report. The rationale was to "beat the Russians." During those waning years of the Eisenhower administration, very little happened; but early in his first year, President Kennedy responded to scientific and congressional advocacy and sharply increased research funding. Now the Congress rallied around a new banner. They were concerned over duplication. Many bills were introduced to correct this deficiency, one finally passing but pocket-vetoed because of poor draftsmanship.

By 1964, circumstances had changed. The funding momentum imparted to ocean science by the Kennedy initiative had dissipated, and the ocean science community was no longer effective in lobbying. The primary outsiders pushing for increased support were industries that had exploded with space-related activity and were looking for other markets should the nation's space kick disappear. But they, too, were ineffective in an unfamiliar arena.

Key initiatives were then taken by a small coterie of congressional partisans who had not given up. Senator Warren G. Magnuson and Representative Alton Lennon, along with some colleagues, were convinced that the field deserved strengthening despite its not having much political mileage for them personally. There were many different reasons. Scientific research was spinning out new knowledge of what lay in and under the sea. Engineering miracles, some from the space program, permitted exploration in what had previously been too hostile an environment. Global demand was increasing for resources such as oil and gas that could be found at sea and perhaps exploited at prices competitive with materials from terrestrial sources. Waterfront crowding, with attendant problems of urban decay and pollution, collided with increased demand for water-related recreation. And finally, it was apparent that all the 112 nations facing the sea had similar problems and similar latent interests. An obvious question, then, was how to develop the oceanic frontiers by steps of public order to prevent stirring up historic rivalries, tensions, and violence.

Those congressional initiatives took the form of a variety of bills, each contributing lumber to the legislative edifice that emerged. Controversy between vastly different versions in the two houses reflected traditional internecine warfare, but it was finally cooled in compromise.

Still unknown was whether the president would sign the bill. During most of the bill's junket through the legislative hurdles, the Bureau of the Budget (now the Office of Management and Budget) was advising opposition or veto, on the grounds that strengthening oceanic affairs had the potential of becoming a "wet NASA," with attendant new pressures on the budget. But partly out of his long-standing friendship with Senator Magnuson, and partly out of respect for the senator as chairman of the powerful Commerce Committee, President Johnson signed. Not only that, but in switching on implementation immediately afterwards, the president insisted that Vice-President Hubert H. Humphrey proceed with dispatch and submit initial recommendations within four months.

Thus began an epic in U.S. maritime history. For four years, proposal after proposal emerged from the president's National Council on Marine Resources and Engineering Development, many to earn presidential support. Neither before nor since have the oceans had such a high-level advocate and venue for policy planning and coordination. Although the council was permitted to die by President Nixon in 1972 when the National Oceanic and Atmospheric Administration was founded and unrealistically claimed governmental leadership, it left a powerful legacy. Its most notable initiatives included an International Decade of Ocean Exploration, earning "brass-ring" eminence by mention in the 1968 State of the Union message; coastal zone management; control over ocean dumping; new (though ultimately ignored) principles for Law of the Sea; a Sea Grant program modelled after precursor land grants; expanded ocean surveys, especially of deep-ocean resources; use of buoy and satellite hardware in exploration; Great Lakes restoration; capability to clean up tanker oil spills; and intensified nonmilitary research.

While the council was active, outside analysts deemed it one of the most successful policy-planning and coordination groups on record. There were many reasons for its success. The atmospherics were right; science was still selling; and the heightened visibility of ocean affairs, facilitated by Cousteau's TV series, triggered popular support. Propositions adopted by the council were linked to social and economic concerns of special interest to President Johnson, rather than to self-serving parochial interests of the marine community. The marine emphasis had legislative underpinnings, backed by the president and senior members of Congress from both houses and both parties. In being chaired by an exceptionally bright and activist vice-president expounding on peaceful U.S. interests in the sea, the council enjoyed political clout. It was served by a creative, vigorous, and politically savvy staff who quickly built an internal information network, then a felicitous outreach to science, industry, and state government so that all parties could be consulted as policies were designed. Powerful allies were established among White House staff, especially to circumvent minefields constructed by agencies jealous of sharing power. Council meetings were held frequently; minutes constituted memoranda of understanding; and cabinet officers were personally involved.

Decisions were driven up the policy conduit for presidential blessing, in keeping with the incumbent's goals. Then these propositions were released to the press for public information.

That record of administrative accomplishment has so impressed ocean interests that proposals continued to surface as late as 1984 to reestablish the council. The lesson, however, has broader implications. What seems demonstrated by the council performance is a systems approach to public administration, of special utility when important policy lacks the momentum usually supplied by crisis and lobbying, and when responsibility is so diffused among different agencies that none can lead. Once more, we discover that only the president can wield the baton of the executive branch orchestra. We also discover that wise, far-sighted, and effective legislation can be generated by the Congress in the absence of presidential initiative, even in the absence of crisis or pressure. The American political system, for all its quirks, flutter, and flounce, can still demonstrate extraordinary vitality and vision. In a technological age, it is being given its most strenuous test.

Information: The Nerves of Government

Having identified the two major players on the national political stage, we next examine the signals that travel through the sociotechnical system and trigger action. In many ways, the government tends to react, to do tomorrow what it did yesterday, perhaps to do it better. At some point, however, either the risks of inaction in the presence of vocal public concern or a vigorous media exposé are too great, or the militancy of lobbies too intense. How political actors then respond is highly varied, critically dependent upon intelligence about the social and political climate. With information on how things stand, political leadership is then called upon to exercise both political power and political will.

Power, of course, is the ability to influence the total environment surrounding the decision theater, trying to force others to give in. Will is the desire to exercise that potential in the face of adversity. Power and will are thus the currency of politics. By its nature, the exercise of power evokes conflict. Leaders must thus evaluate the energies required to strengthen their position: What is the cost in political capital? How much prestige might be lost by compromise, by conflict avoidance, or by consensus maintenance?

In responding, political actors may reveal different levels of power: comfortable in matching the challenge; tightly strained by over-commitment; or bankrupt. Even if President Nixon had not resigned, the Watergate epic would have so weakened his prestige as to make future governance impossible. Because choices could jeopardize a leader's reputation and thus a future ability to steer, politicians evaluate what vital consequences are at stake.

Clearly, this step requires information. Indeed, a wide range and variety are entailed: data to map the network of present players; memory of how the system responded to earlier stimuli; internal and external constraints of past decisions, commitments, institutional strengths and weaknesses; peer group and cultural norms of behavior. What happens clearly depends on the imminence of the next election, on the battle wounds from recent political combat, on the stress level of people, and on the content of media reacting to prior crises. Last and often least is a view ahead, especially the longer view. Information, its generation, storage, retrieval, and diffusion, constitute what political scientist Karl Deutsch called, "the nerves of government." Throughout the decision process, information *about* the system is as crucial as technical information *in* the system. Indeed, participants are often concerned more with the politics of an issue, so as to mold the system to their will, than about the substance. Staff papers may be so squeezed for swift comprehension in a time-constrained predicament as to leave only the political residue.

Sooner or later, however, leadership must deal with substance. Everyone in the system then shakes the trees to gather all the factual apples around. This is equivalent to collecting military intelligence. Relevant are data on the nature of the problem, options, costs and benefits of each, side effects. Then comes interpretation: risks and repercussions. Such policy planning can minimize arbitrary solutions, improve the allocation of public and private resources, extend perceptions as to both lateral and future impacts. Looking before you leap can head off surprise. Cogitation can be an antidote for the blinding effect of political passions.

Requisite specialized knowledge is generally solicited from experts, who, ideally, are free of advocacy by not having a stake in the outcome. As expected, vested interests are aggressive in providing unsolicited advice, carefully sorting facts that support their self-interest. With ploys to gain access to top echelons, those hoping for support may exploit an incumbent's pride, vanity, biases, or need for help in the next election campaign.

There is another subtle problem with political intelligence in that staff subordinates often listen for the preferences of top leadership, then in an uncritical quest for survival in a turbulent milieu, respond deliberately to please the boss. A healthy search for different perspectives and options is blocked. Nowhere is this disability better illustrated than concerning advice to President Kennedy on Vietnam prospects where, as David Halberstam wrote in *The Best and the Brightest,* staff members failed to lay out the uncertainties and future consequences. The costs of error have been staggering.

That hesitancy to disagree has a counterpart: the use of top-level coercion to steamroller dissent. This happens when a political position is adopted by a president and delivered to the Congress as though there were no alternatives. Add to this foible the tendency of leadership to think itself infallible, or at least to create that image.

In characterizing political behavior on issues, we can usually isolate three phases: advertising a position; promoting it; then claiming credit when it has been successfully negotiated. As a result, the information nervous system becomes saturated with rhetorical messages to gain or keep popular support. Such slogans as "national defense," "more jobs," and "protection of free enterprise and individual opportunity" are plastered over the substance of an issue that may have less palatable objectives. The point is that the information system is so clogged with salesmanship that the substantive truth may never be detected. It is a melancholy fact that the more salient the issue, the more tendency there is to merchandise positions.

Almost certainly, the technical content of science policies makes them less comprehensible for the politicians than social policies that can be chosen largely from ideological or purely political considerations. Also, the consequences of error are potentially disastrous. These incentives to collect more and better information are thwarted, however, by the ticking clock or a mind unable to deal with complexity.

More Choices, Less Time to Choose

One of the more tenacious paradoxes of technology we repeatedly encounter is that we have more choices but less time to choose. If that notion is accepted a self-evident, it becomes worthwhile to understand its roots and its implications, especially when dealing with the grand issues in politics.

Technology has expanded our range of options in two ways. The first, a purely technical one, concerns hardware. For example, energy was once extracted principally from wood and coal. Now with our technological virtuosity it comes from oil and gas, from hot water and steam in the earth's mantle, from differences in the ocean's temperature between the surface and the bottom, from the sun, and from nuclear fission. Having more choices, like any embarrassment of riches, carries the burden of needing to distinguish the key features of each: direct cost, convenience, safety, abundance, renewability or nonrenewability, plus a wide spectrum of risks.

Second, technology has also augmented opportunities to choose. That is to say, the technology inherent in modern management, the "squishyware" rather than the hardware, has increased the versatility of infrastructure and of the decision apparatus to cope with a wider range of purely technical alternatives. A rainbow of different delivery systems can be assembled with the ingredients of knowledge, capital, human and natural resources, and a melange of interlocking organizations capable of putting in place and operating virtually any technical innovation that the human mind can conceive.

Despite these two realities, we face a disconcerting hang-up. These choices are complex, technically *and* socially. Moreover, each carries the couplet of potential benefits and of potentially adverse side effects. And perceptions of those benefits and side effects fire up controversy by stakeholders, the beneficiaries and the disadvantaged. With these complications, there is high incentive to cast a wide dragnet for data and interpretations as an aid to rational choice.

The trouble is that such study takes time. And as has been said, time is the one resource in human experience that cannot be magnified by technology. Nowhere is this dilemma more frustrating than in the political arena. For one thing, time is scarce for decision makers because they cannot devote full time to matters of choice. They have other duties besides making decisions: ceremonial functions, offering courtesies to constituents and representatives of powerful interest groups, listening to citizens exercising their rights of petition, or shepherding a clumsy and viscous bureaucracy. And negotiating solutions to conflict takes time. If this process is slighted, a phenomenon like Boyles' law in physics takes place: just as a gas under pressure shows an increase in temperature, so does the heat of negotiations increase when confrontation is subjected to the pressure of too little time for a full exchange of views.

The time-constrained search for better information is nettled by other influences. Pressures to decide may be inflamed by surprise and the perception of imminent peril, in which case swift intervention is required, either because of the relentless march of consequences or because a macho atmosphere requires action. Other threats affect only the individual or organization having the choice to make, and these may arise purely from hostile maneuvering by a political adversary. In short, defending turf takes time!

Quite understandably, politicians constantly assess their power and prestige. Because of the interconnectedness of elements and events within technological delivery systems, leaders detect numerous circumstances that affect their status. Then they become compulsive in engaging every possible situation in which they think they have a stake. Such opportunities to take initiative or to respond to others arise on short notice, with timetables over which they have little control. So officials are constantly dancing to tunes played by others. Whether or not the initiative is theirs, political actors must meet with the press frequently to explain their positions and justify their responses.

We are now at the root of the decision enigma. Whatever the issue at hand, it is so loaded with grave repercussions that it deserves diligent study in a contemplative rather than uncritical, tactical mode. Ideally, there should be an inquiry as to facts, options and their consequences, and criteria for choice. But the issue may also be perceived as a time bomb that must be defused before it explodes. The fateful ticking is not just the noise of relentless doom; it is the sound of a clock cruelly signalling that there is not enough time for careful, deliberate choice.

What happens next is that stress, already elevated by the anxiety of simply having to choose, increases further. Under stress, reality becomes warped. The future is discounted; only the immediate impacts are considered. So both the shortage of time and the abnormal stress imposed by the time bind carry seeds of decision error.

To help uncover the relationship of time and judicious choice, time should be understood as an irreversible clocking process associated with periods of internally coherent activities that occur in succession. Thus, a decision is not a flash of instantaneous action; it is the culmination of a series of deliberate actions stimulated by crisis or pressure a long time before. As this history unrolls—say as a chronology of key events—and is analyzed, we may discover not only what happened, but also why and how. Since later events can hardly have affected their precursors, the chronology may help unpeel cause-effect relationships, illuminating both the anatomy of a particular decision and how the system works generally.

If analysis is then pursued in depth, it may be possible to determine not just whether a time-constrained search jeopardized the validity of a particular decision, but also whether there was inadvertent damage to the system's future capacity to decide. That is, the health of the decision system itself may have been undermined by the exhaustion of protracted conflict and residual bitterness that precludes future negotiations; by expediency or haste in generating coalitions that fail to endure and expose poor judgment; by neglect of facts that, when discovered by the public, saps future credibility; by imperviousness to high risks that, when manifest, suggests lack of discretion; or by excessive commitment to the past. The result might then be a reduced capacity to deal with the future, to withstand the shock of new surprise, to muster creativity to meet repeated novelty, and to build on the event as a learning experience and thus deal with another perplexing attribute of a technological age: the past is no longer prologue.

Decision Making under Stress

Making choices is always a source of anxiety. Partly it is because the outcomes are always uncertain. We can never be sure that we have mapped all the options and conjectured properly about consequences; belatedly we may discover that costs exceed benefits. Apprehension then grows because the reputation and self-esteem of the decision maker are at stake.

Making decisions is also painful because they are often forced by some kind of threat as well as by opportunity. No one enjoys the predicament of intimidation. Indeed, it may provoke many different patterns of behavior in a search for the least costly prevention or mitigation. As social psychologist Irving L. Janis has written, there are five typical responses: (1) uncritical complacency, indifference to the situation, and stubborn continuation of present actions; (2) uncritical overreaction, the impulsive, often aggressive knee-jerk; (3) defensive avoidance or delay, a no-win perception of damned if you do and damned if you don't, accompanied by attempts to shift responsibility to others; (4) panic and a frantic search for options, blinded by prejudices and resolved by latching onto simple, even if wrong, solutions; and finally, (5) cool and thoughtful scanning of options and confident choice.

The first response is a familiar example of bureaucratic inertia. Custom, peer pressure, and the short-term rewards for protecting the past override curiosity, vision, and boldness. Or the resources necessary for a shift in direction may be exhausted; or the future risks of change are deemed greater than the penalties for continuing the status quo.

With the second response, emergency warnings are so provocative that in a particular emotional setting almost any motion brings relief.

By contrast, with the third type of response, there is the familiar tactic of "protecting your ass," a practice made easy in large organizations, where decision-making responsibility is diffused or masked. In every political setting, there is the tendency to procrastinate in the secret hope that the problem will go away. Often, this is accompanied by bland public assurances that the problem is well in hand. But while political inaction in the short run may be inevitable, in the long run it is intolerable—unless, of course, the situation is hopeless, in which event there may be no will to respond. How well this seems to describe the mood that permitted growth of the national debt until it was recognized that interest being paid on borrowed money was the fastest-growing component of all.

With the fourth type of response, when the immediacy of threat is credible, or if the resources to respond drain away, the sense of peril mounts. The search for answers becomes hysterical; simple and hastily contrived solutions become attractive, especially if they accord with prejudices. To some degree, this model describes the behavior both of the operating personnel at the Three Mile Island nuclear plant when disaster was imminent and of the regulatory officials first on the site until the governor of Pennsylvania intervened.

Clearly the fifth mode of response is the most appealing, an immaculate model of rationality devoutly to be sought. Our sense of reality tells us, however, that there are serious impediments. Commitment to such rationality is an occupational hazard of policy analysts, but rationality, like beauty, is not subject to arbitrary standards: both dwell in the eye of the beholder. We must ask, "Rational for whom?" Reality also tells us that rationality is not everything; how people feel from intuition and emotion is also highly significant.

That is why technological choice, like all human decisions, is not a science but an art.

In a technological milieu, consider the following challenges to rational decision making. The underlying technical facts may be harder to understand, partially obscured by scientific jargon. And they may be couched in unnerving mists of probabilities. The range of technical alternatives may be greater. The consequences of error are more lethal to society and hazardous to the prestige of the decider. The social setting may be blurred by new fashions in social preferences, increasing interdependence of the institutions in the delivery systems, and complexity in defining cause-effect relationships. Then there are gaps in communications and noise from shouting advocates in a litigious atmosphere where narrow self-interest excludes dedication to the commonweal.

These are the external sources of difficulty. In addition, there are the difficulties internal to the policy process. Stamina may be inadequate for problem solving, or will may be too weak to prevail over obstacles no matter how skillfully detected. Or there may be too little information to steer by, and the steering mechanism may be disabled by incompetence, error, exhaustion, or self-delusion. Finally and perhaps most seriously, the machinery may have lost its capacity to learn and so possesses neither spontaneous versatility for rearrangement nor resilience to withstand shock.

This caricature of a worst-case decision environment has other harrowing features. Policies do not operate in isolation. Even though each policy may have narrow objectives, it not only impacts its neighbor, but it may inadvertently defeat effective implementation of a second, completely disparate policy. And domestic policies interact with foreign. In a sense, political boundaries at every scale are transcended by technological functions. Technological delivery systems, once compact, orderly, and predictable, become larger and uncertain. New networks and the volume of message traffic outflank the quest for understanding.

Given this grim portrait of reality, it may be surprising that any policies achieve their intended purposes, that any problems ever get solved. Former congressman Charles A. Mosher contends that any theory on how the Congress operates boils down to all congressional activities' being a learning process. Nothing is ever fully settled. To perfect outcomes, we need to crank up enhanced capabilities for pragmatic course correction. Later on, we consider whether this strategy, characterized by Charles Lindblom as one of "disjointed incrementalism," is largely a matter of step-wise political expediency, and if so, whether it continues to work under the new conditions of a technological age.

Given the esoteric tactics adopted in politics as the art of the possible, it is not surprising to read that some wit argued that "those who love sausage or respect the law should never watch either being made."

Very clearly, political instinct dominates methodical analysis. While we grope for more rational exits from technological paradox, we must recognize that the social performance of policy may depend less on technical virtuosity than on political acumen. At a moment of excrutiating tension in foreign affairs, the critical judgment of a leader may be far more significant in averting global catastrophe than the abundant capabilities of nuclear weapons and defenses.

Pathologies of the Short Run

Whatever connections we assume between technology and the future, we must admit they are marked by paradox, by problems as well as by progress. And notwithstanding the seriousness of latent threats to human survival, political leadership is sluggish in response. It is almost as though the policy apparatus were deaf to signals about the future.

Examples abound. When nuclear energy was being pushed thirty years ago as a cheap source of electricity, the safe disposal of the inevitable radioactive waste was ignored. When lobbying intensified for a national system of highways, no voices were raised about the future threat to the passenger railroad. When subsidies were adopted for crops, no one inquired as to the aggregated annual costs or as to the inadvertent incentives to expand production with exorbitantly priced land. When feasibility of artificial kidneys was demonstrated, no one calculated the costs of their distribution. When the nuclear arms race continued in its forty-first year, people still failed to recognize that more arms will not purchase more security. With personal computers proliferating in the home, inquiries have yet to be started on whether this may create a new social division of the information rich and the information poor.

Such a list could be endless, because every technology carries its own load of side effects. Yet, there seems to be little desire, much less the capacity, to look before we leap. Each given the uncertainties of forecasting, why? Why is there so little inclination to look ahead? Why is there uncritical dedication to the here and now, to demands for instant gratification? Why do we knowingly ignore the bills which are sure to come due tomorrow when opting for benefits today?

What lies beneath our social pathology of the short run?

First among causes of this disease is the familiar reward structure in politics. An incumbent's survival by a quest for votes is always a factor in political choice. Short-term benefts are more certain and more tangible to constituents; so for the policy maker, they are more admired. Even in campaign rhetoric, there seems to be a lack of courage and leadership to advocate a healthy balance between the short run and the long.

Yet another feature in the political milieu weakens anticipation. Everything takes time: with the increasing complexity of choice and the shrinking margins for error, rational analysis of tradeoffs would betoken the need for more time to process information. Yet, the percentage of time devoted by elected leaders to decisions has shrunk. Vested interests and constituents demand more attention; telephone and Xerox technologies clog channels with irrelevancies and distract people from their intellectual priorities, leaving them vulnerable to the tyranny of decision backlog. The hectic atmosphere and the pressure of day-to-day survival tactics completely demolish the will to think ahead.

Unfortunately, political leadership receives little encouragement from the bureaucracy for dealing with the longer run. Most large organizations resist looking ahead because doing so opens up the possibility of change, and change is threatening. While all organizations begin life as the embodiment of a new idea, some mature only to invest their creative energies in retaining the loyalty of their adherents and combatting forces inimical to their congealed beliefs. They continue to machine grooves of their initial mission no matter how obsolete. Paradoxically, the more successful is an aging institution, the more resistant it is to new ideas. Policy makers thus become captives of their entrenched bureaucracies and think twice before investing the energy required for internal reform.

Organizations, in and out of government, may also be reluctant to look ahead systematically because classical long-range planning has failed. In being directed to a current crisis, plans often neglect changes in social setting, becoming rigid blueprints without flexibility or even information channels for monitoring and feedback. And the public rejects the notion of planning, partly because of its association with the well-publicized plans of socialist states and partly from a perception of planning as a top-down, autocratic masterminding of life. A serious conceptual gap thus opens up between planners and those being planned for.

Some regard systematic foresight as a danger because it may expose errors of decisions past. Better to let sleeping dogs lie.

Finally, public servants are often deterred from looking ahead because repeated past experience has taught them that the opportunities for new starts are blocked by scarcity of resources. Despite the touted multiplier effects of technology, the system seems to have soaked up all reserves. There is little incentive to defend new options which can only become exercises in fantasy.

All these factors tend to make political process "piecemeal, provisional, parochial, uncoordinated, unsubstantial and lacking in prophetic moral vision," in the words of analyst Warren Wagar.

In private enterprise, as in politics, the reward structure places a premium on the short run. Pressures for immediate performance are intense, measured by Monday's stock quotation, or the quarterly statement of profit and loss, or an impatience for rapid return on investments, especially when interest rates climb. Executive promotions and bonuses are based on accomplishments visible this year. Indeed, officials are not moved to contemplate a future that they are not in: success that accrues too far ahead may only bring credit to a successor. There is small motivation even to contemplate the future, much less to act on that foresight.

To load all the blame on the self-serving traits of business and policy executives, however, is wrong. To a significant degree, the entire culture is at fault. Excessive zeal for the short run has many sources.

First, most people live in villages in that they hesitate to explore the terrain beyond their familiar mental boundaries. This includes a form of temporal provincialism: living in the present. As Walter Lippman said, modern men are predominantly isolationists, preoccupied with the more immediate events which may help or hurt them. They are marked by a vast indifference to the big issues, especially those about which they feel they can do nothing. Indeed, many people are so buffeted by daily crises in simply trying to survive day-to-day that it may be expecting too much for any but an especially attentive sector of the general public to engage these tormenting questions of the day. Suffice it to be entertained by the evening TV news, not informed.

Then there is frustration over uncertainty; the way ahead is always obscured. Even when there are danger signals, pundits and experts disagree, and warnings may be weak, ambiguous, or worn out from shrill repetition. Doubt and perplexity sow seeds of anxiety, and that leads to bald denial.

Coping with uncertainty has a twin difficulty, that of coping with complexity. It is not simply that the technical artifacts may be beyond common understanding. Rather, it is the social complexity induced by technology that is heightened. More and more diverse organizations must be wired together in every delivery system. Given the intricacy, fragmentation, transiency, and opacity of these networks, people discover that they are so imbedded in a maze of constraints depending upon the uncertain initiatives of others that they feel pulled and pushed by forces over which, in the long run, they have no control. In trying to solve these riddles, we stumble over the threshold of exhaustion. So we dismiss the challenge.

Finally, neglect of the future is prompted by a feeling of bliss through selective ignorance, and by the cultural imperative for immediate satisfaction. In no instance is this embrace of bliss by selective ignorance more apparent than in public indifference toward the threat of nuclear extinction. Someone characterized the attitude as a "Titanic syndrome": knowing that catastrophe lies ahead, metaphoric passengers on that ship choose to go first class. So it is hedonism practiced ironically in full awareness of a threat about which so many people have abdicated responsibility for choice to the expert and the politician. Yet both of these suffer from narrowness of perception, albeit in different ways. Neither has been able to break out of the molds or grooves of past study and commitment to examine fresh approaches to conflict management without violence.

There are those, however, who do not surrender to these ubiquitous discouragements. Social gadflies press unremittingly for change, for reform, for incorporating foresight into the decision process to gaze over the lip of the future because of the dangers that lurk there for our progeny. Frequently, their only practical recourse to raise consciousness of risk is to force project delays, initiate court action, and raise the costs of political bargaining. For consideration of the future to be forced only by incandescent political conflict may itself be symptomatic of political failure.

Given these forces that prompt neglect of the future, are we to suffer the ultimate disaster? Are there no remedies to the technology-amplified pathologies of the short run? Reader: please stay tuned.

Orchestrating the Bureaucracy

The federal bureaucracy is enormous; it is diversified; and each agency has a mind of its own. No wonder focusing the energies of federal agencies on a coherent set of goals is one of the most bewildering challenges of modern government. The problem is not just one of a granular, splintered, and competitive bureaucracy. It is compounded by centrifugal loyalties, by what political scientists refer to as the "iron triangles." These define a set of congenial relationships between an agency, its congressional oversight and appropriations committees, and outside constituencies. Because of these reciprocal linkages, unswerving loyalty to the chief executive is undermined, and this can damage internal unity and effective management.

The scope of the executive branch is dramatized in the *Government Organization Manual,* an annual publication that catalogs a taxonomy of all the organizational units and authorized functions of the federal government, as well as the names of current senior officers. At the front of the book is the Constitution of the United States, and its twenty-six amendments, establishing the basic authority of and the limits to governmental responsibility. It occupies 14 pages. The next 860 pages describe some 320 agencies and bureaus created by individual laws to carry out the broad purposes of the Constitution, most set up since 1932. If the manual had continued publishing in the same detail it had before 1966, it would be twice as large.

The point, of course, is to recognize the difficulty in public administration when the apparatus is so massive, when agencies vie for power, and when functions of a compartmentalized bureaucracy are constantly shifted. Under these conditions, how, then, to gain a sense of unity and direction? Gaining coherence requires coordination. That process is needed partly to salve the competition among agencies for power and purse, a rivalry as vigorous as some in the private sector. The infrastructure perceives a zero-sum game where if somebody wins, someone else loses. And so the warfare endures to capture budgetary or policy support and to defend mission-defined turf.

A different problem in coordination arises when initiatives by a single implementing agency spill over as policy and program impacts on sister agencies. Coordination is especially needed because more and more functions cross departmental lines. Consequently, government is less and less able to cope by jamming new functions into existing compartments. So today, almost every policy requires a partnership of several agencies. Farm policy is not set solely by the Department of Agriculture. Also in the act are the Departments of State, Health and Human Services, and Treasury, and the omnipresent Office of Management and Budget. Energy policy involves the Department of Energy, but also the Departments of Treasury, Commerce, Interior, and State, and others. Most federal agencies were created to fulfill a narrow purpose with a limited constituency, and the name of the agency revealed that ostensible purpose. Today, none operate within such homogeneous limits.

Finally, there is the problem of minimizing waste and duplication. Almost every department engages in some form of research and development. Some of it is highly specialized in accord with the unit's mission. But much research is basic enough to have widely diverse application, so that discoveries spurred by one agency might be of significance to five. This situation illuminates the most basic value of coordination—that of exchanging information on who is doing what and where, with a review of possible duplication or gaps.

One principle is clear. Only the president of the United States has supervision over this flock; only the incumbent can orchestrate all of the different instrumentalists to play the same tune, in harmony. But while all agencies report to the same boss, each also feels a linkage to the specialized clientele that it serves. And each agency has learned from legislative discipline that it must also respect transient currents in Congress and the preferences or biases of powerful members and committee chairmen.

So, robust incentives and coordination mechanisms are required. Yet the sectoral fragmentation and procedural rigidity almost defeat intent. More than that, interagency committees have no admirers and few defenders. Such organs have been characterized as "blanketing the executive branch with an embalmed atmosphere," with participants considered as "lonely, melancholy people who have responsibility but not authority to make decisions." One reason for this disparagement of committees is that self-serving agencies use them as instruments of bureaucratic espionage or obstruction. But as unpopular as interagency coordination may be, the alternatives are scarce and not very promising.

One such option is centralization. When federally funded research and development grew so swiftly after the Soviet space shot, proposals were introduced in Congress for consolidation, perhaps a Department of Science. Similar proposals have surfaced regularly, including one in 1985 by a presidential commission. Concentration of too many functions in a single agency, however, has numerous pitfalls. It opens the hazard of loss in control to powerful lobbies. The absence of competition usually degrades quality. Mistakes by an agency having an exclusive franchise could have major consequences. Even the Congress, which offers compulsive rhetoric to exorcise the devils of waste, is ambivalent, especially if consolidation would remove a component agency from a particular committee's jurisdiction.

In short, there is no panacea for orchestrating the bureaucracy. The tensions and rivalries are eternal. Presidents may complain about the problem of getting a grip on the bureaucracy. But their frustration may be a small price to pay to preserve a system of representative government.

Where Thy Purse Lies, Thy Heart Lies Also

One crucial set of policy choices concerns budgets and appropriations. Some of these policy choices involve direct funding of research and development. Others involve procurement. Still others involve funding of subsidies or regulatory functions. All are incorporated in a master catalog of expenditures and obligations that attracts attention because of what it says about tradeoffs and the art of technological choice.

The annual budget saga begins each January when the nation's capital witnesses a ceremonial rite mandated by the Constitution. Metaphorically, the president's budget is trundled down Pennsylvania Avenue for congressional action. As the saying goes, "The president proposes and the Congress disposes." Transit of this vast document, with several telephone-book-size appendices, is usually well lubricated by White House rhetoric to foster uncritical adoption. With all the hoopla and mystique—and only smidgeons of reality—we often lose sight of the fact that by this one act and this one particular instrument, the president has synthesized the multidimensional wants and needs, hopes and dreams, of a diverse American society into a one-dimensional, quantitative priority list.

In keeping with the biblical injunction "For where your treasure is, there will your heart be also," chief executives open for public battle the question of whether their interpretation of complex and competing claims, together with an accounting of resources at hand, meets the test of consensus. Because demands are justified by so many interests, their total inevitably exceeds the size of purse. Then comes maneuvering to reconcile differences, with battle lines arrayed to protect both legitimate claims and sacred cows.

"When I pay taxes, I buy civilization," said Oliver Wendell Holmes. Today, however, the public spectacle of deciding how to allocate these tax revenues is as uncivilized as any other process of governance. Not fully appreciated is the less visible but no less savage preliminary struggle. Under wraps of secrecy, each agency competes for limited resources, defends its slice of the pie, and attempts to persuade first the director of the Office of Management and Budget and then, if unsuccessful, the president, of its merits.

It would be fallacy, however, to perceive the pie and its division as starting each cycle from scratch. To a substantial extent, the budget is a captive of history, bound by enormous fixed charges for debt retirement, obligations for Social Security and veterans' benefits, and past commitments to weapon systems that, because it is argued that they are only partially complete, carry over to succeeding years. Perhaps only 25 percent of the pie remains to be apportioned, and that is what the fighting is all about.

After originating in the bowels of the bureaucracy, budget proposals pass upward through a succession of vigorous reviews. Because each echelon can say no more easily than yes, proposals are in continuous jeopardy until reaching the top for submission to the OMB. Yet in this game, a relatively weak proposition may survive simply because of a favorable signal from senior officers, most particularly the president.

Then it is the budget director's turn to shoehorn the glittering array of departmental choices into a budget whose size was mandated by the "boss." On the basis of the expertise and whims of OMB personnel, intelligence garnered from informers within the government, and often the advice of outsiders who are experts or have extraordinary political leverage, proposals are trimmed further. Military budgets, however, seem particularly immune from such kibitzing, partly because the OMB is thinly staffed to deal with defense intricacies. During this review, the OMB may solicit counsel from the office of the president's science advisor. At this stage, the advisor has an opportunity to advocate special funding, such as for basic research or for the creation of new engineering laboratories in universities, but seldom has a say on big-ticket items like entire weapons systems, as he did in the 1960s.

In the semifinals of this internal competition, if the budget director and a department head disagree, the issue moves to the president for resolution. In some administrations, the list of unresolved issues has reached hundreds of items. More recently, it has been boiled down to a relative few, conspicuous both by their size and their political sensitivity. The ultimate benediction resides in the president's budget, which becomes the Holy Grail of bureaucratic fervor. Convoyed with press releases and furor generated by leaks, the product enters the labyrinthine ways of Congress, there to be dissected, analyzed, and possibly dismembered. The record shows, however, that presidential initiative usually wins, with nothing more than minor symbolic congressional tinkering.

Through this brutal process, how stands the science and technology budget? In trying to answer that question, we discover that no such item exists. Budget elements with science and technology ingredients are spread throughout government, with science nominally represented under headings of research and development, and technology represented under labels that correspond to such purposes as defense, food production, health, environmental management, natural resources, and the like. While all these pieces may be assembled under the rubric of science and technology because the total can be interpreted as one of the vital signs of technological enterprise, such a total is an accounting fiction. That is to say, there is no unified science and technology budget whose size has been arbitrarily established early in the process, and then subdivided.

Totals, however, can be highly revealing. We can track trends of support for research fields, for biotechnology, or for manufacturing engineering, for example, or for nuclear energy versus solar energy research; or compare the totals for university versus industrial performance; or gauge the balance between civilian and military; or estimate the impact of growing or shrinking functions on employment of specialized personnel.

Needless to say, the science and technology community track these developments closely because federal initiatives have such a powerful effect on the national enterprise. During the 1960s, federal funding supported over 70 percent of the nation's research and development. In 1985, that ratio had shrunk to 50 percent because private funding had grown faster than public. But in defense areas which constitute the cutting edge of high-tech, government funding has grown sharply, and represents by far the largest slice of the federal R&D pie.

Two final points. First, many economists argue that the economic vitality of a nation depends on its investments in research and development, although the payoff is always deferred. Economist Edwin Mansfield claims that R&D is responsible for over 50 percent of the growth in industrial productivity, capital investments representing only about 20 percent. What fraction of the nation's wealth is devoted to this endeavor may thus be quite significant. Over a period of some forty years, the public and private support for R&D in the United States has hovered around 3 percent of the GNP, significantly greater than the 2 percent in Western Europe and Japan, but including a far larger fraction devoted to military affairs. Whatever the magic number, it was previously believed that a strong posture should be assured by direct government funding. Now that view has changed sharply, to one of policies intended to stir the private sector to increase sponsorship.

Which leads to the second point. Not all of the budget issues that involve science and technology involve direct expenditures. Some also concern policies which might affect tax receipts or subsidies, or which entail costs of administration, such as the monitoring of environmental hazards. Yet these items must also pass through a screen of technological choice; all involve fiscal tradeoffs.

The year 1986 saw the traditional budget process convulsed by the Gramm-Rudman-Hollings budget instruction. No technology-related appropriations were immune to this harsh discipline—no research, no incentives for improved industrial productivity, no weapons systems, no machinery to protect the health and safety of citizens or the environment. Both branches of government will be severely tested on the critical choices ahead, the tradeoffs, the manner in which expediency will substitute for vision.

6 / Technology and Industry

n Western society, the industrial firm succeeded the artisan and family farmer as a production unit, functioning as a midwife of technology. For along with radical advances in hardware came a revolution in the institutions for its nourishment and its management. The historical progression was triggered by a technical discovery of how to concentrate energy. With an iron boiler, steam could be generated from readily available coal, and the steam could then be fed to mechanical engines to do work. We learned how to package energy. Because these devices could be built over a range of sizes, and because they could be installed wherever desired for the use intended, critical limitations of human or animal labor and especially of water power were overcome. First, engines pumped water from flooded mines. Then they were employed for manufacturing. Then these principles were applied to the railroad and steamboat, farming and the generation of electricity. As engineering and invention progressed, the limits to applications were not technical; they were institutional.

Organizations were thus formed to concentrate capital, for only with ample funds could industrial firms expand operations with intricate and expensive machines. As entrepreneurs saw opportunities blossom, they went not just to banks but also directly to the public, often with get-rich-quick offerings of stocks and bonds. The public soon became co-owners. But raising capital was not the only challenge to the evolving firm.

The next requirement was one of planning:

industrial management became the software of the era. With innovative ideas and capital, firms then had to organize the separate tasks involved, say in converting raw fleece to woolen garments, to identify the essential specialized skills and their functional interconnections. Thus emerged the familiar organization chart.

Also needed were flow charts. With so many and diverse operations, planning was required to synchronize the internal stream of materials as they underwent modification from raw input to finished output. But such planning was also necessary to deal with the external world: to sense the market and tune products to its signals; to assure formation of capital in phase with anticipated expansion; to obtain sufficient credit to pay wages before products were sold. With sluggish sales, market demand required manipulation through advertising, timed so that output would not pile up unsold in warehouses.

Finally, management had to deal with the economic risk associated with uncertainties: in supply of raw materials, in availability and cost of labor, in foreign exchange and interest rates, in fluctuations of the market, and in the growing encroachment of government in a previously laissez-faire atmosphere. In its primitive beginnings, industrial risk management often meant employing political tactics, coercion, or brute force to contain adverse external influences that interfered with the hallowed free market. Such was the first furious and violent reaction to unionization—a response that later had to be outlawed.

In recent decades, the industrial firm has encountered a new challenge. To the concentration of energy and capital, there is now required a concentration of information. To be sure, specialized, proprietary information on product design and manufacturing processes has always been at the heart of successful enterprise in a competitive atmosphere. The race goes not just to the swift but also to the clever. But with manufacturing techniques becoming so complex and so changeable, it is not only a basic patent that must be protected. A considerable investment is also represented by the research and development enterprise now associated with the more vigorous industries. Here, information is property; indeed, in rapidly evolving firms engaged in high tech, it may be far more important than the bricks, mortar, and machines that ordinarily define capital assets. So companies must nourish, conserve, and guard their information resources: the professionals who constitute the walking libraries, highly skilled personnel with empirical talent, the pipelines to knowledge in the scholarly community and the files.

Apart from narrowly technical information, broader knowledge is essential for decision making. Reports are required about the internal workings of the organization, and about how to measure and maximize productivity. Intelligence is needed concerning uncertainties identified previously in the external world, including quivers and spasms in world events regarding commodities, competition, economic and political stability.

No wonder that the computer has become essential to modern operations, so as to store and make accessible enormous quantities of information swiftly, across global terminals, and in a form and lexicon that is readily understood; then to establish causal relationships, and to play the game of "What if?" This intelligence function of data base, collective memory, and the outreach network, like the technical information, is fundamental to industrial management.

To organize, plan, and manage operations universally required a new prototype of production unit, one that economist John Kenneth Galbraith has characterized as "technostructure." It corresponds to those components of technological delivery systems where management mobilizes knowledge, capital, human resources, natural resources, and tools to deliver some specific product or service.

From its early beginnings, this management task was formidable. A high commitment of personal energy and often personal wealth were required, with correspondingly high risks of failure. As the technological enterprise evolved at the hands of a relatively few individuals, why was the game worth the candle? What made Johnny run?

The pat answer was profit, the possibility of accumulating a large personal fortune. For in that milieu, wealth alone could promise power, recognition, social status, and respect. Indeed, institutional goals and individual goals coincided to maximize earnings on investment because the owners, as "capitalists," were the managers. The founders became living legends: Henry Ford, Andrew Carnegie, John D. Rockefeller, Leland Stanford. Not only was motivation of the entrepreneurial individual and of the entrepreneurial corporation identical, but so also was their behavior.

The situation today, however, has drastically changed. What follows regarding behavior of the firm primarily applies to the *Fortune Magazine* five hundred largest corporations. By no means does this denigrate the importance of small business, nor does it neglect those contemporary fireballs at scientific and engineering frontiers, catering high-tech, innovative products. But while these five hundred corporations constitute only 0.1 percent of all business, they hold more than two-thirds of the capital assets and are responsible for over half of industrial production. Collectively, they represent a dominant influence on both the economy and on politics.

For these firms, the historic goal of profit remains. Unlike their precursors, however, maximizing earnings on investment is not the only goal. These enterprises also seek the confidence of Wall Street, which can lead to increases in the price of stock and greater attractiveness to investors generally. They angle for power in the ability to control their economic and political environment, at least to effect stability. They try to minimize a large portfolio of risks. They seek growth in size through acquisitions as well as in their slice of the market. They hope for respect within the business community, by their innovativeness and recruitment of high talent, and ability to attract venture capital. As the goals of private enterprise have changed, so have the recipients of the benefits. At one time, these accrued to the individual owner or owners. Now, corporate profits go to stockholders.

The crux of the matter is that corporations having a suite of goals are obliged to make tradeoffs among them as they plan their strategies. Overt greed does not kindle public esteem. Neither does blatant overzealous intrusion into politics.

The earlier coincidence of individual and corporate goals of profit simplified decision making at the top. Today, it is complicated by the fact that chief executive officers are hired hands—that is, hired by boards of directors. To be sure, such officers usually hold significant amounts of company stock so as to have a direct stake in the fate of the company. Nevertheless, what makes CEO Johnny run in terms of the many tradeoffs against short-term profit alluded to previously may differ from what makes Johnny the traditional rugged individualist owner run. Some part of the decision is influenced by what chief executive officers visualize as the impact on themselves—in terms of respect by peers, respect by subordinates, retention by the board—as well as by the impact on the organization.

Modern chief executive officers must regard themselves as transients because they so often are. Indefinite loyalty to one firm is not a part of their creed. Their behavior is thus heavily directed toward publicizing achievements that would increase their personal attractiveness to another suitor, especially if the transfer involves a form of upward mobility as measured by gross revenues.

Curiously enough, at senior management levels, mobility occurs among firms engaged in vastly different businesses, confirming a perception that the talents which are especially treasured today are oriented far more to general commercial practices and a familiarity with the tax code than to a knowledge of the specialized hardware and techniques around which a firm was originally built. Such patterns are almost universal in the growing abundance of corporate acquisitions that lead to motley-patterned conglomerates.

What makes Johnny run? Today, it all depends.

Business Isn't What It Used to Be

"The business of America is business." Thus spoke President Calvin Coolidge in his best-remembered contribution to politics. That dictum is more a pronouncement of creed than of function. At the time, it was only partly true; now, it is even less so. More accurate and to the point would be an operative statement that, today, "The business of America is technology." While some believe that the business of America is human freedom and dignity, the reality of the 1980s is that technology drives the business machine.

As we have just seen, as technology changes, so does the behavior of its mediating enterprise, the corporation. Goals have changed; the economic dogma to maximize return on investment is now more complicated; management is far more sophisticated. Indeed, the neoclassical model of "the firm" has undergone such revolutionary change that it is useful to elaborate on these previously mentioned differences.

Historically, technological enterprises began as ventures of individuals. Such people were distinguished by fiery ambition, vision, a willingness to take high risks, self-reliance, a keen understanding of human behavior, and high talent for persuasion, organization, and planning. Over-achievers, all. But during the heyday of the capitalists, many were known by other traits. Frequently they were arrogant, unmindful of human sensibilities, autocratic and intolerant of dissent, indifferent to ethical codes, committed to the Coolidge creed that was reflected in their conservative political philosophy. These nineteenth-century industrialists flaunted their wealth and influence.

Contrast that stereotype with the modern entrepreneur or chief executive officer. Whereas everyone knew who was president of Standard Oil, United States Steel, or the Pennsylvania Railroad, today very few can name the president of Exxon, AT&T, IBM, or others of the largest corporations. The principal decision maker is anonymous: exceptions like Lee Iaccoca of Chrysler Corporation are conspicuous because they are so rare. Corporate power is now generally shielded from public view or, when visible, exercised with appropriate gravity and demeanor.

The personal characteristics of chief executive officers contrast sharply with those of their predecessors. These new managers search more diligently than predecessors for security and hedges against risk. Instead of being nonconforming individualists, most are admired as group leaders, able to mobilize the team. Decision making thus revolves more around the committee than the chairman, with the modern corporate officer depending far more on participatory management than on the old-fashioned notion that the leader is the brain and subordinates are simply hands to carry out the orders of the boss.

In a sense, the internal creed of business has changed. At one time, the individual owner-manager looked forward to providing his heirs a legacy of identity, investment, permanence, and reputation. There was an intrinsic longer-term view that the company, which often bore the founder's name, would continue forever in the family. And for that successful business man, there were intangible rewards beyond profit. One of these was the loyalty of lifelong employees. Another was leisure—indeed, conspicuous leisure, manifested by the country estate, the yacht, the private railroad car.

Today, the chief executive officer is likely to be a workaholic with a single-minded focus on the job: the hypnotic lure of continually solving problems, and the career rewards of success. But managers are increasingly isolated from the internal structure, depending upon a well-designed organizational format to function as intended with all kinds of statistical instruments to check vital signs. The manager deals more with numbers and symbols than with real people. He or she dresses, reads, and adopts the conventions and attitudes of a peer group so as to deliberately submerge self-identity.

That change in the persona of the manager is symbolic of other transformations corresponding to the new multiplicity of goals. Success wears many new garments. There is return on investment and growth to sustain a piece of the market, to be sure. But beauty contests are also won by noneconomic achievements: management virtuosity in responding to surprise in markets or to uncontrollable, external events; the provision of safety and conviviality in the workplace; and finally, evidence of social responsibility that earns esteem from the general public because of an outward display of tradeoffs, say of environmental protection for greed.

Processes have also changed. The classical entrepreneur focused sharply on the play of the marketplace, that legendary and transcendent regulator of economic behavior. And the owner-manager fashioned the necessary internal organization and planning mechanisms to produce with high efficiency. To those devices are now added managing information, both as to content and its diffusion; the constant testing of markets and the skillful use of high-tech advertising and public relations to inflame customer appetites when demand flags; coping with shifts in governmental regulations or the political will to enforce them; developing a capacity to influence political decisions regarding taxes, subsidies, regulation, and incentives; exploiting opportunities for partnerships with government in enterprises that exceed the financial capacity or limits to risk of the private firm; and sensing wobbles in overall public attitudes that can affect both short- and long-term company strategies. Indeed, business isn't what it used to be.

The modern manager must constantly be on guard against new threats to success, personal or corporate. In the past, these came largely from competition for markets, and uncertainties over the cost of money, labor, and the supply of raw materials. Today, that catalog has grown. In a far more complex enterprise beyond the span of attention of one individual, there is a greater dependence on others. Authority now gets diffused; so does responsibility. Then arises the hazard of internal mismanagement. This may occur simply from poor judgment, but it may also occur because of gaps in information or even because of mischief. In the firm, as in society, the past is not prologue because of swift changes in the knowledge base that undergirds the enterprise. New discoveries hasten technological obsolescence in both product and production methods. The corporation is far more vulnerable to foreign events including terrorism, to the vagaries of domestic conditions such as inflation, and to whims in popular fashions, including what is considered sexy in the stock market. There is a greater demand for public accountability and a zealous press is ready to pounce on blunders or neglect of social responsibility. No small wonder that Alka Seltzer adorns most executives' desks.

Apart from the evolution of corporate goals, criteria for achievement, new-style management, and creed, there have been changes in social constraints on corporations, in social consequences for corporate actions, and in relationships between industry and government.

The external rules by which business games were once played primarily involved laws of property rights. These were simple, derived from long-standing precedent in English jurisprudence, and predictable. Only the antitrust legislation of the late nineteenth century perturbed those customs. Soon after, the tax code began to envelop business operations, first by additions, and then, in recent years, by complex loopholes that permitted the sophisticated manager not only to circumvent taxes, but actually to exploit the new rules as a means of enhancing profits and growth through acquisition.

There was also a surge of laws for human rights. These concerned child labor, labor relations, and eventually affirmative action and occupational health and safety. Indeed, the broader implications of human rights were recently connected to the health and safety of the general public, over a wide range of possibly adverse effects from poisons that escape to air and water during manufacture, from disposal of toxic waste, and from hazards to consumers in the use or misuse of products. And finally there has been a heightened concern for the natural environment and the imposition of a network of regulations to protect it.

Such drastic increases in constraints on business reflect major changes in the culture itself: a greater social awareness of the impact of technology on human affairs, of the traditional concentration by most private enterprises on making a profit with studied indifference to external effects on the public, and of the corresponding need for greater accountability. Indeed, as tougher ground rules evolved inimical to laissez-faire, business typically responded by screaming and kicking while being dragged into the mainstream of social reform.

At the same time, there have been other cultural shifts highly favorable to business. Postwar prosperity in the Western world brought with it an exuberant consumerism. In the 1980s, this thrust was accompanied by a new popular wave to reduce taxes and the influence of government. In pursuing its own narrow goals, industry was in tune with the notion of "getting government off our backs." Young people expressed concern for jobs and especially for opportunities in the business world that offered seductive "fast lanes."

Indeed, the pecuniary interests of the business sector and the values of society were in resonance in yet another and salient way. Both focused on the short term at the expense of the long. People have enthusiastically adopted a credit-card economy; they want their investments to rise swiftly, Monday morning. In general, people have become willing to defer or even ignore the longer-term effects, whether beneficial or harmful.

To sum up, industrial firms that were once small, closely held by a few owners, managed by one person, and thus highly individualistic as well as flexible, have emerged as corporate giants, complex, clumsy in responding to external shocks, and thus intent on manipulating their environment to guarantee stability. Decisions are likely to be made by committees of specialists. Management control is likely to depend on computer-processed information of all kinds: technical, economic, political, social. And thus, success is likely to depend critically on access to and utilization of knowledge.

Clearly, the business of America is technology. In that recognition, the myth has been perpetuated that the effective management of technology is largely the responsibility of private enterprise: government and business should be as separate as church and state. Curiously enough, the union of industry and government is considered by both liberal and conservative factions to be a deviant sin, although for completely opposite reasons. What is not widely recognized is that government and industry have increasingly become partners—albeit silent partners—in the business of technology. Entrepreneurs do not want to advertise this reality because it destroys the romantic image of the freewheeling, rugged individualist of eras past. They would like to conceal their dependency on government and their initiatives to keep their hand on the steering wheel. Likewise, government officials hide these relationships, mostly because they hope to avoid accusations of undue meddling in economic processes, and sometimes, simply to head off implications of collusion. Along with this increase in partnership has come a relatively invisible struggle for power, between people and vested interests. Only in late 1984 did this burst onto the public scene with a draft manifesto from bishops of the Catholic church warning about social perils arising from economic obsessions and public policy insensitive to trends of inequity.

Scholars in futures studies often resort to scenarios as crisp means to portray various paths ahead. In one such analysis, five scenarios were proposed. First, there is a return to the liberal precepts and practices of the 1960s. Second, there is possible deterioration of the environment and unending social conflict. Third is the possibility that technological "fixes" can be employed to remedy many of the current side effects or overcome limits that engender strife. Fourth is a society that finds strength and stability through spiritual means, the conservation ethic. And last there is the corporate state. In the latter, industry and government are merged, not so much in organization as in goals and creed. Most analysts think this is the most probable future. If so, exploring these implications may be crucial.

What Will Industry Do When Government Gets off Its Back?

Every society cherishes myths. One simplistic image is so congenial to private industry that it is pleased to propagate the notion vigorously. This popular economic model casts the private sector as the swashbuckling, imaginative, risk-taking generator of abundant jobs for workers, income for investors, and the good life for everyone else. A corollary is that business is at its best when completely unfettered. Government spoils the fun. So industry reinforces its free-enterprise mystique by loudly complaining at each and every step by government to tax or to regulate. Because the nation was built on premises of capitalism, any government interference in a laissez-faire environment is argued by Chambers of Commerce as steps toward inhibited productivity, socialism, or worse. To these protagonists, government is the enemy. No wonder they cry, "Let's get government off our backs," and offer enthusiastic support for politicians exalting that rhetorical theme.

In truth, government and industry need each other. The government requires a vigorous economy to foster material progress, minimize social discontent, and provide an affluent base from which to siphon off taxes. Industry needs protection, both from unfair competition domestically and abroad, and from excessive risk over projects of unprecedented scale or over vulnerability to lawsuits from damages stemming from the failure of unprecedented technologies.

Both government and industry crave security, predictability of economic parameters, and relaxed tensions among confrontational interest groups. And both seek stability in world affairs. Both parties seek national eminence, now mostly through powerful technical means rather than through the force of ideas or ideals. With so many identical goals, both are quietly willing to trade off ideological precepts of separation for that nirvana of their common objectives, although in the United States, neither willingly parades the essential compromises in public.

As a result, government has been a willing partner in stimulating the private economy when it flags. One by one, almost every industry and agricultural sector has quietly sought and received government benefits. These include fast tax write-offs for oil exploration wildcatters, subsidies to tobacco farmers, lower interest rates for overseas sales of Boeing aircraft through the Export-Import Bank, tax credits for purchase of capital equipment, direct subsidies for construction of merchant ships to counter lower-cost foreign shipyards, protection of steel producers by quotas on foreign sources, import taxes on textiles, and wheat sales to the Soviet Union. At times, government has been called upon for a complete bail-out, as with Chrysler and Lockheed. Then there have been such illogical incentives as permitting tax write-offs to companies purchasing bankrupt concerns, or contributing other goodies to firms diversifying by acquisition, even if such strategies contributed nothing to enhance productivity.

This government support has not been balanced with inordinate regulation, because government has always been an unwilling regulator: most initiatives by government to protect the public interest by controlling the private sector have occurred only *after* excessive abuses were detected. Monopolistic price-gouging, violent union-busting, occulted disposal of toxic waste, or unmitigated exposure of workers to hazardous coal dust or asbestos initially passed the threshold of ethical tolerance unnoticed by the entire culture. Now and then muckraking initiatives by investigative reporters or by public interest organizations exposed areas where the pecuniary interest of business collided with public interest. Government requirements for safer cars can be traced to heroic initiatives of Ralph Nader in exposing the unsafe GM Corvair. Pressure for environmental protection was mobilized only after the public read and reacted to Rachel Carson's *Silent Spring*.

So what would industry do if government backed off both with its assistance as well as with its regulation? It is not at all certain that industry and agriculture sincerely want the free market that they clamor for: many industries might not survive without artificial government supports. This is especially true in the international marketplace, where many foreign dealers are subsidized by their governments.

Also, notwithstanding the macho legend, most mature industries prefer stability to competition. They strongly dislike uncertainties—about inflation, about the costs of energy, capital, or labor. The private sector wants the Securities Exchange Commission to regulate the morals of Wall Street. Judging by industry's ultimate acceptance of a national environmental policy, it may even prefer the imposition of uniform regulations regarding environmental and occupational health and safety so that everyone plays by the same rules, rather than be exposed to lawsuits for damages.

Especially, business abhors uncertainty in world order, the wallow and lurch of Third World governments. This partly explains the uncritical support most nondefense industry lends to military expenditures. In the business culture, there is widespread belief that foreign policy is best practiced with gunboat diplomacy, that we need to display our technological muscle, rather than ideas and ideals, to assure the viability of U.S. bank loans to foreign creditors.

So there is a quiet recognition by industry that excessive independence may be dangerous to its health. This is all the more true in light of the need to compete on the world market, where most if not all other industrialized nations have been systematic and public about their government-industry partnerships. As one manifestation, the free market has virtually disappeared in international trade. Japan, Inc., is often trotted out as a model, it being suggested that the comfortable relationships adopted there in keeping with the culture are worth studying even if not emulating. We tend to forget the Japanese Ministry of International Trade and Industry relied on state-sponsored cartels to achieve developmental goals as far back as the 1920s.

There is, however, yet another issue, that of social responsibility. Given industry's focus on profits with a corollary of minimizing costs, there is little if any spontaneous incentive for industry to include within its calculus any of the external social and economic costs resulting from its initiatives. The economist would say that there are no methods, much less rewards, for individual firms to estimate and act in the public interest to reduce unwanted side effects voluntarily. Government's intervention, therefore, may be the only mechanism by which these costs can be identified and fairly mitigated.

Put another way, there are techniques for assuring the fiscal accountability of a firm, but not its social accountability. The state acted to assist the private sector by licensing the corporation. It did so because it believed there was a clear social purpose, especially to encourage entrepreneurship. A new type of legal entity was created and permitted to do business like an individual. As further assistance, permission was granted for the corporation to acquire capital. Then, by the rules of incorporation, the state released those owning and managing the firm from individual risk. These firms are regulated by requirements for extensive financial reports on internal operations, but they are not required to issue corresponding reports on external impacts. Probably they cannot be. Nevertheless, the large publicly held firm today is sensitive to public criticism, especially if there are threats to marketing their products or selling stock. As voters, the public cannot be ignored. As investors, the public holds a similar power, but only when there is enough momentum for investors concerned about corporate responsibility to exert their sovereignty. By openly expressing preferences for, and putting a premium on, securities that have been vetted to confirm that business practices accord well with the public interest, investors can influence the corporate boardroom as was done in 1985 regarding firms doing business with South Africa.

Industry's preoccupation with tracing its disabilities to government leads many industrialists to believe their own rhetoric. What is then overlooked are the devils of mismanagement *within* the firm itself. With economies of scale favoring massive size, flexibility is lost. With excessive, "top-down" hierarchical management, skilled subordinates are not consulted, the biases of top management are perpetuated, and at all levels resistance to change increases. With the owners of capital not directly in control, there is a serious loss in entrepreneurial risk taking; corporate officials may put personal economic security ahead of the firm's. Accompanying this condition is the tendency to seek stability at any cost, and with it, artificial protection against competition. With the intensive focus on new production technology, there is further isolation of labor from the decision opportunities and loss in worker productivity. With excessive compartmentalization of tasks comes weak quality control. With dependence on the apparatus of persuasion to counter market weaknesses, there is reduced attention to product improvement and lower cost.

Externalizing blame only inhibits any internal search for true sources of disability or for new ideas—including those inimical to top management's biases. In the early 1970s and the 1980s, exposés published by General Motors' insiders confirmed this disability. On the other hand, many firms have adopted a more candid as well as more sophisticated view of themselves and the world in which they operate. The best-seller *In Search of Excellence* explains how.

Nowhere is the parochialism more evident than with the tax laws. With these introduced under pressure of industrial advocates, there has been a new phenomenon of what policy analyst Robert Reich calls "paper entrepreneurship." Profits have been made by the manipulation of rules and money, not by innovation to reduce costs, attack new markets, or improve productivity. Shrewd maneuvering to finesse tax laws puts a premium on an entirely different type of manager, one more familiar with accounting than with engineering. Business schools tout their courses on efficient administration, using communication technologies and a personal secretary. But managers lose touch with the real world of people and the untidy struggles for *Lebensraum*, and they may have extreme difficulty performing in the spirit of free enterprise that they espouse. Meanwhile, capital employed for acquisitions soaks up capital that might otherwise be employed to enhance technology. As Reich has said, "We have changed from a nation of traders to a nation of brokers." If government were completely off industry's back, there is a major question as to how many firms would survive.

The basic problem, however, is not whether there should be a partnership. That is inevitable. The problem is that it is hidden from view. Because both sides treat this intimate relationship as illicit, there is deferment of a necessary cultural legitimacy that has been witnessed in other industrial nations. One result may be the unwitting preservation of outmoded and counterproductive industrial management.

As the U.S. trade balance tilted alarmingly in the mid-1980s, pressures were reawakened for a reindustrialization of America. With different slogans, this vexatious demand has surfaced several times before. On each occasion, a different brand of medicine was concocted. In the early 1960s, at the initiative of the Commerce Department, legislation was passed providing technical assistance to states to resuscitate dying industries. In 1971, President Nixon asked the White House staff to suggest new initiatives to keep alive the aerospace industry, as its NASA patron attempted to recruit a sequel to the successful Apollo program. Then there were special rescue efforts by the government to bail out Lockheed Aircraft, and later Chrysler. In the 1980s, quick fixes were sought through the government tax code, wage freezes, and rapid reading of books about how the Japanese enhance worker productivity. However threatening these earlier cycles, by 1985 foreign economic competition loomed as a far more critical, stubborn, baffling, and debilitating ailment than earlier concerns.

With the prospects of direct government assistance shrunken even further by the Reagan doctrine, along with increased prospects of tax reform that would eliminate artificial sources of profits decoupled from productivity, industry has been forced to reconnoitre its internal creed, institutional cultures, and practices. How and how well it responds will constitute a major test of its true strength—including in that characterization elements of social responsibility, willingness to share in sacrifice, and institutional creativity. Only if it passes these tests will the general public regain confidence in the integrity of private enterprise enough to permit relaxation of the regulatory constraints that have led to the repeated accusations of "government on our backs."

First Sputnik, Now a Toyota

In 1957, the Soviet Union's successful launch of Sputnik was perceived as an unprecedented threat to U.S. national security because other nations might interpret this success as proof of the U.S.S.R.'s technical superiority. In the midst of a cold-war atmosphere of military confrontation, that potential loss in technological prestige threw the nation into a tailspin. In the 1980s, another external threat to national security has developed. This time, it comes from Japan, and it is economic. The similarities and differences in these challenges are of considerable interest because the second confrontation is not yet resolved, and how effectively the economic challenge can be met warrants investigation.

In retrospect, it is hard to believe that a grapefruit-size spacecraft with a tiny radio transmitter could have so sharply jolted a robust industrial nation into a complete change in its attitude toward science and technology, and so enhance their relationship to national power and prestige. Within months, almost every institution responded. Exploration of outer space, with its commitment of national treasure, was given high priority. A new federal agency was spawned as a symbol of that intent. So were new committees in Congress. The airplane manufacturing business was sharply expanded and now labeled aerospace.

Also signalling a new awareness was President Eisenhower's appointment of a White House science advisor. Universities and their students were given new support through the National Defense Education Act. And federal funds for research and development began to skyrocket, funneled into university and industrial laboratories alike. On coming into office in 1961, President Kennedy announced the nation's intent to land a man on the moon within the decade.

After the first few years of space competition, the dust of national hysteria settled. But two different forces endured to sustain the space momentum. One was the sheer exhilaration of encounter with a new frontier, a challenge that fired the imagination of young and old and conferred reality on what had previously been only the grist of comic strips and science fiction. The other motivation had a more practical foundation. It stemmed from worry over whether the U.S.S.R.'s space triumphs had treacherous military applications. To some extent, that worry led to ironic developments. Sputnik was a surprise in that its development and plan for launching was unannounced. But it was fundamentally part of a scientific study of the planet from space in connection with the giant collaborative project entitled the International Geophysical Year. At what level the Soviets would have unilaterally pursued their advantage in space is uncertain, for they baldly—and effectively—propagandized their achievements as a tool of dipolomacy to intimidate uncommitted nations through implied technological power. Nevertheless, some of their later efforts may have been triggered by our own massive response to Sputnik, a response that the Soviets miscalculated. In any event, the large booster rockets that the Soviets developed to loft heavy space payloads were considered a capability of unknown potential for military purposes. Our ballistic missiles did not need high thrust to propel warheads because we had successfully miniaturized even the most powerful. But at that time, Soviet superiority in booster size was regarded as threatening. The Apollo manned lunar landing mission provided a rationale for a parallel booster development in the United States; under that innocent cloak we built a military space capability which for decades had uncertain application, until the space shuttle project was switched on and, by 1984, proposals advanced for space stations and "Star Wars" defenses.

The point, of course, is that the United States responded swiftly and effectively to the perceived military threat of Sputnik. Based on subsequent achievements of the lunar landing, and the orbiting of satellites for global communication, weather observations, and espionage, the U.S. program can be judged a brilliant success.

In addition, the Soviet initiative drew attention to the entire spectrum of science and engineering, leading to a policy of seeking leadership in every field. To a large degree, that outgrowth also was successful. By the mid-1980s, however, it was clear that the United States had no clear monopoly on space achievements. The Soviets led in manned space stations; European nations and Japan caught up in unmanned rocketry.

In the 1970s, another technological challenge from abroad was detected. But unlike the space surprise, this threat was slow and subtle in growth, was economic rather than military, had "user-friendly" characteristics, and generated feelings of affection rather than apprehension on the part of the public. Symbolically, it was not a Sputnik; it was a Toyota.

The threat, of course, was foreign commercial competition. It began with expanded imports of automobiles. First were VW's from Germany, then Toyotas, Subarus, and Datsuns from Japan. Soon, there were steel nails and steel girders, even plywood manufactured from trees grown in America. Then came the flood of consumer electronics, followed by such professional electronic gear as TV cameras. By 1985, there was scarcely any consumer product not being manufactured abroad, with a corresponding loss in American sales throughout the world. As American firms found the price competition too intense, there were cries for protection. But the American consumer not only found the lower prices of imports attractive; the quality and style were also often superior.

The continued threat of the Toyota is tangible. It is most conspicuously distinguished by an unfavorable balance in trade that soared from $30 billion in 1980 to $130 billion by 1984. Meanwhile, the American dollar continued to be so strong that price competition from foreign goods continued to embarrass American suppliers. As this enigma grew, and as it became apparent that import taxes and quotas could backfire on U.S. manufacturers who sought to market abroad, the quest for answers intensified. For a while, it became chic to analyze the Japanese production culture and advocate imitation.

While the limitations of any witless transfer of Japan, Inc., to the United States were recognized, one feature was readily apparent: in Japan, industry and government had a far more harmonious partnership than they do in America. The Japanese government joins in researching and choosing which world markets Japanese firms will seek to penetrate, provides venture capital under favorable circumstances without expecting instant return, helps nourish fledgling industries of high promise rather than propping up the obsolete or inefficient, assists with licensing of foreign patents, controls debilitating internal competition among domestic rivals, protects certain domestic markets from serious foreign competition, and encourages firms to meet changing market conditions without repeated firing and hiring of employees. Aging industries, on the other hand, are left to expire.

But the Japanese people pay a price. Whatever their high morale, workers live in very crowded conditions, are exposed to high levels of pollution and industrial hazards, are discouraged from cultural nonconformity, are subject to pervasive paternalism by employers, and have limited opportunities for advanced education and for social mobility. Yet in their own tradeoffs, the Japanese clearly like their policies.

No one expects the U.S. response to the Toyota to resemble the muscular response to Sputnik. Nor should the U.S. government alone be expected to take the leadership. Nonetheless, the consequences of uneven industrial vitality are extremely grave. Perhaps half of our 7 percent unemployment can be traced to jobs lost to foreign competition. And these are jobs which have not yielded to governmental or industrial palliatives.

Meanwhile, talk goes on of government policy for "reindustrialization." Not much flesh is wrapped around the bare bones of that slogan; nor does the concept have vigorous adherents. The President's Commission on Industrial Competitiveness developed proposals in 1984: changing antitrust laws to permit joint ventures in research; offering permanent tax credits for research and development; making government data on trade more accessible; increasing protection of proprietary information; restoring patent life lost during the long government-approval process; streamlining patent law; and making trademark counterfeiting a criminal offense. These seem like weak tea for a very sick patient.

It is also recognized that industrial innovation policies to identify products that could win in world-class competition and then to sponsor research with the hope of commercialization are likely to fall short.

Gradually, therefore, there has been an awakening to the stubborn fact that countermeasures must depend on initiatives within the private sector. The weakening of the technological infrastructure needs reversing, along with a recognition that more is at stake than mixing technical innovation with venture capital.

What can industry do? First, it can examine more carefully the relationships of management style to productivity and, where indicated, reform archaic practices in dealing with the work force. Second, it can improve its salesmanship in marketing abroad, especially by countering ignorance of the sales territory and provincialism of attitude. Third, the private sector—manufacturing and banking alike—can reexamine its propensities toward the short run, giving up those tax breaks which afforded instant profits but contribute not one whit to productivity; and it can try to exercise patience in expecting payoffs from investments. Next, the civilian sector of industry should rethink its uncritical support of defense expenditures, by recognizing the tradeoffs entailed. Our mammoth defense budgets diverted capital and top-quality manpower from perhaps more productive endeavors, for the sake of what may be illusions of national power and prestige in a free-wheeling world that cannot be controlled by economic colonialism or big-stick diplomacy.

Fifth, industry should reexamine its obligations to exercise social responsibility. It might ascertain the costs entailed by government constraints and lawsuits because of failure to exercise due diligence and to patrol its own membership. With Johns Manville having concealed known hazards of asbestos, and Union Carbide having ignored what the *New York Times* discovered in the way of documented defects in the Bhopal chemical plant, it is understandable that the public lacks confidence in the industrial giants.

Sixth, industry should reexamine its traditional characterization of government as enemy, its demeaning of the civil service, its attempts to corrupt by using political channels to place ideological clones in the bureaucracy and the regulatory agencies without reference to competence. Most of all, industry must recognize that when the state confers the privilege of corporate status on a firm, permitting it to trade as an individual but protecting its officers from legal responsibility, there should be an unspoken quid pro quo. The firm must be expected to follow the same principles of ethics and accountability to society that are the noblesse oblige of a nation's elite.

Organized labor also has a key role and responsibility in "rebuilding America," as the International Association of Machinists and Aerospace Workers note. Over the past three decades, widespread pressures to increase wages and fringe benefits were not accompanied by increases in productivity; and costs were simply shuffled to consumers without recognition that other nations had entered the game. The year 1985 saw many firms forcing wage reductions to stay in business. If the unions are to recapture the respect and support of citizens and a balance of power, they will have to demonstrate a different, unselfish commitment in a high-tech world, one in which they can contribute to social as well as economic progress.

Finally, the nation as a whole may have to reexamine its attitude toward the bittersweet relationship between industry and government. It may have to accept new rules based on an open partnership, with heightened visibility of these alliances to head off collusion, while permitting the government to continue in its role as a steward of the public interest and of social accountability of the firm.

If High Tech Is the Answer, What's the Question?

In the 1980s, *high tech* entered the jargon of economics. With it came a mystical cloud of potent inferences. Just as technology once seemed the fast track to the Promised Land, so now its offshoot joined the popular lexicon as a symbol of great expectations. The trouble is that few can agree either on a definition of the term or on its social and economic implications. Yet major policy decisions regarding high technology were initially made at all levels of government and in the private sector as though the simple incantation would guarantee the prize, disregarding the possibility that the expected benefits might be wishful thinking.

For practical purposes, *high tech* can be defined as a special class of technologies based on complex technical knowledge, usually at the cutting edge of sophisticated research and development, and considered innovative in the commercial market. High-tech enterprises require highly educated and skilled workers to develop prototypes, but have limited requirements for such talents as the later stages of manufacture and utilization. Generally, the enterprise is woven around a central idea and a central entrepreneur, eager to transfer the innovation into a highly competitive marketplace swiftly. Examples lie in microelectronics, computers, new generations of communication equipment, advanced materials, biotechnology such as artificial organs, robots, advanced weapon systems, and even video games. In short, high-tech applications and processes of gestation are generally exotic.

That sense of novelty adds to the glitter of high tech. But underlying the drive for high-tech enterprise are the same motivations that underlie all technology: the bright prospects of contributing to human needs and wants; the expectation by scientists and entrepreneurs of markets, sales, and profits; or the determination to achieve the highest potency of national security by more sophisticated weapons.

Yet there is another dimension to high tech's mystique. It evokes images of quiet, clean, aesthetically desirable, nonpolluting facilities. It represents an enormous value added, in going from limited requirements for raw materials to compact but expensive products out of the delivery door. High-tech industries need not be sited near the source of materials, nor even near the market. Because they have such flexibility in location, high-tech industries tend to cluster wherever high talent or cheap but literate assembly labor is readily available, or where sufficient relocation incentives have been provided by a host governmental unit.

Now we discover the allure of high tech that has earned it promotion in the political climate. Almost every state and community has recognized the virtues of attracting high-tech industry. There would be the clear benefits of employment, of a cadre of high-learning and high-earning professionals, and of an identity as a progressive, innovative, and hospitable climate that could attract other firms such as those which densely populate Boston's Route 128, Silicon Valley in California, the Washington, D.C., beltway, the Research Triangle in North Carolina, and elsewhere. What blessings high tech would tender, with a minimum of adverse social or environmental costs, or conflicts within the community. Competition for high-tech industry among the states has been fierce, and the prospect of such economic development has been a major reason that governors and state legislatures have established their own science advisory groups, a few imitating the president's science advisory office in visibility and influence.

Curiously enough, the high-tech phenomenon is not new, even though the financial world and the public treat it as fascinating as the discovery of a new comet. Once, the wheel was high tech. So was the printing press, the telegraph, the telephone, mass production of cars, the airplane, the pill. And each time, the public responded with uncritical passion over the ingenuity of the innovator and the auspicious prospects for a new era. And, of course, there were serenades to attract the solitary investor. In earlier cycles, too, cities and states competed with each other through a variety of tax incentives, even gifts, to bring in the smokestacks, then the symbols of progress and prosperity. With General Motors' search for a site to produce a new car, history once more repeats itself.

Much in this new high-tech wave is thus the same. But much is also different. For one thing, now there is a far greater dependency on human capital—on brains and information—than on plant. In addition, high-tech firms are generally smaller than their predecessors. Third, the high-tech firms cater relatively more to the service and information-handling sectors than to manufacturing and resource extraction. Fourth, some of these businesses count on exporting licenses for overseas production and sales, rather than directly on products themselves. Fifth, the tax incentives for venture capital have changed so as to encourage capital formation to serve small business rather than the giants, who in the past could usually raise the money they needed without a middleman. Contemporary giants, however, also invest in venture capital firms to gain insights into the new ideas of the small independents. Also, because of limited profits in the formative years, high-tech concerns have to rely on equity claims on future earnings rather than debt-financing claims on present earnings.

Notwithstanding these contrasts with previous high-tech cycles, so much is the same that it is remarkable how casual some political actors have been in overreacting to promotions or being too late with too little.

Among all its promises, high tech has been promoted most assiduously as an instant answer to the unemployment that developed in the late 1970s. Is it? What seemed unconvincing were the initially enthusiastic conclusions to such basic questions as the following: (1) What fraction of U.S. industry qualifies by even a rough definition as high tech? (2) What fraction will this amount to twenty years hence? (3) Within a high-tech enterprise, what fraction of jobs are professional and what fraction are low-paying, routine, assembly-line operations? (4) How stable are high-tech firms in withstanding competition from at home or abroad? (5) And among those surviving the frequent wring-outs, how likely are they to move where other incentives beckon, including overseas? And most trenchant, (6) how many unemployed in a given community are likely to qualify for such employment; and for those who do not, is retraining feasible?

Digging into these questions, we discover that high tech represents only about 4 percent of American jobs. Department of Labor analysts do not see this fraction as growing significantly during the next decade, notwithstanding increased use of high-tech components such as robots by low-tech, smokestack firms. Within a high-tech company, perhaps only 10 to 20 percent of the jobs are high-paying professional. Given the prior training and experience of most newly unemployed, there is a serious doubt as to whether they could be recycled to fit a high-tech environment. In Washington State, for example, many of the unemployed worked for wood products firms, cutting timber or manufacturing plywood. Others were commercial fishermen. Others clerked in small businesses in the towns debilitated by the closing of the only factory. By neither earlier education nor disposition would many of these individuals qualify for high-tech retraining. Thus, if the most pressing economic question is how to meet the melancholy prospect of 7 percent unemployment for the indefinite future, the answer is probably not high tech.

A second question is whether high tech will contribute significantly to our national security. On the basis of the last fifty years' experience, the answer is an unqualified "yes." But then it may be necessary to unpeel the onion of benefits further. For example, (1) will defense expenditures devoted to high tech attract the cream of the professional crop so as to leave too little talent for the civilian sector? The same hazard was detected and remedied by massive aid to higher education when the space program took off about 1961. (2) In the competition for scarce talent, will wages in the defense sector skyrocket so as to squeeze out potential civilian employers, or excessively push up their costs? (3) Will university grants from the Defense Department seriously distort directions for research from the preferences of scientists, on the basis that whoever pays the piper calls the tune? (4) How will new graduates reconcile their dilemma of wanting to work at the research frontier, but finding that such opportunities lie primarily in defense-related activity that for ethical reasons they disdain?

We should also ask whether high tech can improve the vitality and stability of the national economy, especially in improving productivity and the capacity to compete on world markets. Indubitably, it can. But even here, there are questions: (1) Will introduction of automatic machinery and robots create more unemployment? (2) Will they detract from the challenge of the job for the individual worker? (3) Are there other factors influencing the climate of world trade that are more important than high-tech exports? (4) Is high tech as vulnerable as smokestack industries to business cycles?

And will high tech contribute to the regional economy? In most cases, yes. But how much? (1) What are the inducements that states may have to offer through tax write-offs, gifts of land, loan guarantees, amenities such as roads and water supply, and investments in retraining; and how do these costs balance the economic benefits? (2) Do high-tech firms offer stability to the region, or are they likely to move their operations overseas to take advantage of more favorable wage rates? (3) What inducements as to university-industry partnerships require negotiation, especially so that academic institutions can maintain their independence and integrity so as to be buffered against the short-term expediencies of firms intent on brain-picking? (4) Are states vulnerable to fashions in federal industrial policy that could impose great and unpredictable burdens? (5) Do high-tech concerns require special deals that undermine general policies for industrial development? (6) Are there hidden costs of pollution, especially (as discovered in California) of threats to ground water, that belie high tech's clean image?

From these explorations into the more subtle parameters of a high-tech future, it would seem that high tech has been oversold, especially as a simple, quick fix to the complex, stubborn problem of unemployment. Nevertheless, as with earlier cycles of innovation, the world will never be the same after integrating the present high-tech wave into the culture. It will be intriguing to uncover lessons from this experience to guide future technology-intensive public policy as the next wave, discussed in Chapter 10, envelops society, beginning around 1990.

Making Peace Profitable

When we explore the interactions of technology with people and politics, elaboration of defense technology is of special interest. For one thing, ever since World War II, the Department of Defense has been the most influential sponsor of research and development in the United States. For another, all the major players in the civilian technological game— business, universities, and the public—are intimately involved with and influenced by defense policy, not just the weapons designers, the manufacturers, and the military forces.

Defense research has always constituted more than half the federal research total; by 1985, that sector had grown in absolute terms faster than the civilian, and represented roughly 70 percent. In qualitative as well as quantitative terms, defense research has effects on the entire knowledge generation function. It has nourished the cutting edge of numerous fields to maintain precedence in areas of direct military application as well as in areas having unknown potential but supported to help avoid surprise by discoveries of an adversary. Military research has also generated valuable civilian spillover. But with this commitment, defense research must compete with the civilian sector for the nation's highest talent, and often distorts university programs.

Defense spending had other critical effects on the nation's technological enterprise, particularly by its impact on the technology-based economy. For one thing, its rapid growth since 1980 was a major source of the budget deficit that had ballooned in four succeeding years to double all the deficits accumulated throughout the nation's history. In noting this trend, economists called attention to another brand of side effects: by imposing new demands on available capital, interest rates blossomed, affecting the cost of capital while attracting foreign investments in the United States to the point that the U.S. debts overseas exceeded foreign obligations. In that chain reaction, foreign currency fell relative to the dollar, stimulating imports and placing American manufacturers under severe price competition for domestic as well as world markets.

By 1985, a great debate had erupted on the defense-deficit issue. With its secretary of defense as chief advocate, the administration argued that the enormous military power of an unreliable and expansionist Soviet Union warranted this investment in technology as the principal strategy of national security. More was obviously better. Not only was the buildup rationalized on the basis of an alleged Soviet superiority, but defense initiatives such as the MX missile, the B-1 bomber, and the so-called Star Wars system were also defended as necessary bargaining chips in seeking arms control agreements.

On the other side of the issue, questions were raised as to how much is enough. Almost every skeptic agreed that the Soviets were a serious threat.

But in the matter of nuclear strategy, independent defense analysts such as Richard Garwin of IBM and retired Admiral LaRoque of the Center for Defense Information asked whether new weapons such as the difficult-to-verify cruise missiles destabilize the balance of terror, stimulate a never-ending arms race, and inadvertently increase rather than decrease risks of catastrophe. The Center for Defense Information also pointed out in their testimony before Congress on the U.S. military posture of nuclear forces, FY1986, that the United States was *not* behind. Out of twenty categories of weapons systems, the United States led in fourteen, the Soviet Union in one. Thus was raised again a doubt over Department of Defense credibility.

Other opponents of the defense-deficit policy argued that the domestic economy was suffering. For reasons just outlined, jobs had been lost or exported. Equally serious, in strenuous efforts to limit deficits, the safety net under the poor was being dissolved, investments in education for the future were truncated, the superfund for cleanup of toxic waste dumps was not recharged, and the nation's health was being imperiled because of cuts in federal assistance to those who could not afford the skyrocketing costs. America's basic creed was at risk.

Although the debate was starkly cast in terms of dollars, the fundamental issue may have been neglected; for at the heart of the matter was a tradeoff of risks. What indeed were the risks to military security through Soviet aggression if current nuclear stockpiles were not increased and defense funds levelled off? And how do these military risks compare to economic and social ones in a more broadly defined national security if defense expenditures and deficits continue to mount?

On that dilemma may hinge the key technological choices of the decade.

Perhaps, however, another question should be asked first: Is the defense build-up a response to perceived external threats, or are there other motivations? A number of investigative reporters, scholars, and public interest organizations have addressed the issue and concluded that indeed there is a second major factor—successful lobbying by the military-industrial complex. As to the authenticity of this situation, people forget that, in his 1960 farewell address, President Eisenhower complained of this leverage in explaining why his campaign promises for a balanced budget had been undercut. It was he who coined the now-famous term "military-industrial complex." The combination of pressures from the military, from the contractors, and from a compliant Congress were simply greater than a president could contain, even someone with philosophical roots and first-hand experience in the armed services. While the existence of this political force has been fully exposed, exploring its origins and its influence has not been high on the nation's agenda.

For the contractors, the defense business has been highly lucrative, but the attractions of this avenue for entrepreneurship and investment are usually hidden. It is one thing to make a fair profit; it is another to make it so easily. In the defense business, there are relatively fewer risks and uncertainties of the marketplace. Only a small fraction of contracts must be won in competition; there is only one customer, and that customer's preferences and practices can be more simply and effectively scouted than those of the decentralized and often chaotic commercial market. Additionally, plant expansion is often subsidized by the government, reducing the need for venture capital. Taxes can be deferred: General Dynamics has paid none since 1972; Boeing, none since 1980 despite reporting a profit in 1983 of $289 million on $2.6 billion in military sales (compared to $98 million on $7 billion in commercial sales). Finally, there are numerous examples of the government's acquiescing to price gouging, say of spare parts, or of bailing out vendors by awards based more on balancing support among major contractors than on technical superiority or lowest price in competitions.

But even these considerations do not fully explain the powerful coalition of contractors, technicians, military officers, business in general, members of Congress, and even the general public. In 1983, Sir Solly Zuckerman, for years the science advisor to the British prime minister, addressed part of this puzzle in a book, *Nuclear Illusion and Reality*. Singled out for comment were the technicians, who, he said, are in charge of the world's destiny, but hardly apostles of peace, as many in defense activities like to characterize themselves. Zuckerman did not assert that these people are malevolent; it is simply that technicians ply their trade in weapons laboratories because this employment offers the most exciting and intellectually rewarding technological frontiers. Participants are relatively unfettered by limitations on funds or instruments; and they are not badly paid. In this regard, technicians in the Soviet Union are on a par with those in Western democracies.

Military officers also have a special stake in technological enterprise. Careers can be built on successful innovation. Some may blossom from having bet on the right horse. But there are also times when a new weapons system spawns a new organization whose identity, size, and influence can serve as a launching pad for whoever happened to be its leader when the system ripened. Indeed, folklore in the nation's capital has it that no weapons system, no matter how defective, has ever been killed after it survived the first five annual appropriations (in 1985, there was a first with an antiaircraft gun). Finally, Washington observers report a "revolving door" syndrome whereby retired military personnel enter second careers with their one-time contractor dependents.

Apart from those who have vested interests in the defense enterprise, business in general has favored large military expenditures, sometimes from a sincere conviction of military threat, sometimes as a self-conscious expression of patriotism to gain public approval, and sometimes because this defense contribution to employment leads to increased commercial sales in communities having large military contingents or industries. But the uncritical support by business of defense expenditures may also be explained by two other factors. First, there is a recognition that since 1939 the nation's economic machine has seemed to depend on what Columbia professor Seymour Melman characterizes as "the permanent war economy." It is the technological impetus to the welfare state. And second, there is a deep-seated wish for international order and a willingness to accept assurances by political leadership that weapons are the most reliable strategy toward that end. Given the realities that the United States cannot be the world's policeman nor effectively battle elusive terrorists, that weapons strategy may not really work. By 1985, Business Executives for National Security grumbled more openly about the uncertainties in the domestic economy unless the deficit can somehow be checked. With the nation apparently unwilling to face the simple truth of our war economy, what under other conditions may have been a stimulant may now prove a debilitating drag.

The alliance of those in the defense business exerts a relatively invisible, unified, and powerful influence in both branches of government. If that military-industrial sector had a potent identity in the 1950s, thirty years later it has grown even more powerful. In this maturity, it learned a new technique of influence—to distribute defense subcontracts throughout the country so that the threat of cancellation of any weapons system can be publicized as a threat to jobs in almost every state. Under these circumstances, the Congress is vulnerable to constituency pressure almost everywhere. Pressure becomes excruciating to fund almost every proposal advanced by the Pentagon or by the defense contractors because not to progress from concept phase to development and then to production might, in the short run, be painful. The public readily sees that direct connection and finds its instant self-interest teased. Members of Congress, often against their better judgment, then become allies of the lobby.

Not as obvious, and not as effectively publicized by public interest groups concerned with broader aspects of national security, are the indirect repercussions of a continued military buildup. The Northwest, for example, lost timber businesses and many jobs because the demand for housing had been shrunk through a combination of inflation and interest rates. And both of these economic factors were in some way related to defense and deficit policies. Similarly, with national unemployment bottoming out at an unprecedented 7 percent, enormous social as well as economic costs could be associated with jobs lost to foreign competition.

Again, a sprinkling of corporate executives sensed that connection. Purchasing a full-page advertisement in the *New York Times* to publicize an analysis in *The Trimtab Factor,* they hoped to enlighten business so that it could recognize where its own best interests lay. The response was not reported to be overwhelming.

One great mystery was why the public, at least until 1985, accepted the defense extravaganza and seemed timid about questioning the weapons bazaar. Was doubt thought to be unpatriotic? How could the public be so naive regarding the ploys of the lobbies, which, year after year, made surprise discoveries of new Soviet weapons each time the defense budget came up for a committee vote in Congress? Why did it cave in so timidly to an administration's threats to close bases in the districts of recalcitrant congressmen? Why was the public satisfied for so long to accept the grim arithmetic of borrowing from the future?

Uncritical support by the public for increased expenditures clearly dates back to the middle 1970s. Some insight can be extracted from social indicator polls taken continuously on whether people wanted government to spend more or less on various federal programs. Throughout that decade, the public reported satisfaction with the level of expenditures in such areas as public health, education, and urban development. But on defense, there were violent shifts in attitude. In 1971, only about 21 percent felt that more should be spent. By 1976, that fraction had increased to 70 percent and did not begin to decline until the end of 1984.

For whatever reasons, the general public had been convinced of a vital threat by the Soviets, perhaps because of chagrin over "losing" in Vietnam, perhaps because of the invasion of Afghanistan. Citizens seemed persuaded, like business, that the most reliable countermeasures lay in more arms. That both sides had approximately equal nuclear arsenals and a massive overkill capacity was ignored. Somehow, there was a conviction that the U.S. weapons superiority that had been enjoyed for three decades was the best insurance policy, even if it meant building well beyond some limit of diminishing returns.

Another reason for public support may lie in a basic desire for peace of mind. For many people, that has been simplistically purchased by sidearms. This may be what lies historically behind the power of the gun lobby and may carry over to nuclear arms.

But public support may be based on another critical premise, an outdated psychology of affluence, that the nation can afford both guns and butter. In effect, people reasoned, "We don't have to choose, to make tradeoffs. We have the technological capacity to have it all, even if we have to pay later."

Notwithstanding the public's right to know that such a strategy could not continue indefinitely, few leaders had the political courage to lay out the facts and the hard choices.

Not that there was dead silence. Some in the 1980s—policy makers, analysts, peace activists, and citizens alike—saw the inevitable consequences of the guns and butter fantasy. One sector called for "more bang for the buck." By improving the military technology, weapons performance could be enhanced, and reliability improved. Most importantly, costs could be reduced. These protagonists constantly hammered on the theme of Pentagon waste, a specter to be exorcised by more than incantations. Indeed, documentation seemed compelling, culminating early in 1986 with shocking disclosures by President Reagan's own task force, chaired by defense contractor David Packard.

Another sector pressed earnestly for a nuclear freeze, on the grounds that more arms do not buy more security. Not now, and not ever again. What they proposed was not a unilateral action, but one that was both reciprocated and verifiable. Their arguments were based on the nightmare that history teaches: that nations have usually done what their weapons made possible. No nation with a first-strike capability would be trusted by the other. Yet, in a nuclear exchange there could be no winners. Even survivors were threatened by a probable "nuclear winter." Without some radical change in the trajectory of defense expenditures, the ratchet could only increase risks of destabilizing the long-held strategy of mutually assured destruction—and inflame the side effects of economic and social disruption. The nuclear freeze seemed like a good place to restart arms control negotiations.

Others pointed out that a nuclear war would not be simply another war with larger explosives, and that in a new era, conflicts had to be resolved by nonviolent means. Disappointed with the Arms Control and Disarmament Agency, they proposed a Peace Academy as a new institutional vehicle to drill more resolutely into the enigma of warfare. Against overwhelming odds, that proposal earned statutory backing in 1984, although implementation through funding and appointments was weak.

Throughout this growing debate, sight seems to have been lost of another strategy to ease the pressure for more arms: making peace profitable.

One of the realities of the weapons buildup is indeed the combined pressures from different groups who have a stake in weapons research and development and in procurement. Perhaps it is crucial to identify non-defense areas that would engage the talents of technicians, produce commodities for which there are profitable commercial markets and jobs, and at the same time contribute to the industrial productivity of the nation and to tangible social benefits, both domestically and globally.

Nominations of peaceful targets for this nation's imposing technological enterprise are plentiful: to use technology more aggressively in reducing risks, from exposure to toxic substances to better health maintenance and disease prevention; to look again at a civilian supersonic transport; to resume interplanetary exploration; to rediscover low-cost housing; to enhance telecommunications for social management of technology; to develop more productive agriculture in arid lands; to repair urban infrastructure; to increase sharply the number of teachers (and students) integrating science and engineering in good liberal education. Some may criticize these projects because in so many cases the government would be involved. But so it is in the existing welfare state. The only question is, who gains the welfare—the needy or the defense vendors?

These are not new ideas. For many years, small regional groups have been advocating "conversion." And they have opened a cafeteria of possibilities. The trouble is that no individual firm can take the risk. The critical requirement is clearly fresh national policy. By no means does this reduce the need for a vigorous military capability, in conventional as well as nuclear weapons. What a new policy might accomplish is an exit from the impasse arising because the public has been offered too little undistorted information to recognize what tradeoffs are genuinely involved. Approached more creatively, technology might allow us to substitute for the guns and butter fantasy a strategy that has fewer risks, military, social, or economic. To trot out the old aphorism once more, "If we can land a man on the moon, we can . . . "

7 / Technology and Science

The Well-Tailored Curiosity

n technological delivery systems as defined previously, one major input is scientific knowledge. While everyone shares in the goods and services that constitute the outputs of such systems, only a small fraction of the population participates in knowledge production—that is, in research. To most people, therefore, science is either mystery or magic.

Science, however, need not be inaccessible. Think of it as exploration, one of the most transcendent imperatives of human nature. Fundamental science, along with the research enterprises that enrich it, springs from human curiosity, from a creative urge to discover. As a field of learning we once called natural philosophy, it deals with the flood of information about the world around us.

To capture the full implications of science, we need to identify three stages that link people with their natural surroundings: the attempt to understand, then to predict, and then to control. We first describe what we see, what we hear, what we sense. Then we search for patterns, cataloging casual observations so as to confer order on what might otherwise seem a random array of things and processes. Next, we establish systematic relationships, both as to classification and to cause and effect. The latter challenge is akin to breaking a code.

Motivations for doing this research differ. There is primarily the excitement, the sheer joy, of discovering something for oneself, even more of a thrill if secrets of nature have been uncloaked for the first time. For a scientist who achieves precedence, there are many rewards: recognition by colleagues, self-esteem, and self-fulfillment. And today there may be tangible benefits: increased income, funds to expand the research enterprise, travel to professional meetings, career advancement, enhanced presige and power within the scientific community. Increasingly, as we shall discuss, there are rewards in the commercial transfer of scientific findings to the marketplace. The crux of the matter in this case is the ultimate application of the new understandings. The contributions derived from empirical deduction or rational analysis have been instrumental to survival in a harsh environment, then toward the progress that we call civilization. Such practical use drives scientists and their sponsors in a quest both for leverage to enhance the human condition and for profit.

So the search for meaning may be impelled by the well-tailored curiosity, but it may also be prompted by anticipated dividends. Whatever the motivation, the methods are similar, both the strategies and the tactics. The scientific method involves four steps: generating a hypothesis (about causality), testing by direct observations or by mathematical analysis, revising and refining, then generalizing so as to frame "a law of nature." Without such generalizations, we would confront massive idiosyncrasies. There would then be millions of separate observations and explanations, beyond understanding except by rote.

Once a theory is propounded, then confirmed in a variety of situations, we think we understand. We can then proceed to the next stage, that of prediction. Newton's laws of motion make possible sound conjecture as to what happens not just to one but to any billiard ball when struck by another. By generalization, we can calculate trajectories from parameters of force and mass. Then we can proceed confidently to the third step, that of control. For example, by matching booster to payload and selecting orbits, we can design spacecraft to carry out a variety of useful functions.

Deciphering nature's code is a game anyone can play. Over the last century, however, the research frontier has been populated largely by those with preparation, and more recently, only by the prepared who also have command of the powerful research tools of laboratory and computer. The process thus requires education, usually specialized and advanced. Through such a background, the investigator becomes familiar with the fundamentals of the discipline, with the literature, and with the bounds of what is known that forms a springboard for research. Then comes a process of search, often learned from apprenticeship with brilliant teachers. Some of it is random, most highly systematic. The historian Thomas Kuhn contends, however, that the brick-by-brick approach to science has been far less fruitful in triggering major discoveries than have flashes of insight. These often break with traditional patterns of paradigms of thought and represent the grand accomplishments of science that earn Nobel prizes. There is no shortcut, however, to having a prepared mind.

At this stage, a distinction needs to be drawn between research and a related activity called development. It should also be recalled that science is different from engineering, that neither is the same as technology, and that the all-inclusive term "science and technology" embraces more than research and development.

Research is often thought of as divided between basic and applied. The more fundamental the research in generality of potential application, the more it is considered basic. Most often, basic research stems simply from the desire to fill gaps in the knowledge base. Applied research, on the other hand, is clearly motivated by anticipated use. It draws on fundamental concepts that are then refined, enriched, and focused on a specific deployment. The line separating basic from applied is fuzzy; research performers and research sponsors may call the same project by different labels. Academic faculty who depend for promotion on new discoveries are likely to identify their research as basic. Exactly the same work may be called applied by a governmental or industrial sponsor who must justify its support within the funding institution in terms of agency mission. Development is a further step beyond applied research to fit its results to a particular application, at full scale, compatible with all its real-world constraints.

Distinctions can be usefully drawn between science and engineering. Differences are apparent in motivation, scale, substance, and style. Very simply, scientists seek to understand nature; engineers seek to control it. Engineers employ scientific principles in their design and deployment of complex structures and machines for specific human use. Usually, they must assemble a number of components to achieve function, yet even as they do so, must make compromises because of conflicting requirements. In contrast to scientists, engineers are more concerned with synthesis than analysis, with tradeoffs between safety and cost, with the constraints of building codes and environmental laws, with the performance of a system composed of numerous components that must articulate harmoniously for some common purpose. Because everything engineers do is ultimately for people, they should be acquainted with the laws of human behavior as well as with the laws of nature.

Finally, although technological enterprise embraces research and development, as a social process it entails a great deal more. Involved are engineering design, industrial management for economy and efficiency in production, and social management to extract benefits with a minimum of external ill effects. Thus, despite popular usage, research and development cannot be equated with science and technology.

In technological delivery, the path from laboratory bench and mathematical theory to the industrial enterprise is a continuum. The internal linkages are made up of information, first packaged as scientific papers published in professional journals or as gossip and lectures. But then the information is picked up by a second party, usually operating in a different institutional environment. But because knowledge from discovery is most effectively transferred to application through the mind of a single person, the practice of "hot pursuit" has grown. Here, the individual making a discovery has the opportunity to make the applications personally. Government and industrial laboratories have long been hospitable to this process because it works so well; the Bell Laboratories are often cited as a model. Now, that practice is being imitated in universities and in nations bent on increasing technological virtuosity.

Curiosity is being more finely tailored, everywhere.

Counting Noses, Counting Heads, and Counting Money

Earlier, I drew an important distinction between "science in policy" and "policy in science." This section is largely devoted to the latter, or at least to the social significance of the research enterprise. To help the reader grasp the issues entailed, some facts and figures follow regarding the size, scope, content, subdivisions, and ubiquity of the research enterprise, as well as changes therein.

First, a nose count. In 1906, some 4,000 distinguished scientists earned listings in *American Men of Science*. By 1982, that number had grown to 130,000 men *and* women—in other words, from 47 per million population to 561. Not ordinarily included in this list are the engineers who often work anonymously in applied research and development in industrial laboratories; census tabulations reveal about 300,000. If junior staff is included, the United States has roughly one million engineers and scientists in the laboratory. This probably amounts to 30 percent of all the practicing scientists and engineers in the nation.

On a global basis, Western Europe, Japan, and the Soviet Union field about an equal number. And the rest of the world perhaps the same. Thus, the United States has roughly 30 percent of the world's research talent. That cadre, however, amounts to less than 1 percent of the U.S. work force. To students of the sociology of science, these researchers compose the knowledge elite, with all of the nuances that designation entails.

While this snapshot speaks to quantity, there is also the dimension of quality. A head count is not the same as a nose count. One objective measure of quality may be Nobel prizes. Since 1960, U.S. scientists have received roughly 50 percent of the awards in physics, chemistry, physiology, and medicine; on a per capita basis, this stature is exceeded only by the United Kingdom. Of equal significance is the trend. Before the war, by far the greatest number of Nobel laureates came from Western Europe. In the 1930s many of these had to escape from totalitarian regimes, particularly under Hitler, and took refuge in the United States. Their legacies contributed indirectly to the domestic training of young minds as well as directly to scientific discovery. That focus on quality has been a hallmark of American science ever since. Indeed, a key plank of American science policy has been to educate our highest talent, to attract a significant fraction to scientific research, and to fund the research of the most creative in a commitment to maintain a lead in *all* fields of science.

A further measure of technical creativity can be found in patent awards. Originality as well as utility must be demonstrated. And while these innovations are different from scientific findings, they define the cutting edge of the technological enterprise. Although the United States was a late starter in industrial development compared to Britain and Germany, many of the most significant inventions spurring technological enterprise worldwide were patented here: the telephone, electric lights, the automobile, and the airplane are conspicuous examples. As in science, a pronounced international lead developed after World War II. Military hardware has the same distinction, almost across the board. That is one reason why a direct numerical comparison of weapons with the Soviet Union may be invalid.

In this mapping of science, the next question is where these people do their work. Here, it is necessary to distinguish between research and development. As Table 7.1 indicates, slightly more than half of all research occurs in universities, while somewhat more than four-fifths of all development activity takes place within industry.

Who performs research is vastly different from who funds it. Table 7.2 shows these relationships, separately for research, and then for research and development. Table 7.3 portrays trends in distribution of source.

These tables make plain, first, that development is far more costly than fundamental research. Second, most fundamental research is conducted in university laboratories; most development is conducted in industry. Third, the federal government is the source of roughly 50 percent of total support, a fraction that has dropped from a peak of over 75 percent in 1962.

Another point should be recalled as to the federal government's sponsorship. Whereas the tallies here represent what could be considered the R&D budget, as discussed previously, that identity is essentially an accounting convenience. There is no R&D budget as such. Each mission-oriented agency supports research and development item by item, in pursuit of its wide range of objectives. The budget is thus built from the ground up, not from an arbitrary pie that is subsequently divided into small slices, by agency, by function, or by field of science. The Department of Defense is by far the major R&D sponsor.

This leads to a further unwrapping of the science package. The national R&D enterprise is composed of many individual projects, perhaps some

Table 7.1 Locales for Conduct of Research and Development (percentages)

Employing institution	Research	Development
Universities	54%	3%
Industry	21	84
Government	17	11
Other	8	2

Table 7.2 Distribution of Funding for Basic Research and for Research and Development (billions of 1984 dollars)

	Performer of research				
Sponsor	Universities	Industry	Government	Other	All performers
	Basic research				
Universities	$1.22	$0.0	$0.0	$0.0	$ 1.22
Industry	0.26	1.88	0.0	0.14	2.28
Government	4.03	0.43	1.80	0.55	6.81
Other	0.34	0.0	0.0	0.25	0.59
All sponsors	**$5.85**	**$2.31**	**$1.80**	**$0.94**	**$10.90**
	Research and development				
Universities	$2.08	$ 0.0	$ 0.0	$0.0	$ 2.08
Industry	0.43	48.65	0.0	0.30	49.38
Government	5.50	23.35	13.17	1.85	43.87
Other	0.60	0.0	0.0	0.65	1.25
All sponsors	**$8.61**	**$72.00**	**$13.17**	**$2.80**	**$96.58**

150,000. This number can be adduced from unclassified work in progress regularly put on file at the Science Information Exchange, for many years managed by the Smithsonian Institution and now under the aegis of the Department of Commerce. Cataloging who is doing what, where, and with whose funds is an enormously useful tool for research administrators eager to prevent unwitting duplication and for researchers wishing to know who else may be plowing the same field.

Sometimes it is important to know about the balance in support for research and development as between different fields of science and different end applications. The former is more amenable to definition. For one thing, science over the last century has been distinguished by subdivisions of knowledge. That separation of the entire corpus of scientific thought into various fields evolves from sharp distinctions in fundamental principles that underlie each. This is not to say that boundaries are watertight. Increasingly, knowledge in one area finds relevance to others. Multidisciplinary enterprises, such as biophysics, biostatistics, and physi-

Table 7.3 Public and Private Research and Development Funding, 1960–83 (billions of constant 1972 dollars)

| | Source of funds | | % of GNP from fed. govt. | % of GNP from all funding |
	Federal government	Industry		
1960	$12.67	$ 6.57	1.7	2.6
1970	16.32	11.42	1.4	2.4
1975	14.54	12.58	1.1	2.2
1984	16.82	27.20	1.1	2.7

cal chemistry, have become legitimate regions of science. But the subdivisions so often represented by separate departments in a university do define the basic territories, as well as uncloak the sociological problems for faculty who try to break out or cross over. Younger faculty are not only discouraged; at promotion time they may be punished.

Parenthetically, disciplines can be mixed in several ways, sometimes described as layer cake, marble cake and mocha. Experience has confirmed that there are both intellectual and administrative problems and barriers regardless of baking style.

Compartmentalization also stems from the enormous volume of activity. As an indication of this activity, over the last century the number of scientific journals has grown from roughly 300 to now almost 20,000 worldwide, publishing some 700,000 articles each year. For purely practical and pedagogical reasons, people working at any place on the frontier are obliged by the expanding nature of science to work and teach in narrow sectors.

Statistics gathered regularly by the National Science Foundation afford a bird's-eye view of the fragmented territory and permit an appreciation of relative intensity of effort, whatever the explanations for differences. In 1983, for example, the proportion of research by field was as follows:

Physical sciences	28.6%
Life sciences	42.1
Mathematics/computers	3.2
Engineering	11.4
Psychology	1.7
Social sciences	2.2
Environmental sciences	9.7

Perhaps the most striking conclusion to be drawn from this inventory is the overwhelming strength of support for the natural sciences and engineering as compared to the social sciences. That disparity became even more conspicuous during the Reagan administration, which was outspoken in its unwillingness to keep up with rates of inflation in the social sciences as it did elsewhere.

All of this leads to a final observation, that with government supporting such a large fraction of basic research, it has an inordinate influence on the matter of balance. Even assuming that the institution of science has been able to maintain its internal integrity in that scientific findings have not been warped by the preferences or biases of the sponsor, there remains the obvious implication that science and politics are inextricably linked. Nowhere is this more obvious than in the impact of the government agency's mission on the type of research it supports. That the government is the predominant patron of academic research is a matter of grave concern to university science administrators, who experience the whims and the uncertainties of federal funding, the burdens of accountability, and the surges of political fashion. The problem of funding is not confined to support for research. Over the last decade the pinch within universities has related to obsolescence of equipment because of government parsimony in that area. This problem has become even more painful now that what could be termed "little" science in the university has become "big" science, as needs grow for elaborate and expensive astronomical observatories, high-energy accelerators, and super computers.

At one time, this overwhelming influence of government on the independence of academic research seemed eased by the availability of undesignated funds from private foundations. Opportunities were thus afforded particularly for longer-term and unorthodox research. That source has dried up somewhat; at least, it is not expanding in proportion to the costs of research. The new entry as patron has thus been industry. Notwithstanding these much publicized arrangements, private funding of university research is not significantly greater now than three decades ago. But as grateful as the universities are, they now face a host of new dilemmas in maintaining an arm's length of independence from pressure for undue concentration on profitable products and demands by industry for constraints on results they regard as proprietary. Another problem for researchers is the unspoken demand of sponsors (public or private) for quick results. Answers are often expected before proposals for renewal are drafted. All of this induces a distortion in research styles, especially with regard to taking risks.

Universities know, and the public may discover, that the salubrious climate of unstinting support for the production of knowledge by the great research universities in the 1960s is, like other federally supported programs, in jeopardy. Consciously or not, the nation is making tradeoffs. The benefits of the longer-term investments of twenty years ago should soon be revealed in a cascade of innovation. Overall, the Reagan administration has continued support. But the current funding clamp on social sciences and the emphasis on military sponsorship is bound to impact performance; it may take two decades before we see how.

Science Is Culture, Too

Scientific research is well established as the mainspring of knowledge generation, the fuel of technological change. But that is not its only attribute, and perhaps not the most important. Science also has a profound engagement with culture, affecting what we believe, how we think, and how we behave.

Consider some of the basic tenets of science that reinforce humanist traditions. For example, there is the need to understand the world around us and our place in it. Science does not replace religion, which historically met that need; indeed, science and religion can play mutually reinforcing roles in personal philosophy. However, Western thought is committed to a rational explanation of nature and to the role of fact in portraying its secrets. In science, therefore, truth is proclaimed on the basis of evidence rather than inherited belief, divine inspiration, or superstition. Facts must withstand public scrutiny, with validity being subject to test by independent observers rather than being established by weight of authority alone.

In this tradition woven about the freedom of inquiry, science has violently collided with religion. Witness the execution of Galileo and the mortal threats to Darwin. That contest continues to erupt—for example, on the issue of creationism versus evolution. Nevertheless, modern science vigorously resists any constraints on its performance, especially those arising from civil authority. Even policy concerns about unrestricted research on genetic mutation have stirred resistance to outside control; the scientific community asserts its own ability to patrol its members adequately so as to mitigate risks to the public or to progeny rather than be subject to legislated discipline.

Clearly, these points of view have found a place in our cultural framework. Logical processes are admired, and healthy skepticism of authority has become a solid element in the democratic creed. By no means, however, is commitment to rationality universal, permanent, or isolated from other doctrines. Jurisprudence, for example, teaches that truth emerges primarily from battles of protagonists. Nevertheless, Professor Harvey Brooks has argued that science strengthens an optimistic view of intellectual enlightenment, as well as helps satisfy the quest for human progress. Despite the caricature of the mad scientist, seeking an evil use of learning, science and scientists have consistently and conspicuously tried to apply new understandings to benefit humankind. As we shall see, that challenge is not theirs alone.

In addition, with advances in research, well-entrenched scientific truths and cherished dogmas become vulnerable as new discoveries refine or completely dislodge earlier findings. Knowledge is in a constant state of flux. As compared to earlier times, modern society has learned to live with change, much of it wrought by science. Indeed, in some elements of culture, change is welcomed or even promoted. But for many cultures, such lurching ahead has been uncomfortable, partly because social institutions have been uncongenial to change.

It is significant that even without permanence in scientific findings, there is a remarkable stability in the overarching structure and processes of the research edifice. That says something about its internal coherence and cohesion, which enable it to survive the shocks of new discoveries. Even society itself can today withstand scientific revelations without stampeding to punish the bearer of such tidings. This is not to say, however, that society is indifferent to challenges science hurls at fundamental values on such questions as transplanting animal organs to humans, making abortion and birth control safe and accessible, sustaining life artificially in the terminally ill, threatening human survival with the development of nuclear weapons, or leaving to future generations a legacy of environmental poisoning. Science cannot settle these ethical questions, but their being raised so dramatically points to further interactions between science and culture.

Because of these dynamics, science fosters an atmosphere conducive to looking ahead. In contrast, we find that the humanist tradition generates tendencies to look backward—to key ideas, fundamental values, and heroic figures in history. No wonder clashes occur in the way different individuals and societies look at the world, conflicts conspicuous enough to be the subject many years ago of C. P. Snow's work *Two Cultures*. What emerges from that tension is a recognition that there are several ways to view human reality. Throughout history, the problem has been to find a balance, in practice and in education. Perhaps today, the culture has gone too far in conferring authority to scientific results simply because of the sometimes mistaken emphasis on numbers.

These two approaches merge in one other phenomenon, the extent to which science links humankind with the natural environment. Indeed, a fundamental concept in nuclear physics, the Heisenberg uncertainty principle, states that the act of observing fine scale in the atomic nucleus can actually change the subject of study so as to create uncertainty as to what reality is. The view of the earth from outer space that science and technology have made possible dramatizes the fact that everyone is a passenger on the same spaceship, along with all living things, and that we are therefore subject to a common fate. Research constantly reveals how interconnected are the elements of an ecological community, and how artificial penetration of that harmony may incur disruptions of potentially calamitous proportions. The transformation of forests and grasslands to deserts, the decimation of some living species and endangering of others, unveil webs that connect living creatures with their environment. So science reinforces cultural inheritance as well as practical measures of respect for nature and its conservancy.

Increasingly, too, science and culture interact at the personal level. In the scientific community, there is a boundless premium on integrity of findings. Falsification of data, dishonesty, plagiarism of others' work, and theft are so unacceptable as to be rare. The open publication of findings, eligible for independent substantiation, cools any temptation. These values and high expectations for human behavior reinforce the moral foundations of culture generally. The razor's edge of ethical behavior is approached, however, when researchers and their sponsors view discoveries as having such immense social benefit that their exploitation will be profitable and therefore adopt secrecy in research so as to preserve proprietary rights, even sometimes denying access to colleagues who by the traditions of science would expect to have access.

Finally, there is the contribution of science to global comity. Natural phenomena are universal. They spill over national boundaries. Notwithstanding appeals to pride of race, culture, or tribe, no group can indefinitely monopolize either the truths revealed by science or the research capabilities. Scientists are in constant communication with each other, worldwide. Through invisible colleges, publications, international conferences, nongovernmental international bodies, and exchanges of scholars, they promote global understanding. Even during the coldest of wars with the Soviet Union, meteorological data were not blocked at the borders.

In that appreciation of one world, scientists have been conspicuously at the forefront of initiatives to control the nuclear threat. Perhaps it was out of guilt about creating weapons of mass destruction in the first place. In 1983, scientists heightened public awareness of another planetary effect in the aftermath of a massive nuclear exchange—a nuclear winter that would threaten even the survivors of such a catastrophe.

That dedication to the preservation of the species is the strongest noblesse oblige of science. In its pursuit of knowledge, science may inadvertently open Pandora's box. In that respect, the future is dangerous. But no matter how science may perceive its role, it does not bear the full moral responsibility for application of its discoveries: society, through its political institutions, also has a crucial role to play, one that it can execute only when it understands these subtle connections.

Life at the Frontier

The "frontier" of science is not simply an abstract boundary where knowledge stops and the unknown begins. It is also a cultural-social-psychological environment in which the individual scientist lives and works. To gain insight as to those primary features is to appreciate the intangible challenges and stresses of research as a vocation, indeed, as a calling.

To earn elementary status as a scientist generally requires the union card of a Ph.D. This achievement is a testing ground for the capacity to concentrate on a single key question, and to find answers which pass a well-guarded threshold of academic achievement. Threading through, under, and around that academic maze is as much a test of stamina as it is of intellect. The thesis has to pass muster for creativity and maturity. And the candidate must deal with academic politics to avoid undue friction with personalities on the review committee. But in a healthy atmosphere, both student and teacher learn from the research and from each other, the student as apprentice, the teacher from the perspective of a younger person who may be better trained. In any event, the experience in graduate study is a neat indoctrination for what follows in practice.

Once in the research mill, a scientist is constantly on the prowl for funding, either submitting unsolicited proposals with hope of support or else answering requests for proposals. These funding opportunities come from agencies with money but frequently with strings attached. So choices have to be made as to whether to pursue the unknown out of curiosity or to veer toward where the dollars lie. Such choices become especially painful when investigators committed to research for human progress discover that funding for their specialty is available primarily from the Department of Defense. Unfortunately, to succeed today requires entrepreneurship that would have been considered gauche in an earlier age; indeed, the preoccupation with funding induces a melancholy diversion from the substantive qualities that motivate entry into a field.

There are other sources of anxiety. One often hears the footsteps of others doing research in the same narrow track, with the hazard that someone else may reach the finish line and gain the rewards of precedence. There are no prizes for second place. The race becomes all the more demanding because of the frantic pace of the entire research enterprise. New knowledge accumulates so swiftly that the old is continuously perishable; its half-life may be only five years. Just keeping up with the literature is a problem. What makes this race doubly strenuous are statistics that in some fields creativity diminishes with age. Thus, if a researcher cannot demonstrate talent in youth, the possibilities of later success are fairly remote.

Then there is the reality of criticism and peer judgment. New discoveries must withstand scrutiny and be confirmed by other scientists. There is always the risk of being found wrong or even refuted. The public, incidentally, loves to witness such brawls. It is here that scientists earn membership in the "scientific community"; in specialized niches they join an elite and global "invisible college." Each has its own lexicon and syntax, so that scientists may lose touch with scientists in other niches as well as with society.

Yet another problem in the research enterprise is the evolution of little science to big science. Until the last few decades, most research was conducted by individuals; teams were rare. The reverse is now true. Today, also, elaborate and costly instruments are essential. As a result, energy must be invested in the management as well as in the conduct of research. Skills are required in planning, dealing with staff, monitoring budgets, maintaining equipment, preparing and issuing administrative reports, and stroking sponsors so as to increase the probabilities of grant awards and renewals.

In universities, the situation carries an added perplexity because research is usually combined with teaching. The scientist must ration time, in that promotions and tenure depend on "publish or perish," while simultaneously the classroom imposes demands on time to prepare lectures and counsel students.

Finally, there is the noblesse oblige in science and engineering to participate voluntarily in the activities of professional societies: reviewing grant proposals or papers submitted for publication, serving as program chair or officer of such organizations, or serving on advisory committees to government. At some point, these voluntary associations go beyond responsible public service; they become so gratifying to the ego and so exciting from rubbing shoulders with prestigious scientists or policy officials that they begin to demand every splinter of time not utilized at the research bench. Advising becomes a second vocation.

All of these circumstances add to the risks and the stresses of life at the frontier. Given this setting, it is not surprising to find in most scientists specific personality traits. We should expect an inquiring mind and high intelligence, usually revealed in childhood. These are fed by dexterity with numbers, by analytical skills and creativity. Add to this inner-directedness, self-discipline, and the willingness to trade off short-term benefits for longer-term goals, high vitality and ambition to succeed, perserverance and tolerance for frustration in dealing with cranky machines if not people.

The rewards, however, are clear. Peer recognition is cherished, indeed possibly the most powerful of motivations. Nobel laureates gain the top prizes. Nevertheless, with all the stresses and strains, including those of family relationships, life at the frontier gets mixed reviews. Airplane pilots jokingly describe their work as hours of crushing boredom interspersed with moments of sheer terror. Scientists might describe theirs as hours of demanding, exhausting, and often frustrating labor, interspersed with moments of unmitigated joy.

From Truth to Power: Science and Politics

In the United States, the connection between science and politics has been especially congenial. Scientists as well as statesmen, Benjamin Franklin and Thomas Jefferson saw a blend of democracy and science as common harbingers for human progress. The two concepts shared an identity in creed: emerging truths must be tested by critical inquiry; content is constantly revised and revitalized; order was to be established by public examination, not authoritarian edict. Advances of science and of the democratic tradition were expected to have a mutually reinforcing, synergistic effect.

From the nation's origins, scientific thought contributed to this political philosophy, but the operational connections were scattered and widely spaced. The Constitution itself contained the patent clause, which reflected an important relationship between invention and the national welfare. The Coast Survey, the government's first scientific agency, was not established until 1807; West Point, the country's first engineering school, in 1802. The National Academy of Sciences, which was to honor individual distinction and serve as a focus for technical advice to government, was chartered by an act of Congress in 1863. The National Bureau of Standards was created in 1901; the National Advisory Committee on Aeronautics, the precursor to the National Aeronautics and Space Administration, was founded in 1915. During World War I, the National Academy of Sciences established the National Research Council as a specific advisory organ on war-related projects, although the council then failed to function vigorously.

The trigger for a much closer and continuing relationship between government and science was World War II, which led to the creation of a presidential advisory apparatus to tap scientific genius for weapons development, intensive mobilization of that talent, and the historic decision to build nuclear weapons, code-named the Manhattan Project. Thus were founded the Office of Scientific Research and Development and the National Defense Research Council. Subsequently, in recognition that the world had been changed by the technological pulses of World War II, the connection between science and politics was systematized. President Franklin D. Roosevelt requested the former head of his OSRD advisory unit, Vannevar Bush, to study government's responsibility in husbanding the nation's science resources. And in his landmark report, *Science: The Endless Frontier,* Bush recommended institutional support through what was to become the National Science Foundation.

Meanwhile, the defense agencies were attempting to continue both the support for and communications with the scientific community that had been of such critical value during combat. In particular, the Office of Naval Research built a sponsorship of academic science that satisfied both investigators' demands for independence and the skepticism of upper military strategists and Congress that these investments were worthwhile.

What was emerging was a new policy: because of rapid advances in science and the potential for military surprises from new discoveries, government should become a patron of basic research. Indeed, with the United States' having already pulled ahead in many fields where leadership before the war had resided in Europe, goals were quietly set for stimulation and maintenance of that leadership across the board. The final thrust came on October 4, 1957, with the Soviet Union's successful launching of Sputnik, followed by the orbiting of a dog, Muttnik. By 1963, funding of the research enterprise had grown by a factor of five; the federal government, which before the war had mainly supported research in agriculture and a little in public health, was now providing 75 percent of all research funds, nationwide.

Such a radical change in policy was naturally accompanied by heightened political attention, in the bureaucracy and especially on the floor of Congress. For congressmen, there was a fresh opportunity to gain power and visibility. One incentive was the chance to control increased funds, some earmarked for their districts, there to earn constituency approval. And there was incentive to gain publicity from hobnobbing with famous scientists and sharing the umbrella of their prestige, which had suddenly been heightened by the national concern over competition with the Soviets. A classic example of congressional exploitation of this situation was the frequency of hearings on the fledgling space program called by the House Science and Astronautics Committee. Its chairman, Overton Brooks, from the bayous of Louisiana, basked shamelessly in the new spotlight of attention and influence; never mind that he did not believe in evolution.

Conversely, scientists delighted in the attention they received at highest levels of government; they began to feel they had influence on the levers of power, and were especially hopeful of bounty, not for themselves but for their fields of science.

Harvard professor Don K. Price captured both the spirit and the substance of what was happening in his book *The Scientific Estate.* What he saw was a new alliance between science and politics that could be distinguished as a spectrum of relationships, extending "from truth to power," made up of four groups of participants: the scientists, the engineers and professional managers, the administrative bureaucrats, and the politicians. At the first end, there was a dediction to truth. At the other end of the spectrum, there was concern mainly for power. The closer activities were to the role of truth, the more they were entitled to freedom. And the closer these activities were to power, the more they were required to be publicly accountable. Across this spectrum, exactness diminished inversely with the importance of public policy, for in the latter there were perpetual ambiguities that always nettled the scientists, and the problem never stood still. Thus arise further distinctions: in a sense, scientists could control their subject matter and their own fate; politicians could not.

Apart from its subject matter, science is a way of thinking. So is politics. But the two frames of reference are substantially different. In an old allegory by nuclear physicist Leo Szilard, when two scientists converse and one is baffled, he asks later, "What did she mean?" In a similar situation with two politicians, the follow-up question is, "Why did they say that?"

Between 1959 and 1964, three incongruous roots of policy for science emerged. Insiders of the executive branch were pushing for support in all fields as a de facto policy of maintaining U.S. supremacy; there were reasons of both national security and national prestige in the race with the U.S.S.R. Insiders in Congress argued for greater control of the purse strings, to the point of considering a Department of Science so as to consolidate widely distributed functions and subject them to central management. The scientific elite were advocating yet a different policy, a carte blanche annual increase, free from any governmental interference.

No wonder, then, that a nervous gavotte began with scientists and politicians that never became a comfortable dance. Some would say that is just as well. For only by its independence from politics can science be free.

The same attitude, however, was never true in dealing with applied research and engineering development. Far larger projects were involved: development of the B-1 bomber and the cruise missile, or construction of a massive facility for launching spacecraft. Individual congressmen had more at stake. So did the large industrial firms bidding for contracts. Pork-barrel politics at its best (or worst) took hold. Not only was there squabbling to get a larger slice of pie, but there were battles over making the pie larger. That condition became manifestly clear in the Reagan administration, when expenditures for defense research and development grew by 60 percent in four years, far more swiftly than inflation.

One last point. Although the direct participation of scientists in White House affairs peaked in the mid-1960s and then slowly diminished, a different set of connections to the agencies continues. These are the hundreds of advisory bodies appointed by the National Research Council, now operating under joint aegis of the National Academies of Science and

Engineering and their sister agency, the Institute of Medicine. Most of these committees were created at the instance of some particular agency to provide advice on a technical question of limited scope. Some, however, were appointed with far broader hunting licenses; indeed, some were mandated by legislation. Most have served with distinction, and all have been marked by a precaution: appointments to these committees have been screened by the host institutions to head off conflicts of interests by advisors, or, at the least, to make known to all parties any direct connections or investments of the advisors with private organizations so that it is clear where advice may be tainted with self-interest.

Early in 1985, the connections between science and politics took a new twist with proposals by the President's Commission on Industrial Competitiveness to create a cabinet-level Department of Science and Technology. To be consolidated were NASA, the Department of Energy, the National Science Foundation, the National Institutes of Health, NOAA, the National Bureau of Standards, and research components of all other agencies except Defense. Whatever the arguments for greater management control—and these are arrayed both pro and con—any such creation must be regarded primarily as symbolic of a new national priority: to enlist science and technology more effectively in meeting foreign economic competition. The political history of other science-based agencies—the AEC, NASA, the NSF, and others—makes clear that their origins can be traced to a perceived need for enhanced governmental attention. And as has been said by political scientist Harold Seidman, the medium of organizational structure is the message of national priorities.

In 1958, Senator Hubert H. Humphrey believed that the Soviet space challenge warranted departmental status for science and technology, but the timing, senatorial politics, and weak constituencies mitigated against support. The strongest arguments against consolidation, however, were concerns that separation of research from the substantive missions of individual agencies would cripple the performance of those agencies because of the loss or interruption of prompt information transfer associated with internal research functions. In addition, scientists worry about excessive concentration of research sponsorship, which could inadvertently squelch new starts or the competition of ideas. Contemporary proponents of a department are concerned about the same problem of knowledge transfer, but they want to strengthen the pipeline between government-supported research and industry. Perhaps overlooked are mechanics of the transfer process; knowledge diffusion involves special talents and infrastructure on the part of the recipients that no amount of organizational reform by the knowledge generators can provide.

Tightly laced interdependencies between science and government have grown now for five decades and are subject to continuous review and change. Altering these for purely commercial purposes might well be approached with great caution, if for no other reason than to protect the geese who lay the golden eggs.

What's on Tomorrow's Agenda?

Reports to the public constantly filter out of the laboratory about tantalizing new scientific discoveries, clever inventions, or promising engineering developments. Most have the property of eliciting a "gee whiz" response. Whether from the stimulus of novelty, the solution of a complicated puzzle, new understandings of natural phenomena, or the admiration of revealed genius, these announcements stir excitement. Some part of the response certainly comes from expected practical benefits.

Because innovations that can be transferred to the marketplace have a good track record of commercial return, entrepreneurs constantly monitor university laboratories and patent awards to sniff potential for exploitation. For a century, the larger or more enterprising firms have not waited for random invention or its transfer. Beginning with Thomas Edison and with the General Electric Company in 1890, firms have built their own laboratories to make invention happen. Meanwhile, there was much combing through ideas that were born elsewhere but deserved backing.

In the last few decades, the bright and creative in these industrial labs have often left the larger companies to begin their own small businesses, and have successfully competed with the industrial giants. In the 1980s, both large and small firms installed new linkages with the universities, to permit legitimate and systematic peeking at what was happening at the frontier, to gain an advantage in being able to transfer such discoveries to the marketplace swiftly, and to gain an edge in recruiting the most promising students.

Along with these hands-on activities, there is another body of analysts who gather information, analyze, and report on prospects in what is called technological forecasting. The commercial market for such advice and reports on promising hardware grew swiftly, and soon it included intelligence about the marketplace, public policy, and the geopolitical context which could influence corporate strategy. Many research institutes now cater to that demand.

Because of its intense interest in every facet of technological affairs, government also monitors the science and engineering future. In the military establishment, there is always a gnawing anxiety that a potential adversary might uncover something new of significant military value. In that recognition, nations have always carefully shielded new developments by security measures, to preserve their potential of surprise by superior weapons. The massive Manhattan Project went on for years without leakage of its secrets. Now, restrictions have been cast not only over applied research sponsored by national security agencies, but also over esoteric basic research—in mathematical cryptography, for example—that has military significance.

In addition, government agencies which sponsor scientific and engineering research constantly monitor progress in all fields to judge which areas warrant special nourishment, which investigators are most promising, and which proposals should be denied because of unnecesssary duplication. Agencies must also be responsive to breakthroughs or surprises, in energy conversion, in disease prevention and treatment, in food preservation, in discovery of toxic waste—indeed, in every sector of government responsibility.

Notwithstanding these powerful motivations to look ahead, government interest in technical trends has not been distinguished outside the intelligence community. With the 1976 science policy act, however, the president's science office was enjoined to prepare a systematic *Five-Year Outlook* that would compile information on what loomed over the horizon. The statutory charge concerned not only new or emerging hardware but also new and emerging policy issues related to science and technology. By 1985, three editions of the outlooks had been released, all prepared by the National Science Foundation with the assistance of the National Academy of Sciences.

General topics identified for increasing emphasis were first classified according to governmental interests:

—National security: electronics, materials, aeronautics, space, nuclear test verification.
—Space: shuttle development, remote sensing, international cooperation.
—Energy: supply of fossil fuels, synthetics, nuclear safety, solar, fusion and conservation.
—Natural resources: water, desertification, loss in tropical forests.
—Environment: acid rain, air quality, toxic wastes, ground-water contamination.
—Transportation: energy efficiency, safety.
—Agriculture: productivity.
—Education: cognitive skills, computers, science literacy.

There were not many surprises. Each edition also identified a number of generic issues in science policy deemed to require research:

—Maintaining a healthy base of science and technology, assuring adequate funds, countering pressure for short-term payoffs.
—Fostering industrial sponsorship of research in the civilian sector.

—Assuring adequacy of human resources.
—Contributing to industrial productivity.
—Attending to international aspects of cooperation, restricting information transfer to adversaries and competitors, helping build infrastructure in the Third World.

Finally, there was a list of research topics that had earned citation as of special interest in the five following years either because the field had matured to the point of hatching major discoveries or because attractive prospects of market deployment contributed special momentum to the research enterprise:

—Computers: artificial intelligence, electronic funds transfer, enhanced computer security, increased use of optical fibers, expansion of electronic mail, wider use of commercial and public satellite communication services.
—Molecular structure in biology: applications to immunology, neurosciences, enzyme production, organ transplants.
—Medicine: epidemiology of cancer, understanding and treatment of mental illness.
—Geosciences: Control of toxic substances in the environment, earthquake prediction, inadvertent climate modification, radioactive waste disposal, nonseismic means of oil exploration.
—Robotics: improving industrial productivity by overcoming present limits to locomotion, tactile sensing, speed, vision for quality control, and programming in a new environment; studying impacts on the labor force.
—Psychobiology: comprehending the biological basis of human behavior in learning, thinking, awareness, and language; the significance of the right/left differences in brain function.
—Genetics: understanding DNA of bacteria and viruses, modification of plants to resist drought and disease.
—Lasers: expanding versatility for communication, drilling, cutting, welding, uranium isotope separation, medical diagnosis and surgery, spectroscopy, and military applications, possibly for missile defense.

Clearly, this is only a snapshot of frontier research. But such a shopping list indicates where the present excitement may be found, either because of intellectual ferment or available funds.

Conspicuous by their relative absence are topics in the social and behavioral sciences. Nevertheless, the grand issues involving science and technology will be aired in a political arena, and competent choice depends as much on understandings generated by the social and behavioral sciences as by the hard sciences. To mention just a few of the more compelling questions that occur to me:

1. What has the effect been of violence on TV? Has it shifted public preferences to an arms buildup and to the death penalty?
2. What are the most productive strategies for managing conflict by nonviolent means?
3. What processes induce sharp pathological shifts in human behavior, such as led to the Holocaust and to mass suicide in Jonestown?
4. How can critical thinking be measured or taught?
5. What are the sources of criminality and how can such antisocial behavior best be mitigated, or prevented?

With all the funds invested in research, there are inevitable gaps. What is most troublesome is that these gaps may have the most to do with society's future capacity to cope—with itself. Would it not be interesting if perhaps 0.5 percent of all federal funds for research and development were turned over to a citizens' advisory body for allocation? If we put aside traditional processes of choosing projects on the basis of peer review, with its politics and inevitable parochialism, or on the basis of commercial incentives, would a change in process change priorities? We know from NSF-sponsored opinion polls which broad areas the public thinks deserve increased support. It would be fascinating to see what research a citizen body would actually recommend.

8 / How Decisions Are Made

Is the Question "Can We Do It?" or "Ought We to Do It?"

mericans are in constant motion. Thus observed de Tocqueville 150 years ago, when he wondered if such a dynamic society ever had time to think. If anything, that compulsion to act rather than to meditate has intensified. With technology, we seem to enjoy the luxury of choice, yet reality tests of that experience do not generate confidence that the quality of our decision processes has kept pace.

In a boisterous, sometimes chaotic and crisis-ridden atmosphere, competence in technological choice is bound to be affected. Cool judgment yields to impetuosity. From a subconscious desire to escape the labor of thinking or the pain of discord and confrontation, or from pressure to tackle the next dilemma in an endless queue, there is a natural tendency to dispose of an issue as swiftly as possible. Each one is thus reconnoitered only within its provincial boundaries, as though it were isolated from everything else going on. Moreover, analysis may be given short shrift simply because of too little time.

So, in a time-bind, the politics of the issue lure more attention than the substance. In that myopia, many of the wrong things can happen: shortfalls in achievement of goals, harmful side effects, delay, conflict to the point of deadlock, or the high costs of limiting damage or correcting mistakes. Indeed, the decision machinery itself can be maimed or political power enfeebled.

To avoid these penalties of poor judgment, one strategy is to bring within the ambit of decision making three broad elements of social context. These concern (*a*) public attitudes, the cultural tilt

Table 8.1   Frequency of *New York Times* Coverage of Environmental Issues

	1960	1962	1964	1966	1968
Issues/Key Words					
Environment	1	1	0	30	22
Water pollution	63	81	80	162	186
Air pollution	73	69	85	287	130
Waste	0	0	0	0	0
U.S. environmental problems	0	0	0	48	49
Total	137	151	165	527	387

of the moment; (*b*) other policies or practices along the boundaries of the issue under study, neglected because they are seemingly independent; and (*c*) the power distributions, institutional structures, and behavior patterns that mold the decision environment. The first may be overriding; the political behavior of a society usually reflects the prevailing cultural profile, even the instantaneous mood.

Politicians respect this condition. By instinct, now supplemented with polls, they listen carefully for opinions on which to base tactics for new policy. As Senator Daniel J. Evans once said, "You check out the surf. If you can time position your surfboard, you can ride to success with modest effort. Too late and you are left behind. Too early, and you get a watery thrashing."

One of the most dramatic examples of that metaphor occurred during the 1960s in regard to environmental policy. Perhaps the initial trigger for action was the 1962 publication of newly perceived threats. In 1969, the National Environmental Policy Act (NEPA) was passed. That interval of seven years is extremely short as legislative gestation goes. Yet the act has proved to be one of the most influential in modern political history, reflecting a major change in values when dealing with technology. Only because of an aroused public sentiment to impose political limits on technology was that swift action possible.

One indicator of significant changes in the focus or level of social awareness can be found in news coverage. Newspapers have sensitive antennae, always prepared for a story. In our information-laden society, material is seldom in short supply, and managing editors select from this material what in their judgment is of greatest significance or interest to readers. So the media, in their daily scanning of the menu of key events, act as referees on which ones have the greatest portent.

Indeed, headlines may be predictors of the future. The fate of an issue may be tracked over a period of time by noting when it first erupted in the

1970	1972	1976	1980	1982	1984
153	203	88	115	134	432
758	592	617	265	169	175
696	354	294	230	139	103
0	177	175	207	354	383
335	127	80	7	36	0
1942	1453	1254	824	832	1093

media, counting the frequency with which it is subsequently attended, then observing by its neglect when the issue is declared dead. Using key words on environment, it is possible to tell from an index of the *New York Times* when this concern first made the scene and how issues flourished (see Table 8.1). At some threshold of public attention, the issue seemed to demand action at the highest level. The National Environmental Policy Act of 1969 was the result.

What was happening? Because the average citizen has difficulty understanding technical details of chemical and physical threats to the environment, and because there were so many alarms, some universal concern and intuitive understanding must have been operative between 1962 and 1969. However explained, there was a major cultural shift. What had been an era of technological optimism expressed by "Can we do it?" precipitously changed to "Ought we?"

To appreciate how dramatic was such a change in outlook, we should recall that during the 1940s and 1950s, there was unquestioning faith that "science is good for you." People mainly saw the benefits, profound and ubiquitous. Only when contrary evidence touched a deep, even spiritual, concern for nature and then for human life were perceptions awakened that some perils had been present for a long time, either hibernating or being ignored. Once alerted, people tripped over bushels of trouble that had been stealthily accumulating in their back yards.

The threats were not abstract. Family and friends were vulnerable. However, the situation was far from hopeless. In almost every case, some form of mitigating or remedial action could be found. And there were public-spirited pathfinders, activists committed to informing the public and then mobilizing clamor for political action. Organizations such as the Natural Resources Defense Council, the Environmental Defense Fund, the Sierra Club, the Cousteau Society, and others had plenty of ammunition.

Curiously enough during this warm-up period, there was no single, conspicuous environmental crisis. Incidents were more frequently reported, to be sure, some of them unprecedented, like the Torrey Canyon oil spill in 1967 that produced a resonance in 1969 when one occurred in the Santa Barbara Channel. Whether or not accidents or perils were more numerous, public concern was being aroused by the media. Many new environmental groups got into the act, some responsibly and some hysterically.

With that growing public sentiment, the stage was quickly set for political action. Legislative history reveals that many different bills were serving as prologue for the 1969 policy. Not only that, a bandwagon began to form of congressional leaders who sensed which direction opinion was running. Some were candidates for president and eagerly grasped this broadly based issue as their own. Senators Henry Jackson, Edmund Muskie, Gaylord Nelson, and others took strong initiatives. After his 1968 election, so did President Richard M. Nixon.

The maturing of society from its preoccupation with technology's toys to a concern for consequences had a sequel in 1971, when the Congress killed the supersonic transport (SST). Hindsight confirms the wisdom of that move: even the winner in the design competition, Boeing, was relieved of the public embarrassment of having to abandon its model and adopt the loser's. Meanwhile, it was discovered that the projected SST fleet would consume 25 percent of the nation's petroleum to keep flying, a demand that would have been prohibitive with the hike in oil prices. More than anything else, the values held by the attentive and activist sector of society made possible the legislative prize.

By 1980, however, sharp swings to conservatism made it highly doubtful that, without a major environmental crisis, the NEPA legislation could have been threaded through opposition by business and a popular ground swell newly focused on economics. More jobs, threats to a materialistic life style, deficits, interest rates, the balance of trade, and demands for less government partly drowned out concern for the environment. If the SST issue were to come alive in the near future, even its fate might be different.

Are there lessons here? In hindsight, the Environmental Policy Act seems a minor miracle in arresting dangers to human health as well as to environmental integrity. Through the provisions of that policy, many hazardous situations have received attention and been dealt with so as to head off disaster. Yet we find that public sentiment is somewhat fickle. Durability in attitudes is shaky, and cyclic behavior may be the norm rather than the exception. There is a second lesson of political behavior. Politicians became advocates of the NEPA legislation because of the anticipated political benefits in the short run. In this unique situation, the public benefited both in the short *and* the long run. That, too, may be an exception.

Thus, decisions prompted by violent swings in popular acclaim warrant careful scrutiny. Moving uncritically in response to wild swings in sentiment is especially worrisome with technology-intensive public policies because of the heightened possibility that the public really doesn't understand the tradeoffs. For example, according to polls reported in the Bureau of Census's *Social Indicators,* popular support for defense funding increased sharply in the middle 1970s, although national security was not suddenly threatened. President Reagan adopted and pushed that theme vigorously. Yet early in his second term, more and more people seemed to become aware of the vital tradeoffs entailed when considering other threats to national security which must be equally guarded against and which the nation was being asked to sacrifice for weapons. Now, in another time, the public which was asking only "Can we do it?" of MX and Star Wars began once again to ask "Ought we to do it?"

Case Study: Harmonizing Economy and Ecology

Harmonizing economy and ecology: to some, that precept, outlined in the preface of the National Environmental Policy Act, is romantic nonsense. For two decades, society has witnessed bitter controversy between advocates of these different viewpoints. Each side has waged war with such emotional zeal that the roots of the conflict must lie well beyond a simple collision of ideas. At stake is a collision of values.

To be sure, a robust economy promises a rainbow of material benefits: jobs, profits, better health, comforts, and opportunities for self-fulfillment. On the other hand, a wholesome ecology betokens a joyful and healthful aesthetic environment. It upholds a compact between humankind and nature from which people derive sustenance along with satisfactions of the spirit: stewardship of an inheritance for the benefit of progeny. No wonder both prizes attract adherents.

The trouble arises because we cannot realize the childlike but impossible dream of having it all. Amidst the chagrin and anxiety of cruel reality, we have to choose. Always, this means making tradeoffs. In getting down to brass tacks, we recognize that contests between economy and ecology seldom erupt from purely philosophical differences, although they are at the root of conflict. Most often, they center on concrete technological initiatives. Examples abound: expanding the Kennedy airport; building an oil pipeline across Alaska or a canal across Florida; constructing a nuclear power plant in California or in New Hampshire; extracting oil from shale in Colorado; arresting air pollution from a copper smelter in Washington State. What triggers intense concern are the perceived, or real, consequences: unwanted impacts to either economy or ecology, by action or inaction.

If the notion of harmony is taken to mean congenial accord, and if its virtue is a self-evident article of faith, then we must search for common premises that could link economy and ecology. From connections between technology, science, culture, politics, and risk, eight cognate properties can be distilled from arguments advanced earlier:

1. Because all technologies create side effects, managing technology to extract socially satisfactory outcomes requires a doctrine of anticipation— to estimate both lateral and future consequences. This is not an exercise in crystal ball clairvoyance, a forecast of what tomorrow will be like. Rather, looking ahead is anticipating plausible future effects of today's choice. Such a doctrine implies the will to look ahead and ask, "What might happen if?"

2. The introduction of any new biological species into a healthy ecology is certain to induce change. Thus, while the undisturbed natural setting can be employed as a benchmark when evaluating human impact on the environment, some disturbance is inevitable.

3. To expose the content of both economy and ecology, scientific and factual information relevant to a particular technological initiative should be mustered to estimate both direct and indirect effects. Also required are credible methodologies, resources for their exercise, and analysis independent from vested interests.

4. Alternatives must be sought and exposed. For seldom does purposeful technological enterprise entertain but one unique course of action. Harmony thus requires examining options without premature commitment to one or contamination of the process by too acute a bias of value preferences.

5. The reality of conflict must be faced squarely, as between use of resources and their preservation, incompatible uses, the short- and long-run benefits and costs, and different stakeholders.

6. All parties have rights, and all parties have responsibilities. In a free and pluralistic society, perceptions of social and economic effects will vary enormously among different parties in the decision chain. All parties should have ready access to an effective information system that translates implications for the public as well as vested interests.

7. While there are ethical as well as substantive grounds for involving affected parties, that participation early on could mitigate conflict between those imposing and those exposed to risk. If excluded from the acts of choice, people may be reluctant to transfer responsibility for their exposure to risk to those whose guiding values may be foreign and whose self-interests they do not trust.

8. Because technology is mediated by politics, and compromises are reached by bargaining, special steps are required for representing future

generations who cannot be around that table. Only government can fill that role as surrogate and trustee.

As these arguments indicate, our concern should be with the *process* of illuminating impacts, with ground rules to facilitate choice, rather than with absolute criteria to be applied when exercising choice. Here, government has a clear responsibility—and not only as a power broker, as an umpire in balancing influential economic or ideological interests. It should function as a steering system. It must foster public understanding of social goals and their perplexing contradictions, of obstacles to achievement of these goals, and of crisis-avoidance strategies. Most of all, it should help illuminate the tradeoffs entailed in alternatives, especially between short-term economic rewards and long-term preservation of capital, our genetic and environmental legacy. That tradeoff theme intrudes stubbornly every time we retroactively diagnose policy shortfall.

As we have seen, there are several reasons for neglect of the long run. In brief, most people live in the present and manifest a desire for instant gratification. Others feel impotent; since they cannot affect the long-term outcome, why even try? Discounting the future may also stem from the stress of living in a complex and insecure technological society, as psychological research has amply proved. Under the tyranny of the clock, with more choices and less time to choose, with the consequences of error so serious, anxiety is bound to rise. Under that stress, attention is concentrated on the immediate moment. As the intensity of stress increases or its duration is prolonged, the entire decision process may be crippled.

In contrast, all societies clearly treasure their children. The issue raised by the contest between the short and the long run is fundamentally one of sacrifice, the sacrifice of present satisfactions for the benefit of progeny. Insurance companies and investment counselors have taught how economics and concern for offspring can be combined. But the issue of the willingness to sacrifice for society as well as for the immediate family still only flickers over the horizon.

Thus, the problem for society as a whole can be stated bluntly. Economy is a calculation about short-term needs and wants that can be quantified and satisfied immediately. Ecology, on the other hand, is about long-term atmospherics that ordinarily cannot be quantified. Therein lie the most trenchant contradictions, the ultimate limits to harmony.

From the arguments just spun, it should be clear that harmonizing economy and ecology does not mean development of new principles for social or institutional conduct, or a new set of laws. Rather, achieving harmony is a special type of political process that depends upon democratic principles, ready availability of unbiased information, a cultural dedication to future generations, and public education in the notions of critical judgment and the social contract of civic participation. To design environmental policy, perhaps we can learn from striking parallels with the practice of engineering design discussed previously—how to reconcile conflicts in requirements.

The eight guidelines for establishing harmony outlined above were all employed in drafting and passing the National Environmental Policy Act of 1969. Through its almost revolutionary section 102(2)*c* calling for environmental impact statements (EIS), foresight is mandated by a systematic estimate of "What might happen if?" Options must be identified, with speculation on social, economic, and environmental consequences. The process also calls for public hearings, providing the opportunity for all stakeholders to be heard if not listened to.

Since enactment, over ten thousand such early warnings have been prepared at federal levels, and perhaps an equal number at state and local levels. As with any radically new set of social rules, there have been problems. Many EIS's simply justified a course of action already decided upon, rather than searching for an optimum course. Many were so encyclopedic as to defy comprehension, a form of intimidation with paper. Many were incomplete, and these were often challenged successfully in the courts on procedural grounds. Nonetheless, a substantial fraction of the EIS's achieved the legislative goals.

At its inauguration, this environmental impact process led to inflamed discord, partly because it exposed a long-standing history of technological initiatives secretly planned and autocratically implemented without consultation with affected parties. The step itself both slowed implementation to allow for reasoned thought and mediation and exposed the decision-making processes to the light of day. It formalized the opportunity to inquire "Ought we to do it?" as well as "Can we?" And it opened the door through the courts to permit objections over defective process to be raised in an orderly, albeit litigious, way.

Refinements are surely necessary. In light of the previous concepts, two possible reforms emerge. First, citizen involvement might be sought more aggressively at the front end of the entire process, rather than awaiting completion and airing of an EIS. Second, the quest for other techniques of conflict resolution, such as mediation and arbitration, should be intensified. Under such conditions, consensus on tradeoffs should be found sooner, at lower transaction costs, and with less frustration.

Information to Steer By

With all the complexities relating technology, society, and politics, along with the untidy shoving and shouting of democracy, we should recall that the bottom line is to make policy decisions which lead to socially satisfactory outcomes. The emphasis, therefore, must be on informed choice. Questions then arise as to what information is required. Perceptive choice involves two different kinds. The first is information *in* the system, the purely technical data associated with the specialized techniques and artifacts manipulated to generate the desired output of goods or services. The second category involves information *about* the system.

Here, four streams of information are required. One is intelligence of the outside world, the social-economic setting, and the events which energize the culture. Of special importance are the cardinal values of the society that impel or constrain the sociopolitical apparatus. The second is essentially a static map of the technological delivery system, its internal organizational elements, their characteristics, interrelationships, and communication networks. The third type of requisite information constitutes a memory of how that TDS performed. In other words, system dynamics must be exposed to capture past organizational behavior in relation to input and output. Such a representation may be qualitative rather than quantitative. Indeed, with all social processes—and technology is here considered to be one—comprehending the relationships qualitatively may be all that one can do with confidence. But it may be enough to illuminate the situation under study.

Fourth, making informed decisions requires an inventory of the challenges that lie ahead, the opportunities for and obstacles to goal achievement. The problem, crisis, or threat for which policy is being fashioned must be analyzed, along with the strength and tactical disposition of advocates and opponents, with estimates of future changes in the situation, and both direct and indirect impacts.

This information inventory may seem pedantic. But the effective performance of technology in a democratic society fundamentally depends on large numbers of people making thoughtful, realistic choices—with the aid of appropriate information. Jefferson's epigram that "people cannot be safe without information" has special poignancy today.

There is, however, one pitfall: the assumption that with adequate information, decisions will be made rationally. Not that choice is often irrational. But we must ask, Rational for whom? Only by this disaggregation can we become aware that in solving policy riddles there are no "right"—that is, rational and neutral—answers.

Because steering technology is largely a political act, the challenge is not simply providing a narrow inventory of technical data for those in responsible policy positions: citizens as well as politicians should have a hand in writing the script, information that contributes the perspective essential for comprehension by policy officials and citizens alike, and for action. This means not only having good technical information—objective, authentic, and timely—but also having knowledge *about* the system in a form that is readily accessible and understood. By way of example, this involves alerting the public on major bills, their assignment to committees, and schedules of hearings, along with calendars of committee and floor action; compiling summaries of relevant facts and testimony which reveal the public stance of lobbyists and executive branch agencies; providing *independent* analyses of issues and options and technology assessments (discussed later) that portray what might happen, if, to whom, and when.

Then, with common information, and with social systems acting as communications networks, we might learn to manage complexity first by a shared cultural stance. Information could lead to understanding, dissolving unproductive myths, biases, prejudices, political science fictions, ignorance, and hasty or reckless responses to threat.

In a society deafened by sales pitches—including those from government—we discover the salient role of media and its critical function in diffusing facts and untainted analysis. In its role as information processor the press is crucial not only to preserving our democratic creed but also to the study of technological delivery.

If widely accepted social commentary is correct, we have graduated with the aid of technology to an "information society." Yet, on deeper inquiry, that aphorism may be found untrue and possibly dangerous. The explosion of information has not conferred the benefits on the general public that it has on special interests. The information needed to map the kinetics of change is largely the bailiwick of powerful lobbies, facilitated by former insiders now associated with Washington, D.C., law firms. But these fact-finding operations usually focus on narrow issues, with only a passing interest in the larger picture. Even presidents and members of Congress, with all their staff assistance, may be lacking one key ingredient of the information mix: insights about changes being wrought by technology, the insights necessary to comprehend why the future isn't what it used to be.

Helping Politicians Shoot Ducks

Duck hunters and football fans know well a principle derived from country wisdom: "You can't hit a moving target if you aim at it directly." Instead, you must point the gun or throw the forward pass to where the target will be when the missile gets there, a practice known as "lead." Although seldom recognized as such, most policy objectives are moving targets. In political navigation, therefore, ignoring those kinetics almost certainly will result in policy shortfall.

Lead is fundamentally a predictive capacity put into action. It should be imbedded in policy design because of the protracted interval between problem identification, policy solution, and implementation; for during that time, the technical content and the context of a decision may substantially change. Given the technical uncertainties and complexities, and the random interactions among participants, there are huge problems in generating credible lead. Yet the primary test of a decision's validity is its long-term performance: in meeting intended goals, in generating limited adverse repercussions, in not permanently denting the decision system itself or inflaming unmitigated and continuous strife.

Unfortunately, the chaotic atmosphere of most decision theaters dampens lead. Decision makers want to be statesmen in honoring the longer-term and less parochial avenues to choice. But they find themselves squeezed by a vise of contradictory pressures from constituents and lobbyists, all demanding instant results.

Two types of antidotes are available. One is the doctrine of anticipation; the other, the practice of monitoring and course correction. Both have their virtues and their shortcomings.

In the practice of anticipation, we define the issue, nominate the options, and estimate the consequences of each. Policy analyses are often entitled "Issues and Options." Repeatedly missing, however, is a vital fourth step, the citation of tradeoffs. Many are subtle or hidden; the obvious ones still require political bravery to resolve. Providing the policy official with a bold and explicit, rather than implicit, scorecard of effects over different time horizons can be salutary in focusing attention to the way ahead and forcing movement.

This is a strategy of foresight. It is a necessary but not a sufficient condition of lead. For one thing, there is the widespread pathology of the short run; people tend not to look ahead except possibly in terms of how a future event may affect their immediate kin. For another, uncertainties and surprises make foresight, like weather prediction, a matter of probabilities.

So instead of looking ahead, we can monitor the local situation, using social feedback to spot existing policies that are not performing satisfactorily. Then we try to correct course. This process, too, is not without its problems. There is no well-developed mechanism for systematic social feedback. Most serious, we find that short-term amendments to short-term policies based on expediency are unlikely to prevent high future costs.

In making policy, leaders have often ignored the more portentous signals about the future. Take the energy crisis of 1973, arising from the Middle East oil moratorium. By that date, our imports had grown to 50 percent of the supply; a crossover had been reached worldwide between the rate of increased consumption and the rate of new discoveries; in the United States, the birthrate of cars exceeded the birthrate of people; U.S.

manufacturers were promoting large V-8 gas guzzlers, all the worse for lowered efficiency induced by antipollution devices. The danger signals of vulnerability to a cutoff were present. In such cases, the warnings of approaching crisis are credible, readable, and subject to prophylactic action. If these are ignored, neither strategy mentioned above will work. Why, then, can't we generate lead in dealing with signals about the future?

For one thing, listening may be deficient because no auditors are prepared or motivated to appreciate what is heard. Part of this condition may be the inability of the decision system to learn from past experience, or it may be a result of bias or inherent hostility to new ideas. Or hearing may be impaired by the culturally set reward system, which neither favors longer-run elements in tradeoffs nor fosters conservation of resources for anticipatory or corrective action.

On the other hand, transmissions may be weak or ambiguous, either because early warning messages are absent or because there are no messengers, say from a political constituency for the future. And communications may be masked by the noise level of conflict or the overload of other simultaneous warnings or crises.

Finally, because different participants have such different perspectives, communications bog down as though adversaries spoke separate languages. More technical information does not necessarily contribute to political enlightenment; moreover, the frames of reference of experts and politicians differ.

All of which points up the information problem. It is not just what one person says; it is what the other hears. In an age of pride over communications technology, there is a tendency to believe that enhanced processing capabilities will prove that more is better. I doubt it.

If we dissect the political process, we discover that there is no information shortage. Decision makers are deluged with unsolicited traffic from vested interests. Like everyone else, they are clients of mass media. The stream of relevant readings and reports is unrelenting. One remedy to that vexatious burden is resort to interactive information systems wherein a client does not interrogate an information bank directly, but deals with an information broker who has no stake in the outcome, who has subject expertise and also an understanding of the milieu of the client. Such bilingual translators seem in very short supply.

One further reality lies in the high proportion of oral communications rather than written. Politicians seem inclined to favor this mode as both more efficient and more easily subject to a test of confidence in source. But it also makes judgments highly vulnerable to being influenced by whoever had the last word before a vote. No wonder that direct access to decision makers is the prize most zealously sought by lobbyists everywhere.

Virtually all of this information traffic deals with the short run. Given the problems of prudent choice, the need to integrate the future in decision calculus is compelling. Helping politicians shoot ducks is what makes technological choice more an art than a science. Political and business leaders must teach themselves something about this strategy of foresight. Then they must teach the electrorate.

From Knowledge to Understanding, with Intermediate Steps

Making decisions about the grand issues of our times would seem to demand the wisdom of a tree full of owls. With the modern epic called the "information society," there is the strong belief that such a condition is being satisfied. That may be an illusion. As said before, we may have opened up a paradox of more knowledge but less understanding. Indeed, we may need to explore more exact definitions of information and wisdom and, in the context of technological choice, their connections. Consider five possible links in such a chain: with evolutions from data to information; from information to knowledge; from knowledge to understanding; and then the crowning achievement, from understanding to wisdom. By no means are these stages mutually exclusive, but it is instructive to treat them independently. To begin, let us contrast the two extremes.

Data are the basic ingredients of science, the raw evidence from observations or theoretical calculations of natural phenomena. Indeed, science is almost meaningless without measurement. In the physical and life sciences, data are usually collected with the aid of instruments; in the social sciences, by gathering statistics and by polling. With both techniques, data are collected systematically within a defined scope, with variables qualified by the context of observation—that is, the boundary conditions—and by estimates of accuracy. Almost always, data are preserved in permanent records, either stored or indexed through computers. They are tangible and can be copied and widely disseminated so as to be separated from their origin, but usually retaining the identity of the author. Quality and objectivity can be tested through the reproducibility of data by different observers. Although data do not directly entail inferences or speculation, scientific experiments most often are driven by an intent to confirm a hypothesis. From the standpoint of ultimate application, data are passive and morally neutral because prior to use they can have no social consequences.

Wisdom, on the other hand, is a far less tangible and abundant commodity. It is even mysterious. With few exceptions, it resides only in a person, does not appear to be reproducible or teachable, and is best recognized in terms of its practice. Variously, it has been described as "common sense in an uncommon degree," "the right use of knowledge," "pursuit of the best ends by the best means," "the abstract of the past," and "a keen insight into cause and effect." Buried in these phrases are notions of favorable social outcomes. So, unlike data, whose physical presence endures perhaps imperceptibly, wisdom is manifest only when exercised. Seemingly, there is a combination of intellectual prowess and reason with an intuitive sensitivity to socially relevant application. Although wisdom is always subjective, somehow there is the intimation of a higher level of unselfish involvement, in contrast to what is shrewd or cunning.

This distinction between data and wisdom may help illuminate intermediate conditions.

Information, for example, is one step removed from data, although it is always its offspring. In its being better organized, refined, subject to internal tests of validity, cleansed of anomalies, and qualified as to scope, information is almost always more compact and directly useful. Indeed, the prospect of some social utility for data strongly influences their processing. Nevertheless, information still retains many properties of data. It is portable, reproducible, maintains identity as to origin regardless of user, is neutral. It is subject to computer storage and retrieval, but may also be filed in the human memory.

The next stage in this progression is knowledge. Now information has been further structured, condensed, highly refined, and subjected to human reasoning and empirical tests of validity. Most often, it is fitted into some taxonomic classification such as the scholarly disciplines. Knowledge is more than information processing, and a blizzard of data is no substitute for thought. Knowing, incidentally, involves learning, and it is this aspect that is of great portent. Prerequisites are the prepared mind and an appropriate lexicon simply to understand. Now critical judgment begins to play a role. Thus, knowledge may be squeezed for answers not only to "What?" and "When?" but also to "Why?" and "How?" That is, causality. While knowledge is presumed to be neutral and ubiquitous, it does partake of the identity, bias, or qualifications of the user. Indeed, some of it may be simply subconscious folklore.

The step to understanding now involves the direct interaction of information with its client. New requisites beyond those for just knowing include the wit to recognize the significance of the content, the memory capacity to test as well as to retain essential features, and the talent for analysis to extract meaning, that is, to make connections. Understanding may also entail a broader base of knowledge. The structures of mind go well beyond simple classification and cataloging. Mental models or paradigms are required to correlate heuristic information from disparate sources and identities, derived from experience as much as from formal education. Such enlightenment may flash from subliminal inspiration as much as from formal study. Unlike generic knowledge, which has few proprietary boundaries, understanding is a completely private property that can never be confidently shared. But what a bouquet of satisfaction when two or more individuals realize that almost magical bond.

The leap from understanding to wisdom is one both of degree and of kind. Wisdom may be understanding in action, exercised largely through decisions. Here, we make further connections, not just between bits of information but between separate understandings. And we reconcile their gaps. Facts and values are synthesized, especially parameters of intellect with emotional, intuitive, and spiritual dimensions of the human psyche. Both hemispheres of the brain seem involved.

Almost always there is imagination: in pattern recognition and especially in the ability to foresee future effects of current initiatives. In some respects, wisdom reveals command of a metaphorical art of dead reckoning. Unlike understanding, the level of wisdom cannot be foretold in advance; its virility must await the passage of time.

But what has this to do with relating technology to people and politics? For one thing, we can differentiate the involvement with the five elements just set forth as between technicians, policy makers, and citizens. Especially, we need to ponder how to foster that sector of wisdom we associate with foresight.

Scientists, for instance, have a solid command of their subject, from data through a particular kind of understanding. As experts, they can answer intricate narrow questions regarding the natural phenomena that constitute the core of their study. There is no expectation that they will deal with consequences, because utilization lies functionally outside of their purview, in technological delivery. Some, however, may choose to exercise that role.

Professional engineers, on the other hand, are obliged by law to exercise social responsibility. While they often lack the breadth of fundamentals extracted from scientific research, they apply practical knowledge to meet conditions of ultimate use. Almost always, the satisfaction of utility requires tradeoffs because different requirements of functional performance, cost, durability, and public safety are difficult to reconcile. The resulting compromise exacts judgment that bridges knowledge with wisdom.

In technological delivery, we see that much greater breadth is demanded at the decision stages of the information transfer process, including extracts from economic and social context. It is here, too, that we begin to see a sharp distinction in the *kinds* of decisions that must be made by different players, especially if measured by the type and potency of consequences.

In the spectrum from truth to power by which Don K. Price characterized the connection of science to politics, there is a continuum extending from the technical data of scientists to the social wisdom of policy makers. Somewhere in between, there is a vital role for citizens. Generally, they lack the expertise associated with a particular technological issue. And they lack the power of elected officials to make those technological choices of greatest portent. Yet people are involved either as direct beneficiaries of an initiative or as bystanders exposed to side effects. In either case, they want a say; with representative government, they have that right. More than that, there abides in the body politic a fund of common sense that, in the long run, seems to be the best protection against ignorance, blunder, and folly. In the absence of understanding comes fear and hate, neither of which leads to felicitous experience.

The public need not arbitrarily exclude itself for want of formal education. Very few policy makers were trained as scientists or engineers, yet, in contributing to technological choice, they assume a responsibility for prudent action on the basis of incomplete knowledge but with a reliance on understanding and wisdom. To aid in that political navigation, policy makers are heavily supported by staff, formally inside or informally outside the decision theater. Some may be technical specialists. But a significant number serve as translators, that is, as knowledge brokers in an interactive information system. They must be able to interpret technical information, then to recast it in colloquial terms to facilitate understanding by the principal. Such comprehension deals not so much with the technical content of a decision as with its consequences.

The citizen who feels left out because of technical naivete is no more vulnerable to misapprehension than the politician. But the political leadership grapples with complexity through preparation and through studying the alternatives and consequences laid out by advisors presumably having no stake in the outcome. The policy maker can thus move from the rigors of information to the crucial stage of choice: to understanding. Then we expect the revelation of wisdom that, like a healthy body, may come from regular excercise.

From this model, we see that two critical elements are missing for citizens: a preparation of mind essential to knowing and the aid from interpretive, background critiques that facilitates the illumination of tradeoffs. Only with such prerequisites can the public become partners with the policy leadership, so as to zero in on the future effects of current choice. Therein may lie the most potent handle that society might grasp if, indeed, it seriously chooses to manage its technology.

9 / Technology and Citizens

The Media: Lenses, Mirrors, or Filters?

iven the number and diversity of partners, including the public, that interact to deliver any technology successfully, somehow they must be synchronized; and synchronization demands powerful communication networks. Some conduits distribute technical data; others, administrative. Almost always, this traffic is specialized in content and selective as to recipient. Superposed on these discrete linkages are the mass media.

The mass media, print and electronic, are the primary means by which all parties involved in technological transactions can gain a common data base. That is to say, the media that lace the planet with resources to gather, sort, and disseminate information are the most universal of all facilitators. It is here that modern technology has had such a profound impact in that worldwide reporting makes events which occur anywhere known almost everywhere, and almost immediately.

Without such a lacework, the social functioning of a democracy would be impaired. If the public is ignorant of the issues and of a calendar for their resolution, decisions will be left to an elite operating through private networks. Only the institution of a free press can help people keep government honest.

The media, however, do not serve only the general public. They enrich the perspective of all key actors on the technological stage. Presidents read newspapers; they listen to TV commentators. Indeed, government officials concerned that their messages to top levels might be intercepted by bureaucratic staff deliberately seek press exposure of their interests. Even lower-level officials in government exploit this route. In scanning the news, policy makers compulsively track reports of their personal activities, to check on the quantity and the authenticity of coverage as it affects their power and prestige. Some rely on editorial comment as a form of social feedback.

Business depends on the media as an alerting mechanism, part of an intelligence function to detect circumstances that may influence day-to-day decisions. While much fascination attaches to the drumbeat of economic indicators, stock and currency prices, there is intense scrutiny of snippets from anywhere on the planet that would signal opportunities or dangers ahead.

Scientists and engineers read as citizens, but they also scan the news for general content which casts perspective on their enterprises. They look for fluctuations in overall research funding, the priorities of a current administration, the commercial climate for innovation, and new discoveries in fields other than their own.

To elaborate on the vital role of the mass media would be to state the obvious. The key questions revolve around what news is selected for dissemination, and whether it is independent, balanced, accurate, objective, and adequate to inform citizens in an open society of the choices ahead. That requirement is more than catering to public appetites.

Because the media are swamped each day with far more bulletins than space permits for printing or time permits for TV reporting, innumerable choices must be made. Managing editors become gatekeepers, exercising judgment as to what people want to know and on what they believe people should know.

So the media act as a lens. Yet no lens can capture all the action. Questions arise as to whether the press concentrates on drama, on the bad news, or on the sensational with which the public seems obsessed. Such accusations are perennial criticisms from politicians stung by adverse publicity. Every president cringes when the press does not indulge in puffery; then they indulge in a familiar paranoid theme: "If you're not for me, you must be against me." Presidential staff, including a recent science advisor, indulge in similar press relations as cheerleaders and self-appointed critics.

Apart from the concern over media selectivity, there are periodic debates on objectivity. Does the press act as a filter, slanting news according to the biases of editor or publisher? Do reporters, like all thinking individuals, bring their own baggage of attitudes, which inevitably color their reports? Is the press subject to intimidation by advertisers who reflect conservative political philosophy, or by government agencies that threaten reporters' careers by withholding leaks from those not readily tamed?

Accusations have been leveled, for instance, at media alarms over environmental threats, reflected for example in public loss of confidence in civilian nuclear power. Yet those who criticize the press for this alleged distortion have never proved falsification. At the other end of the ideological spectrum, some suspect the press of acting as a transmission belt for government propaganda. And, indeed, the government has coopted an unwitting press, as when it impetuously adopted a policy for the swine flu vaccine, or in its desperate rationale for yet another technique of hiding the MX missile. To the public, such technological issues may seem complex, if not downright arcane. And the public cannot seek alternative sources of information as can researchers in technological enterprise.

Whatever level of literacy in science and technology the general public has reached is not from formal education. Rather it is from the mass media. That responsibility of the press has been almost completely ignored. Since the heyday of the space program, the media has indulged in so-called science reporting, all too often with a "gee whiz" attitude, concentrating on new discoveries or developments that will intrigue a public that has an appetite for novelty and surprise. Interpretations of how new developments, indirect consequences, or accidents affect people have only occasionally found a place in TV specials, and newspaper editors still worry about boring readers with interpretive studies on the social impacts of technology.

More subtle, but nonetheless a problem with complex technological issues, are the distortions from deadline pressures on reporters, or from contractions to fit sound or video bites into broadcast time. Such limits of time or space make it impossible to sketch the context of an issue, the facts, the complex implications, and alternative perspectives. During interviews, reporters insist on black and white answers to fit the medium, thereby fostering blandness and banality in explaining technology-laced policy. Moreover, when political leaders face the camera, they artfully project confidence in having every situation well under control, along with having command of all the technical facts but which they say, unfortunately, circumstances do not permit sharing.

Why do both TV and newspapers such as *USA Today* adopt such modes of compressed reporting? More than any factor, it is the perception, confirmed by commercial success, that the public has no patience for detail, complexity, or ambiguity. And here is yet another paradox to add to earlier enigmas: that the nation with such a high fraction of university graduates has developed no appetite to comprehend more than emotion-laden headlines.

In short, message content is vulnerable to biases of the reporter and of the reporting organization, to tendencies to highlight the sensational, and to the influences of powerful sources who try to misuse the press for propaganda. In addition, the media has its inherent limitations when it conveys snatches of information without helping recipients understand.

Whatever historical power the press has held to influence public opinion has greatly increased with new technologies. Modern society, because of its complexity and interconnectedness, critically depends on information for effective functioning. No wonder that political campaigns devote such a large fraction of their funds to TV ads. Consider, also, the crucial role played by TV in the transition in Philippines leadership, both in Aquino forces seizing a domestic station and the publicity given the entire process by foreign TV cameras.

Direct or indirect constraints on the freedom of the press may signal the health of the entire democratic process. With editorial control over the national news media so centralized, our high-tech information system is vulnerable to subversion. In a technological society, where control of information linkages becomes easier, the public needs a press that will report when the government lies. At a more subtle level, if we are not careful with television, we may lose the knack of critical judgment, healthy skepticism, and demand for evidence before making up our mind. Until the educational system catches up, people need the press to explain how technology impacts their lives, both in benefits and in penalties.

Since the media need customers, some of their behavior can be explained as purely commercial. Every night, on TV at least, the public votes by twisting dials. But while appreciating its primary fare of entertainment, the public also knows that TV can inform and function as the glue for coherence in a pluralistic society by giving everyone a sense of where we are. Think of the potential contributions to democratic process if media beyond the *Washington Post* and the PBS network would inform citizens in advance of crucial decisions, with brief scoping of the issues, a list of key facts and uncertainties, and a scorecard of alternatives and estimated consequences in the long as well as the short run.

Today, technology both fuels policy dilemmas and provides leverage for the media to influence the outcome. If the public fully appreciated that situation, it might well demand a somewhat different balance of television programming for the seven and a half hours a day that pollsters confirm is the average viewing time per household. People might recognize that our precious system of freedom succeeds only when every component maintains both its competence and its integrity. With that caveat, the media could well become the nation's most salient mentor in science policy.

The Technology of Politics

Politicians, in the modern sense of elected officials, have always depended on technology to reach public office and to keep it. Gutenberg's printing press was probably the first such piece of hardware. It is hard to imagine that the revolutions in France and America could have succeeded without it. What has been termed the fourth estate—the news media—could not have originated as an institution in our society without printing presses.

Beginning in 1932, political leaders began to exploit other technical levers. Franklin D. Roosevelt took to the radio to cool hysteria over the economic crash. Through "fireside chats," he hoped to boost morale, to tutor a nation on its social and economic ills, and to sell his brand of medicine. The instant news of the Pearl Harbor catastrophe and keen interest during the subsequent four years in the fate of American military engagements crystallized for all time the pervasive and influential role of electronic journalism. In Germany, radio broadcasting was also being exploited as a powerful instrument of politics, but in service of a different creed. Adolf Hitler fully understood radio's appeal to those who were more easily turned on by a hypnotic voice and the shouts, songs, and applause of supporters than by dull print. How much his takeover of German politics can be attributed to radio propaganda may never be understood, but he was not alone in recognizing the potency of the new medium. Winston Churchill dramatically rallied the support of his beleaguered people by radio. When peace was restored, newspapers and magazines had a strong competitor for news and political commentary. Their one conspicuous advantage lay in supplementing text with photographs. Such graphic messages not only compressed content so as to speed comprehension; pictures hooked the heart as well as the mind. Then came television to conquer mass communication.

Meanwhile, regarding the technology of politics, other technical means and innovations were adopted. Harry Truman used the rear observation platform of a railroad car to carry his personal campaign to previously inaccessible districts. Soon after, the airplane performed a similar service. Indeed, the speed associated with jet travel made it possible for congressmen to return home frequently, even to the west coast; their historical remoteness from voters during congressional sessions was permanently ended. To some extent, this altered strong party allegiances, replacing them with a direct and idiosyncratic loyalty of representatives to their immediate and provincial constituencies.

Recourse to weekend jaunts home for members of Congress was nudged by another technology, air conditioning. Until its installation on Capitol Hill, heat and humidity drove elected officials out of the capital for the summer. With artificial cooling, the entire legislative calendar changed; and activity was discovered to saturate the newly available time.

But more and more, television played the pivotal role in politics, with the 1984 presidential election marking a watershed in the use of technology for political campaigning. The union of big money and subtle technique brought television to its zenith as a medium for merchandising candidates. The amount of money spent on TV advertising was staggering, some $150 million nationwide.

In addition, the technology of polling reached a new level of intensity and credibility. Applied social science was employed both to forecast trends and, by exit interviews at the polls, to explain why people voted as they did. Indeed, the two technologies of television and polling had a subtle symbiosis. The content and style of campaigns, especially the techniques used in TV ads, were designed, polished, and then revised with information continuously gleaned from interim tests of the public sentiment. But on election night, the combination of polling and TV news also erased all suspense over the outcome, especially for residents in the West.

A major question is whether the hoopla and the hype contributed to public understanding. Both scholars and citizens seem agreed that few care about the issues. People were not asking what might happen, if? They were voting their feelings, based largely on images of personality, powerful images brought into the intimacy of the living room in a manner that required little effort to translate the message into action. It was the same technique that had successfully sold deodorants and flea powder.

Even the TV debates between candidates were judged by the public on the basis of how the contenders looked and acted rather than on the substance of their arguments. The potency of this medium was demonstrated first in 1960 with the debates between John F. Kennedy and Richard M. Nixon. Because the debate format had a long and respected history, there was every reason to applaud its restoration as a stage on which the grand issues could be identified and the contenders challenged to explain their stand and their reasons. Not so. The medium swamped the message. And that curious phenomenon was reinforced in 1980 with Jimmy Carter and Ronald Reagan. Television was now the most influential instrument in American politics, and the campaign managers of 1984 saw the opportunities. If scores were kept on the relative skill of the candidates' handlers, clearly the Reagan staff won.

The point is that there may be a significant mismatch between TV projections and reality, and for that disparity no knob on the TV set permits correction. Indeed, the brevity of news clips or ads, the invocation of "evil empires," and the absence of truth squads permits escape from challenge to distortions, disinformation, contradictions, and recourse to emotional bumper-sticker slogans. Television thus exploits uncritical, passive attitudes of the electorate.

When acknowledging the potent role of technology in the game of politics, we must note another connection, the striking influence of TV pulpits, especially those of Evangelical Christians. In America in the last decade, these churches have grown faster than other denominations, partly because of the new adherents attracted by TV. That distinction is matched by an almost unprecedented involvement of religious groups in domestic politics, supporting particular issues and particular candidates. In ideologically congenial alliances with political organizations, they effectively use another technology, the computerized mailing list.

The point, of course, is not simply that TV is a medium of overwhelming potency. Its effectiveness lies not in the hardware but in the skill with which it is exploited. Does its increasing influence suggest that future candidates will be chosen primarily from rosters of movie actors? Or that victory goes to the side with the largest purse? Or that truth and logic no longer count, that slogans, bands, flags, and balloons create the most persuasive images?

That all depends. Behavioral scientists are sure to debate the implications. For there are contradictions. TV *has* portrayed real events with substantive content and tweaked the American conscience. Witness the reporting from Vietnam and from Teheran; the reactions to the movies on nuclear war; the raising of public awareness of the disparities and miseries of the poor, the handicapped, the disenfranchised. The question is whether enough people are having their consciousnesses enlarged by these technological images of reality to offset the exaggeration and persuasion in the drumbeat of television indoctrination.

To date, the technology of politics has been most conspicuously employed to persuade. Observers seem unanimous in concluding that it has been enormously effective. Will the same technical instruments associated with political power be employed to improve the quality of political decision making? Whatever the answers, the technology of politics may be as significant to the future of technological choice as are the politics of technology.

What If Orwell Had Written 1974?

The year 1984 ended with collective sighs of relief that the Big Brother scenario portrayed by George Orwell had not happened. When the movie *1984* was released shortly thereafter, it elicited a big yawn of indifference. People already knew that Orwell was wrong; and in seeking entertainment, many people avoided the film because it might trigger feelings of guilt about that indifference. But those hasty and emotionally loaded conclusions may have missed the point.

Orwell's novel was not meant as a prophecy. Rather, the date was a metaphor for the future, a warning that unless society learns to manage technology, some people will find ways to use it to manage us. Through pathological twists in governance, we can lose our precious gift of freedom.

If that seems like political science fiction, it might be instructive to review Orwell's plot and to guess what might have happened in the decade preceding his 1984 scenario to lead to "groupthink" and to slavery. What if Orwell had written *1974?*

For instance, how would the gang in power have gained control over public information so as to manufacture the false news of combat without challenge? In that technetronic era, let us assume an initial condition of an aggressive and independent news media. Inquiring reporters told it like it was. Perhaps commercial advertisers then began to complain of comments inimical to their chants of "consume" and "keep government off our back"; or of reports of consumer fraud, tax evasion, contractor over-charging, or bribery of government officials that seriously undermined confidence in business.

We can imagine also that the government might have complained about the nagging criticism, about independent views that to those in power smelled like ideological bias or political opposition. What particularly upset government was exposure of lies—lies about foreign military expe-ditions, the state of the poor and disadvantaged, the predictable impacts of short-run economic policy, the concentration of personal data on com-puters, and the general situation at home and abroad. Politicians didn't care one whit for investigative reporting that exposed promises not kept, policies that flagged, or special treatment for narrow but affluent con-stituencies. Moreover, in Orwell's development, we have to assume a partnership between government and industry that might be termed the corporate state.

Both parties thus began a subtle campaign to constrain the free flow of information. It was not the brainchild of political leadership but of those carefully hidden behind the scenes in both government and industry who yearned not simply for power, but for absolute and unchallenged power. Commercial enterprise squeezed publishers and editors to paint more favorable images, using economic intimidation but also increasing direct sponsorship of public interest TV programs whose content was more congenial. Government increased the number of handouts to those report-ers who were often too busy to write their own copy and who enjoyed the media opportunities to hobnob with the leadership. Then the White House began to offer special wire services, with its own brand of the news, to small-town newspapers that could not afford their own capital reporters. Leaks were more deliberately controlled, favoring reporters whose careers depended upon wooing influential sources and withholding access to those who simply wanted the facts. Finally, penal sanctions were ordained against government employees or retirees who blew whistles.

In Orwell's fantasy, technology made those ambitions to manage the news realizeable. By 1974 television had become the primary source of information, in a few nationwide broadcast and cable networks. Decisions on the content of the programs were concentrated in the hands of a few individuals; the anchorpeople became the wardens of communication. By subversion of these information managers, the inauguration of groupthink was easy and almost unnoticed.

In an open society, how could this have been accomplished? Coercing the gatekeepers head-on held great danger of premature discovery and failure. But there were other promising options. Like most business enterprises, TV networks were investor-owned. So, a campaign could be mounted by some well-recognized leader having a power base of ideological, unquestioning adherents to buy stock in the networks. When enough stock was in the hands of this group, management of the networks would then permit selection of anchorpeople of more certain loyalty to the management's ideological profile. Alternately, there could be a classical takeover by a wealthy corporation or by a coalition of wealthy investors whose political polarity was congenial to the administration in power and who expected reciprocity in favors.

The point of this allegorical preface to Orwell's novel is to suggest that technological ways and means are increasingly available to those who would, at the very least, avoid accountability. In 1985, the preconditions of Orwell's fanciful 1984 just portrayed were actually present in the United States. Life in the Soviet Union and other police states confirms that Orwell's nightmare can be realized. As Walter Lippmann has so eloquently said, freedom is not guaranteed by the genes; it is provisional, vulnerable, and subject to continuity only when guarded. The challenge to contemporary society to preserve the system of freedom encompasses the institutions of education, the press, and religion in a high-tech world. Later we consider the strengths of these institutions to protect our most treasured values.

We, the People

Is our contemporary nest of dilemmas largely a response to the impact which technology has on society, as Alvin Toffler asserted in his classic, *Future Shock,* or is the reverse closer to reality, that culture drives technology? Perhaps the truth lies in between, with pulses travelling in both directions, even ricocheting off each other.

To grasp the significance of such a dynamic sociotechnical environment, we need to define ourselves as well as the hardware in these transactions. In short, we need to characterize the social attitudes of "we, the people." This is far more difficult than depicting technology. Even as a social process, each technology for manufacturing cars or delivering health care stirs instant recognition; descriptions are relatively free of subjective interpretation, and indicators of what is going on are fairly explicit, often subject to quantification.

Detecting the principal, albeit transient, currents in a pluralistic society requires research techniques that are often controversial, measurement of parameters that are often fuzzy, and then generalizations about an extremely diverse people. Nevertheless, the Bureau of the Census canvasses and catalogs social indicators of American life along with topics of deep social concern. Gallup and other pollsters collect and publicize similar data. Authors such as Daniel Yankelovich in *New Rules* and Robert Naisbett in *Megatrends* report their own versions of what they think is going on or what is on people's minds. These social indicators are similar to the more familiar economic indicators of GNP, inflation, interest rates, balance of trade, and stock market levels that are cited by the media with feverish intensity a dozen times a day. In contrast, social indicators are ignored. Partly, that is because changes may be slower and thus lack headline appeal. But that comparison may itself say something about contemporary attitudes as to what is more important.

Three classes of social indicators have been developed to tell us where we are now, where we are going, and where we want to go: those that define social system performance, those that report social and technological trends, and those that poll public perceptions about the future.

Indicators of social performance can readily be described in hard statistics. Some of these simply represent the inputs of dollars in various categories of national endeavor. But the outputs earn special attention. We can measure the size and age distribution of the population; the number of single parents; the changes in female employment; the use of automobiles in terms of annual mileage; preferences in other transportation modes; educational attainment and quality as indicated by test scores or student-teacher ratios; employment; industrial productivity; time devoted to religious services; or the fraction of citizens who vote.

Indicators of well-being go further by interpreting whether people are better off or worse. Numbers can be recruited to describe material affluence, rates of infant mortality, crime, available housing, diffusion of social services, and much more.

Many of these social indicators reflect the force of technology. People live longer because of scientific death control: immunization, better nutrition, and medical care. Fewer are born because of scientific birth control. As a result, the proportion of older citizens has increased steadily. Many young people still die in automobile accidents, although the rate seems to have stabilized. Surveys also show that people increasingly turn to television for news and for entertainment, on the average, fifty-two hours per week. Convenience foods and time-saving devices make it possible for more women to join the work force and make single parenting practical. This development, incidentally, extended major contributions of technology to the changing role of women. That change began when they were freed from chopping wood, carrying water, and shopping daily for want of refrigeration.

While these connections with technology seem obvious, we must be cautious about coming to conclusions. Cursory reviews of social indicators do not directly reveal associations or cause-and-effect relationships, so inferences must be regarded as speculative.

Finally, indicators of public perceptions offer insight into the most elusive ingredients of the quality of life. Polls solicit individuals' purely subjective feelings on sensitive aspects of their own situation. Here, we learn about their definitions of "the good life"; their feelings of satisfaction, alienation, or vulnerability; frequency of traumatic events in their lives; their confidence in leadership; their preferences for national spending priorities; even their means of obtaining information about the world around them and how they play.

If we examine how people behaved in voting booths in 1984 as well as what they said to different pollsters, we can charactize the mainstream of sentiment.

First, people were greatly concerned with their personal economic situation: they wanted stronger assurance of jobs, less inflation that eroded purchasing power, and lower interest rates to foster continued consumer borrowing. They were driven more by a yearning for self-fulfillment than by social commitment.

Next, they wanted to lower the widely perceived risk of nuclear war. But because this issue seemed beyond their grasp in terms of a clear, simple, and confident solution, they accepted the premise that national security was best guaranteed by continuing an arms buildup. That symbol of national power may also have been spurred by the embarrassments of Vietnam, and the hostage situation in Iran.

Individuals and corporations yearned for peace of mind, simply stated as a penchant for stability. They wanted an end to one-term presidents, a buffering from the noise and confusion of world politics, a renewed statement of a few basic values that might provide compass directions to tranquility amidst the perplexing ambiguities of modern technological life.

People wanted to be left alone, especially to escape what was perceived as a growing burden of governmental paperwork, zealous bureaucrats, excessive taxes, rules, and constraints. To some extent, they felt both alienated by the remoteness and impersonality of government and impotent in affecting the grand decisions. Accompanying this concern was a backlash to the growth in social welfare services and costs, from 13.4 percent of the GNP in 1960 to 27.5 percent in 1976. Even though people universally agree that "the rich get richer and the poor, poorer," concern for social equity seemed to have hit the stops of economic self-interest. A deep current of "rugged individualism" reminscent of the 1920s seems to have been reawakened; perhaps fundamental attitudes undergo conspicuous swings in the same fifty-year cycles that economist Kondratieff says characterize economic behavior.

Paralleling this desire for less government, and perhaps at the root of that desire, was a lowered confidence in government, in its competence and accountability in both the executive branch and the Congress. Paradoxically, people recognized that all technologies had insidious side effects and expected government to mitigate these hazards, even though protection of the public interest entailed more regulation.

While the question of confidence in government is conspicuous because the public rated it the lowest of all institutions (barring labor unions), polls showed a drop in confidence in *all* institutions, banks and industrial firms included. Nevertheless, there was continued belief in the virtues of private industrial entrepreneurship as the most effective way to foster efficient management, quality, and productivity. What was so perplexing was the loss of industrial markets to foreign competitors, not only on the basis of price, but on innovativeness, quality and high style. Attempts at explanation as to remedies through free trade or import barriers only added confusion.

In spite of the stresses and frustrations that surround the lives of most people, there was a dominant mood of optimism, a trait deeply rooted in the American character. In stark contrast, however, were feelings about the nation. The public seemed pessimistic about the troubles that surround the planetary condition and the apparent inability of institutional leaders everywhere to cope with modern technologically oriented life.

One result was the increased concentration of single-issue politics, the attempt by people to play out a role as citizen activists by getting a handle on those questions that concern them directly and are amenable to both simple solutions and elemental political action.

Thus the issues which grabbed influential sectors of the public in the 1960s—disenfranchisement, disservice, disamenities, demands for consumer and environmental protection—appeared to have lost some of their appeal and influence. The unwritten but salient agenda of the 1960s—the desire to gain purchase on the power structure or to symbolize a resistance to technological elitism—may nevertheless have been inherited by the new public interest lobbies.

We can illustrate the last point with two examples. First, the concern for the environment and for conservation of natural resources that peaked in the 1965–75 period resulted in massive regulatory legislation. In the mid-1980s some of these acts are being allowed to lapse without reauthorization. Enforcement of others, such as those under the aegis of the EPA, was flagging without significant uproar. Public interest groups seemed exhausted from a decade of litigation, and citizen concerns turned inward and toward their pocketbooks. The "me, now" philosophy of young people in the 1970s seemed to have enveloped the entire culture. While it might be true that, with this shift in attitudes, the environmental legislation of the 1965–75 era could not have been enacted in 1984, it is also true that there is no march to cancel it, either. Not even the most hostile of industrial opponents to EPA have proposed its abolishment.

A similar phenomenon could be observed with energy supply. In the aftermath of the 1973 oil moratorium and the sharp increase in prices, there was a stampede for energy policy. The objectives were to accelerate oil exploration, to underwrite new energy sources such as solar and synthetic fuels, to build up strategic reserves, to publicize the benefits of conservation, and to reward (with tax credits) conservation measures. But a decade later, after high prices had stimulated exploration and increased supply, prices stabilized and dropped. The pocketbook previously strained to fuel the family car or the furnace no longer was being molested. Some degree of relative stability seemed, temporarily at least, to envelop Mideast politics. Despite credible predictions about a renewed energy crisis and its implications for the Third World and for future generations, the public's attitude was ho-hum.

Changes in the intensity of public interest in these two technological issues of energy and environment are striking. Partly this may be the psychological reality that interest in any single issue is not sustained at a high pitch for long. Partly, however, these two issues share a common thread of requiring tradeoffs, not just between economy and ecology, but between the long- and the short-term consequences. In that negotiation, shorter-term elements win.

Thus a fundamental conflict over technology may be built into the culture, because society has neither the desire, the competence, nor the institutions to look ahead so as to identify tradeoffs up front. So, social attitudes of technological clientele influence the grand technological choices. But these attitudes are often baffling. Consider the belief that our society is driven exclusively or largely by a cult of materialism associated with the proven dogma of free enterprise. Despite the past success of the capitalist production system, polls indicate that less than 15 percent of the population assert that for society as a whole, "things are getting better." It is also striking that with questions on expected business conditions, respondents are highly effervescent. From 1954 to 1969, 60 percent of respondents were "optimistic." Sharp fluctuations then ensued, with optimism expressed by as few as 15 percent to as many as 50 percent; but from 1976 to 1982, the fraction of optimists plummeted downward to a plateau at 15 percent. In this respect, the United States shares a spirit of general economic pessimism with the rest of the world. We seem to have passed the era when people generally thought that their children had prospects of being better off than they themselves.

It matters little whether this attitude is characterized as "pessimistic" or "realistic." What is at stake may be a social perception well ahead of political rhetoric and even the expert economic forecasters. If we are entering a new era, perhaps one of uncertainty and scarcity, the elements of technological choice will surely become more critical. That is why, sooner or later, we will have to face up to the challenge of "what do we do?"

Where People Come from Makes a Difference

The idiomatic question "Where are you coming from?" is not simply a geographic inquiry. It is a statement that how individuals intuitively "feel" about an issue has a great deal to do with their position. Call it subliminal perspective, mind set, bias, or whatever, such deep-seated attitudes are powerful. They are not ingrained from the individual's analysis; they stem from fundamental and cherished personal values. Moreover, these values are likely to influence not only *what* a person thinks on a particular issue, but also *how* he or she think about it.

Naturally, some attitudes are rooted in self-interest. "Where a person stands depends on where he sits" is an ancient maxim of political life. People can be expected to subordinate certain personal preferences to those of an employing institution or of the institution they represent, or sometimes, in politics, to those of their party. Thus they adopt a coloration associated with both the goals and the values of their host. Lawyers adopt this posture as a reality of professional life. As advocates for their clients, they may find themselves in hot contests with close attorney friends representing the other side. Within government, the same situation occurs when representatives of two agencies Indian wrestle strenuously, each knowing that such vigorous defense of their organization is expected and not representative of personal animus.

There is, however, a second aspect of diversity. Pluralism may spawn discord either over ideology or over specifics. Not surprisingly, tension over science policies arises from both sources.

During and after World War II, for example, technology was uncritically glorified by almost everyone. While advocacy of a "technological fix" for social problems continues to this day among those having a personal stake in technological enterprise, it is no longer universal. In the 1960s, along with the counterculture, there arose a highly vocal attack on technology. To these activists, technology was the source of so many social ills that the only solution was to turn it off. A fertile literature erupted with this motif: *The Greening of America, The Pentagon of Power*, and others. Philosophical correlates were eloquently presented as *Small Is Beautiful* and *How to Avoid the Future*.

Such skepticism about technology took a different twist with the release in 1972 of *Limits to Growth*. That study and its sequels, sponsored mainly by the Club of Rome, presented results from computer modeling that suggested that somehow technology was pushing natural limits to the carrying capacity of the planet. Burgeoning world population, limits to food production, a finite capacity of the environment to absorb pollution, and the economic and political instabilities of uncritical expansion of industrial production combined to signal dire trouble ahead. While the study was heavily criticized on methodological grounds, it served as a powerful warning that, unwittingly and irreversibly, we may be fouling the nest. At the very least, the future deserved more serious attention than it had been getting, especially in making science policy, a concern that ultimately led to the Council on Environmental Quality's publication in 1979 of *Global 2000*. Some people took an interest in the future. For a few this was philosophical, but most engaged specific technological initiatives: to clean up dumps around the Love Canal, to ban supersonic jet noise at Dulles International Airport, to protest corporate indifference to asbestos hazards.

In the 1980s, the situation changed again. Now we find contests over different philosophical and ideological abstractions; again, many have technological underpinnings: arguments about abortion, about proposals to base national security largely on the superiority of high-tech weapons, about extending the theater of combat to outer space, about arms control, about dealing with energy-triggered inflation, and about the effects of robotics on unemployment—to mention just a few. With some exceptions, these issues cluster around values of the economic imperative, national security, and ethical and religious convictions.

Clearly, where people stand on these issues is more sharply conditioned by their beliefs than by reason. Not that one is superior to the other. Pragmatism forces us to expect both. Indeed, the decision process must somehow accommodate three elements: reason, belief, and intuition. The point is that because of the disparity in where adherents come from, policy making must take into account the notion of multiple perspectives.

Some of these value preferences of citizens enter into the process through the overt acts of lobbying and voting. But some are inconspicuously present among the key actors in the decision process, and silently influential in every element of the technological delivery system. Because the role of personal values is so obvious, we need to recognize the implications of values further engraved by the institutional setting.

Policy analysts Graham Allison and (more recently) Harold Linstone have made a convincing case that three sets of actors on the technological decision stage should be expected to have vastly different viewpoints. The political actor, the bureaucrat, and the expert are likely to disagree at almost every step of the decision process. They fall out over the nature of the problem itself, the weight of different facts in the presence of uncertainty, and the options and their consequences. Although any three individuals might be expected to disagree, here the differences are systematic and chronic. Because all three actors are on the stage together, progress demands that they reconcile their differences. How that is done makes an enormous difference in the quality of choice. When their differences are not harmonized, in the presence of a crisis such as a decision to launch the shuttle, we suddenly become aware of the divergent views within publicly tranquil organizational boundaries.

It is interesting that neither Allison nor Linstone included in his cast of stakeholders those affected by the decision, instead of only those engaged in the decision process. Yet there may be serious discrepancies between the values held by society and those held by the leadership elite. It is not only diverging self-interests that induce discord; there is also the problem identified before, that those in power are often surrounded by others of similar persuasion so as to be isolated from dissent. Indeed, while disagreement with peers is considered simply gauche, for subordinates it may be dangerous, and disagreement from outsiders is often steamrollered because it is politically threatening. The problem, then, is not one of malevolence or even indifference. Purely and simply, it springs from hubris, the trap in Greek tragedy of arrogance that causes successful leaders to be certain that they always "know best."

Experts are also vulnerable to this condition, in relation to what some consider the great unschooled public. They tend to ignore the fact that their attitudes toward risk differ radically from those of the nonexpert. The expert tends to overconfidence in numerics and in the capacity to control risk absolutely. Unfortunately, the finer his specialization, the more the expert loses breadth and objectivity. Unwittingly, an expert may be swept along with forces with whom he has become allied by virtue of sharing a stake in the outcome. Experts have difficulty appreciating why citizens are suspicious of putting faith in those who are not exposed to the same risks, especially when dealing with technical matter they cannot understand. This is in part why citizens and experts disagree so sharply on the risks of nuclear power.

One last point. There is bound to be a difference in perspective between those alive today and those in future generations who are subject to the delayed impacts of today's decisions. It is very difficult to find advocates for progeny, although parents and grandparents are inevitably concerned about their offspring's fate.

These differences were tested by some informal polling by the author among different age groups, with some interesting results. Respondents were asked to rank priorities as to generic impacts that should be addressed in every policy analysis. In doing so, they were to play three different roles: as a contemporary decision maker, as a citizen, and as a citizen fifteen years hence. Note that we were not concerned with the intensity of each impact, but rather, how urgent each was to investigate. Each hypothetical party, therefore, ranked what was for him "the right questions." The results are presented in Table 9.1. They disclose a vast gulf separating policy makers from voters, and another one separating present from future voters.

Clearly, in the struggle for power, the citizen places a high priority on participation in the decision process. Politicians, on the other hand, are more interested in protecting their stature and the stability of the process. They disdain boat-rocking. Neither politician nor citizen shows much appetite for the longer-term, iffy questions. To be sure, it would be naive to expect a universal tradeoff of the present for the always uncertain future. So what is the delicate balance between "me, now" and "we, tomorrow?"

What all of this suggests is the urgency of finding a way to integrate these perspectives in the decision process, so as not to abdicate consideration of those affected by the choice who may not have an equal voice at the locale or moment of decision. Again, the shuttle accident dramatizes the ubiquitous gaps in the decision process. In practical terms, this means providing more continuous access for the contemporary stakeholder to express views as the decision is being made, rather than after it is made. And it means building in consideration of the future.

Technology and the Law

While public policy for science and technology is primarily forged in the executive and legislative branches, the judiciary also has a powerful role. It has proven of extraordinary significance when citizens through public interest organizations held the executive branch's toes to the fire to follow legislative instructions. Yet there is a long and important history. Formal connections between science, technology, and the law stretch back to the Constitution, in the patent and the commerce clauses. But long before, the English and then colonial common law was well exercised where damage from technological enterprise led to suits for compensation. Indeed, there was recourse to the law in anticipation of damage, as for instance when riparian rights to fresh water were threatened by potential upstream pollution.

Over the years, the legal system has advanced with changing technology. Cases have included the protection of patent rights for inventions and proprietary technical information; charges of civil or criminal negligence where apparatus was not installed or operated with responsible concern for public health or safety, or where installations infringed on rights of neighbors by creating nuisances or reducing economic value; situations where business practices or promises appeared fraudulent.

Table 9.1   Ranking of Priorities in Impact Analysis According to Role

Issues to be considered	Sequence of perceived impact	Policy maker 1985	Citizen circa 1985	Citizen circa 2000
Preserving power of policy maker	1	1	14	17
Resolving conflict among interests	2	2	10	11
Achieving immediate intended benefits	3	3	1	12
Continuation of existing power structure	4	4	12	13
Implementing policy efficiently	5	5	2	9
Correlating policy with existing law	6	7	13	14
Protecting private initiative	7	8	5	16
Achieving future benefits at low risk	8	9	11	3
Preserving freedom	9	6	3	2
Maintaining law and order	10	10	4	6
Preserving citizen access to policy apparatus	11	11	9	5
Protecting the environment	12	13	8	7
Preserving quality of life	13	14	6	10
Maintaining information flow	14	12	15	15
Maintaining accountability of leadership	15	15	7	8
Preserving options for the future	16	16	16	4
Protecting capacity to image future	17	17	17	1

In recent years, further ground has been broken because of dilemmas stirred by scientific advances, because of unprecedented types or degrees of technology-induced risks, and because of the massive surge of regulation at both federal and state levels to limit environmental and social impact. Never before, for example, had there been litigation on the propriety of disconnecting life-support medical apparatus; on the rights of various parties with regard to embryos and fetuses produced by artificial insemination or in-vitro fertilization; on the exposure of citizens to potentially harmful radioactive fallout from nuclear testing before aboveground testing was prohibited by the 1963 Test Ban Treaty; or on a public utility's defaulting on bonds for construction of nuclear power plants where investors were led to believe they would never be exposed to monetary risk even if the plants were never built.

One of the more striking developments has been the recourse to the courts by activist public interest groups over concern that the government itself has violated the law. For example, class-action suits were brought on behalf of hypothetical parties, not because of alleged exposure to injury, but simply because that prospect was raised by incomplete or deficient impact analysis as mandated by the National Environmental Policy Act. These suits concerned process and not substance; decisions were not rendered on whether a challenged initiative violated some desired or mandated standard of health or safety. In addition, there were class-action suits because government implementation of standards for health or safety was sluggish, or its penalties for violation insufficient.

Meanwhile, there has been an explosion in litigation to collect damages in cases of alleged technological negligence. Most conspicuous are those of medical malpractice. But there have also been other types of claims, such as those related to weak fuel tanks in automobiles where their vulnerability to rupture in collision was known by the manufacturer, to exposure to asbestos that went uncontrolled for decades after manufacturers knew of the health hazards, or to exposure of U.S. soldiers to the defoliant Agent Orange in Vietnam. The list is endless, perhaps somewhat inflated by an overzealous legal profession that lacks the restraints found in other countries as to splitting monetary awards with the injured party.

One field of jurisprudence affecting technological enterprise deserves special mention, that of tax law. Over the years, Congress has yielded to a phalanx of pressures to benefit narrow groups, to the point that tax law proliferates loopholes and changes so swiftly as to be almost unintelligible to professional practitioners. But it is through these devices, such as limited-partnership tax shelters, that funds for venture capital in technological enterprise are generated—to what long-term social ends, such as enhanced productivity, is now a matter of public debate.

In this account, the point is to emphasize the growing role of the third branch of government in technological delivery, reflected in system dynamics, in establishing norms for social responsibility and liability, and in reflecting the culture's concern for the extension and preservation of human life. In many respects, the courts have not only served their customary functions of protecting the rights of citizens, but have been interpreters of cultural shifts or surprises prodded by innovation. In some respects, they have functioned as surrogates for future generations.

There are, however, two major distinctions between the courts and the other two branches of government that bear on their influence on policy. First, the courts are passive rather than active; that is, they enter a transaction only on the initiative of a concerned party, not as self-actuated monitors of social problems and generators of mitigating policy. By reacting, though, the courts have the effect of setting policy. Second, in the design of policy the other two branches look ahead, or are presumed to, while the third branch looks backward. That is to say, in jurisprudence, recourse to precedent is imperative. Great weight is attached to prior opinion on cases even remotely similar which have blazed a trail of citation against error or inconsistent interpretation. In a sense, this is ironic, in that many suits accuse the government of failing to exercise foresignt through impact analysis to head off some potentially harmful initiative.

Nevertheless, in their landmark opinions, the courts have been extraordinarily influential in correcting course, both in signalling a drift from constitutional doctrine and in recognizing changes in cultural norms that require a reinterpretation of doctrine.

In addition, there has been frequent recourse to the law by public interest groups as a mechanism for delaying technological initiatives believed to be inimical to the public. Indeed, there is some question whether recourse to the law as the primary medium of conflict resolution has been excessive. Some activism through the courts may simply be an attempt to break out of feelings of powerlessness and futility, to get some handle on the elusive power machine and force up the transaction costs of adversaries to get attention if not remedy. Unfortunately, this strategy may only alleviate narrow and parochial symptoms without mitigating root causes.

There is a collateral problem in the disproportionately large number of lawyers in the United States—roughly 2.8 per thousand population, as compared to one-tenth that number in Japan. Their zeal has certainly contributed to clogging the courts and has brought contending parties to their limits of endurance and purse, left litigants bitter and exhausted, and exacted higher costs at every stage of technological enterprise. And the entire high-tech culture seems to have adopted a chip-on-the-shoulder attitude of "Let's sue."

Clearly there is need to develop more congenial procedures, especially to create a precrisis rather than a postcrisis atmosphere. Arbitration and mediation have been engaged as cooler alternatives. They deserve renewed dedication. One route to harmony lies in anticipatory analysis to identify issues before they reach typical stages of ignition, steam-roller tactics, and shouting. For with a high noise level, especially from single-issue advocates, everyone loses a capacity for gaining a shared cultural stance and for hearing signals about the future in which all parties share a common destiny.

Living with Technology and Not Liking It: Ethics for Today

As I have argued, all technologies have dual consequences. The primary effects almost always are intended to contribute toward human progress. Most do. But inadvertently we spin a disquieting burden of second-order effects, many benign, but many also inimical to well-being to the point of unprecedented danger. Forty years ago, Winston Churchill highlighted these twin technological faces of Janus. "The empires of the future," he said, "are the empires of the mind." But he also warned, "The Stone Age may return on the gleaming wings of science."

Notwithstanding that threat, history teaches us that we are not about to throttle down scientific discovery. Indeed, philosopher George Steiner suggests that the urge to discover is as universally irresistible as was the curiosity of Bluebeard's wives, even when they knew that the consequences of its satisfaction might be lethal. As Aristotle put it, "All people by their nature desire to know."

The corollary of that statement is that the adverse effects of knowing, through science and technology, are inevitable. Once more, then, we return to the theme of social management of technology: generating a strategy of anticipation as a countermeasure to technological harm. But as essential as is this doctrine of looking ahead, it is not sufficient. After making the most sagacious of guesses, by what rules do we choose the best course of action?

This second step of technological choice often depends not on science but on conscience, on fundamental ethics by which to judge our goals and our deeds. Such critical principles are shaped by the customs and laws of the community, by the study of human behavior and the humanities, and by religion. What is involved is a capacity to judge ourselves, our conduct and our character, in the light of novel situations generated by technology. Issues of contraception and abortion, artificial prolongation of life, control of toxic substances, prevention of nuclear war, inadvertent changes in climate, computer-generated dossiers—all represent some of the most obvious and highly publicized of the new dilemmas. And they demonstrate why two elements must be combined: rational understanding of the technical content, with some basic rules or norms to tell right from wrong. Both are fused by the imperative of a decision. So, technological choice as practiced by U.S. presidents, company presidents, engineers, lawyers or physicians, and individual citizens involves a combination of moral principle with information.

Further examples abound:

1. With the development of artificial hearts, new diagnostic tools, and new surgical procedures, some few lives may be prolonged. But with medical costs increasing 35 percent over inflation in five years from new technologies alone, we must ask whether the nation can afford such expensive innovation, and whether we have introduced a two-tier system that denies care to the indigent. The latter question is all the more inflamed as health care delivery assumes the trappings of business, wherein it is simply not profitable to care for the poor or for those whose serious illnesses are not fully covered by insurance.

2. Then there is gene splicing to create artificial organisms. Since this era opened in 1975, we have been offered the prospects of artificial human insulin, microbes to detoxify chemical waste, and an agricultural revolution in grains which extract nitrogen from the air instead of from fertilizer. Some two hundred companies have invested one billion dollars to exploit this intriguing potential. But over this bustle of activity hover concerns that genetic manipulation may escape control. Responding to the scientific community's initiative to police itself, the National Institutes of Health set safety guidelines for university laboratories. But now industry is

heavily involved, with prospects of field testing and commercial-scale production and distribution, and under pressure for swift profits from venture capitalists. So, the EPA, the Food and Drug Administration, and the Department of Agriculture have had to assume unprecedented responsibilities for public safety. The problem is exacerbated because nobody really knows what novel organisms might do outside the laboratory. Biochemists who generate them have no expertise as ecologists, and ecologists are unable to predict the survivability of even familiar organisms in a new environment, or even to explain events after the fact. And even if the United States monitors its own enterprise, will other nations who compete for these financial prizes do so?

3. Electronic invasion of privacy continues, now with computer matching of IRS data with information on default of government loans to college students. What limits should we place on such surveillance?

4. The federal government continues to subsidize the tobacco industry, despite the fact that more people have been killed from smoking than from all the wars of this century. The industry continues to support medical research that helps keep alive the myth that the dangers of smoking are still in doubt. The jobs and profits associated with the $10 billion annual revenue of the industry generate many friends in politics as well as in banking. Deciding when enough is enough is clearly not a matter for science.

5. A completely different ethical issue is opened up regarding national security. The growing investment in the Strategic Defense Initiative ("Star Wars") in a tightly stretched budget clearly drains funds from other programs. At the same time, SDI proponents admit enormous uncertainties because computer programs cannot be field tested and debugged. There are no absolutes in purchasing national security, and so the collective social judgment is required as to tradeoffs in risk.

6. Then there is the problem with military command and control systems intended to enable the president to respond to nuclear attack. Researchers contend that these arrangements are unreliable, obsolete, and vulnerable to sabotage, to the point that, when a confrontation becomes unbearably tense, the military's unstated strategy may be to mount a first strike on its own to decapitate Soviet leadership. Under any circumstances, the constitutional responsibility of Congress to share war-making powers is circumvented. That the public has been encouraged by government to believe that all is well opens up major issues of ethics.

7. Indeed, the military experience opens up a plethora of ethical questions, such as improper and excessive charges by contractors. But ethics in the defense establishment has other manifestations. Weapons systems continue to be funded long after field trials fail; and congressional initiatives to create an independent office for weapons testing so as to remove

the jacket of self-interest by in-house, contractor, and congressional advocates have been hamstrung.

Such a catalog of modern dilemmas is endless. The point is that technology seems to entail a sequence of three axioms: (1) all technologies have side effects; (2) many if not most side effects are potentially harmful so that conscious decisions are required to mitigate or prevent those unwanted; and (3) critical choices entail moral standards in tandem with rational analysis.

It is this last point that is often overlooked. No matter how well assisted by computers, technological choice is not a matter of cold logic. Yet, those in the most sensitive positions of policy making seem not to want to hear about the role of ethics.

To be sure, elected officials are in a constant bind between popularity and conscience. For one thing, they are subject to a hefty cultural tide of materialism that infects all major policy issues. As political reporter David S. Broder said, "President Reagan was not elected by people who were questioning the ethic of get more, make more, spend more, take more. The nation is not crying out to have its conscience pricked" on issues of social equity, justice, or even freedom. That same tilt is revealed in the annual Gallup poll on what Americans think is the most important question facing the nation. For twenty-eight of the thirty-four years betwen 1938 and 1972, the key concern was peace. But for the decade from 1973 to 1983, the issues were inflation, the high cost of living, and unemployment. The replies in an annual survey of college freshmen of the value they ascribe to their college education also fit that pattern. In 1967 they stressed "developing a meaningful philosophy of life." In 1984 the motivation was "being well off financially." Economic self-fulfillment has replaced commitment as the basic framework of personal philosophy.

Clearly, the tension between self-interest and social interest creates an ethical challenge. Such an atmosphere also influences attitudes regarding down-to-earth risks. When we recall that acceptance of risk or standards for safety are social judgments, then it is clear that society's risk tolerance and equity in dealing with its innocent victims is an ethical question.

If we examine the professions, we expose yet another dimension of moral standards. Are lawyers prospering unduly from a technology under stress by acting as ambulance chasers every time there is a technological failure? Attorney T. G. Dignan, Jr., questions the ethics of his own profession by asking, "Is this a priesthood ensuring its eternal existence by first suggesting an evil, then for a sufficient offering, investigating it at length, and finally exorcising it by the device of more Pagan rites?" Because lawyers profit from contingency fees on damages awarded in successful lawsuits for negligence, they concentrate on, and thereby draw attention to, those issues where generous awards can be assessed on firms with deep pockets. The public is readily instructed on how to use the adversarial system selectively.

The engineering profession has a different problem. Engineers are involved in every stage of a technological development, from design through production and service. They are thus obliged to assume responsibility for the public interest, a role that they accept willingly. There are, however, a number of consequences that flow from that situation, some incongruous. For one thing, this responsibility for public safety is a humbling experience because each engineer knows that despite every precaution, accidents like *Challenger* and Chernobyl do happen. Indeed, sometimes the only way to learn about weaknesses in a new technology is by experiencing failure, as is so well documented in the British engineers' study *Engineering Progress through Trouble*. In the face of such realities, whose life and property is at stake is clearly an ethical issue, especially when juxtaposed against the economics of safety enhancement.

Engineering publicist Samuel C. Florman contends that it is not up to the engineer to decide what is good for society, but that opinion ignores the fact that such judgments are made every time an engineer employs a margin of safety. Florman does explain, however, the philosophy that undergirds many professional attitudes: "Engineering is dependent upon a society that functions effectively. Most engineers work in large organizations and participate in mammoth undertakings. Thus they learn to value cooperation and recognize that their work requires an established social structure—if the trains are to run on time, the power plants to operate, and the factories are to produce. Law and order must prevail." Therein lies a possible flaw in engineering ethics—as is evidenced, for example, in the uncritical support by most engineers of a military buildup. To be sure, many work for or with the military. They are thus likely to be allied philosophically with and adopt the perspectives of the people who wield power rather than with the people over whom power is held. No wonder, then, there has been more reluctance by the profession to examine issues of arms reductions than among physicians.

On the other hand, there are concerted efforts to combat this provincialism. The American Association of Engineering Societies, a consortium of the major engineering professional organizations, discussed at its 1982 public affairs forum requirements that individuals be educated in the humanities so that they have the ability to weigh the ethical as well as the technical aspects of scientific advancement. In 1980, the American Society of Mechanical Engineers celebrated its centennial by reaffirming its fourteen goals, the first of which is "to broaden the horizons of individual engineers and foster effective means by which they may relate their work and talents to the interests of society." And finally, in a 1985 study of engineering education, the National Research Council urged "post-ponement of extensive disciplinary specialization until the graduate level so that students receive greater exposure to non-technical subjects."

All of which reveals the current high level of interest among engineering educators in dealing with ethics. They have not had much recent help from the government. In 1976, the National Science Foundation funded a research program, Ethics and Values in Science and Technology, to examine issues of professional conduct. In 1985, the Reagan admin-istration threatened its disestablishment. That melancholy stance is con-sistent, moreover, with other political actions to throttle down further the miniscule support for research in the social and behavioral sciences. The share of these sciences in basic university research has fallen from 4.9 percent in 1980 to 3.6 percent in 1984. If it had not been for Congress, cuts would have been even more severe.

What is so ironic is that we find this dampening of the social sciences occurring at a time when more, not less, attention seems warranted for collaboration between those who look at the world through the lenses of philosophy, literature, art, history, and religion, and those who see only the mechanical dimensions of human progress, in which they often have a self-interest. The rift between the humanities and technology is widened when community-oriented people and professionals are drowned out by a chorus of single-issue advocates, each wanting "theirs."

It may also be that the vaunted information age has become an era of ignorance. At the least, we may be heading toward another interval of "know-nothingness," where critical thinking by independent judgment, including challenge to political authority, is considered by those in the mainstream to be subversive. It may be that the computer age fuels that tendency in the mistaken belief that mechanical contrivances can solve our problems, military, political, economic, and social. As Harvard president Derek Bok has stated, with all of its power in teaching science, medicine, business, and law, the computer cannot contribute much to learning that has no formal rules: moral philosophy, historical interpretation, literary criticism, and social theory.

As we ponder the education of future leaders amidst the miasma of contemporary fads, there is reason to be concerned about the response of our institutions to the materialism of students and prospective employers, which threatens academic integrity. Early in 1985, the Association of American Colleges said, "The curriculum has given way to a marketplace philosophy where wisdom and experience should prevail." In its study, the association advocated renewed attention to nine elements: (1) inquiry, abstract thinking, and logical analysis; (2) literacy; (3) an understanding of numerical information, including the concepts of risk and uncertainty; (4) historical consciousness; (5) science, including the social and political implications of research; (6) values; (7) art; (8) international and multi-cultural experiences; and (9) study by a concentration in depth so as to deal with the central core of a particular subject, its methods, tools, theory, and complexity.

The role of critical thinking, the AAC's first item, is of special importance not only for college students but for all citizens if they are to assume responsibilities in a democratic society laden with science and technology and hyperbole. All the erudition in the world is ineffective without openmindedness, a recognition of the importance of evidence and its impartial sources, deferred judgment, skepticism of authoritarian dicta, provisions for public accountability of all institutions that wield power, and a foundation of moral philosophy. All of the great philosophers have stressed this combination. So did the founding fathers. Thomas Jefferson urged that the education of common people be attended to so as to rely on their good sense for the preservation of liberty. Said he, "There is no safe deposit for the functions of government but with the people themselves; nor can they be safe with them without information."

Psychologist Edward M. Glaser feels that critical judgment can be developed by teaching and practice under exacting guidance. The value of such dialectical thought is to weigh and reconcile juxtaposed contradictory arguments, so as to arrive at the truth or at least a synthesis that could foster reconciliation. Critical thinking, however, operates in the presence of an ethical perspective that simultaneously tests the conscience.

Here, we conclude with a reminder that one of the most telling demands on that conscience are the tradeoffs entailed between the present and the future, the value we place today on our progeny—their environmental, political, economic, social, and cultural inheritance.

These dimensions about the future have not been written into our Constitution. The founding fathers lived in a time of religious devotion to strength of character such that they assumed such practices would continue. A vigorous recourse to law has proved that error. But the law cannot do it all.

I, for one, believe that a major source of guidance lies in religion. Strange, isn't it, that we may need to consider the addition of the religious institutions to the model sketched previously of technological delivery systems that entail software of human activity as well as hardware. For if it is true that technology adds power to the destructive potential of the human psyche, increases choices which generate personal dilemmas, tends to make the rich richer so as to blunt notions of social equity, and poses strenuous tradeoffs such as the sacrifice of an existential moment for benefits to future generations, some code of conduct based on moral philosophy plays a crucial role. Only religious institutions have the capacity to set the stage for individual behavior that can lead to shared images of person, of reality, and of the collective future.

The quest for truth and justice, for fulfillment of human possibilities, the demands of sacrifice, the responsibilities for transmitting the inheritance of life and freedom as a legacy to be conserved and enriched—these are not to be found in educational curricula, nor in the sometimes vain enterprise of knowledge production, nor in a vigorous recourse to the law. And there is not much encouragement to be gained from further political and social reform. Indeed, many in moments of candor admit we have been losing ground.

How can the attitude be developed, as Alexander Solzhenitsyn has argued, that man's task cannot be unrestrained enjoyment of life and the search for the best technological ways to obtain material goods? Fulfillment comes from the satisfaction of leaving life better than one found it. In a dangerous technological world, one of the bounties of a free and democratic society remains that of choice. It is only by attention to life of the spirit and an illumination in moral responsibility that we can ultimately achieve victories over doomsday.

10 / Technology and the Future

Looking before You Leap: The Role of Early Warning

or some two hundred pages, we have been engaged in a vital if perplexing exercise—probing the circumstances of life in a technological world. As author, I had two specific goals: first, to serve as navigator rather than sage in exploring the interactions of technology with people and politics and thus to cast a richer perspective on the sources of our current predicaments; and second, to reassure readers that, even without technical training, they can contribute to the processes of choice. Readers now have a right to expect the author to spell out what we should do.

Not that anyone expects a single simplistic, miracle cure. The problems are too complex, too stubborn, too deeply rooted. Nevertheless, as each problem area has been separately examined in the preceding chapters, I have outlined steps to advance the art of technological choice: for the two hundredth anniversary of the Constitution, the president should order an updated study of national goals and directions; industry should reexamine its internal practices that put us at a disadvantage in technological competition rather than castigate the government while seeking special privilege; indeed, a more visible and accountable partnership should be fashioned between government and industry; people should regain confidence in themselves to participate in twenty-first-century democracy by trying to understand the connections of technology and politics and committing themselves to doing their homework. And all sectors should seek to ease the seduction of the short run. This chapter contains additional explicit and strategic proposals on how, collectively, we may cope.

Coping means dealing with the future effects of contemporary decisions and the consequences of myopia. Accordingly, one new element must be added to the tangled framework of connections with technology sketched earlier: the relationship of technology to the future. Concurrently, it may be helpful to restate salient arguments previously made, summarizing them as principles for the social management of technology.

As we have seen, technology has a bewildering capacity to generate side effects. These are often surprises because they were obscured at the moment of choice; they may also be delayed and, when they erupt, may be found capricious and remote from the district where the technology was stationed. All of which renders side effects unpredictable and uncertain. The problem is that these impacts—economic, social, ecological, and political—may be harmful, at some time, and to some sectors of the public, including innocent bystanders. And once harmful side effects are detected, corrective measures are often found to be economically costly, politically strenuous, or ecologically infeasible because the effects are irreversible. At that stage, remedies frequently amount to damage control; they are attempted in hopes that society is both resilient enough and rich enough that it can sustain the shock and the expense of inadvertence.

Life has many parallels. Almost every individual decision has the potential of launching a bombshell. Then, when confronted with egg on our faces, we ask what went wrong, and why. Many situations simply cannot be anticipated. Some are uncontrolled reactions by others to our initiatives. Perhaps when we employed foresight, we stumbled because of human fallibility. Or our own criteria for choice may have changed between the time the decision was made and later, when the impacts were felt; what was tolerable at one time was ultimately not endurable. Often, however, the trouble lies in the way we make decisions. From the crunch of too little time, from blinding prejudice, from impetuosity, from laziness, from unrelated stresses that lead to discounting the future, or from anxiety over our ignorance about both substance and process, we did not even *try* to look ahead.

And so the bills for today's decisions come due tomorrow. In the case of technological choice, the price of myopia may be so high as to be socially unacceptable; human survival may even be at stake. At the very least, when considering technological initiatives, we should look before we leap.

Perhaps the most dramatic example of that exercise was the Nuclear Test Ban Treaty of 1963. Previously, both the United States and the Soviet Union, as well as other nations, had been testing nuclear weapons in the atmosphere and under water. Radioactive particles were spewed aloft, carried around the entire planet, and subject to a slow fallout. The health effects were frightening. Ingested directly in food or indirectly through milk from cows that fed on contaminated forage, or present in fallout on the skin, these particles exposed people to an elevated risk of cancer. The unborn were vulnerable to genetic defects. Notwithstanding the short-term military imperative to test new and more powerful weapons, amidst a cold war between powerful adversaries, the lethality of the long-term consequences to all peoples was intolerable. Since the treaty, all testing by signatories has been conducted underground.

Here, the decision process was elementary. All that was required was to ask, "What might happen, if?" That is, if above-ground and underwater testing continued. The facts regarding the risks of exposure were available and by then a matter of public knowledge. The answers to that question were so alarming that when President John F. Kennedy took his initiative to negotiate the ban, proposed in different forms previously, public acceptance of the tradeoffs involved was immediate and enthusiastic. Parenthetically, it is baffling that neither leadership nor the public has expressed a similar interest in catastrophic effects of a "nuclear winter."

Can this test ban be considered a model of looking before you leap? Yes, but with reservations. Seldom are the consequences of an action (or continued action) so stark, so certain, and so universally harmful. Frequently, it is not possible to fully define the current situation, much less guess at a future one. Facts are missing or ambiguous or even suppressed. There are heated conflicts among interested parties over who wins and who loses. Interpretations are contradictory. Complexity and inter-dependencies make difficult any definition of situation boundaries for analysis, yet it seems fruitless to deal with "the whole thing."

While such exercise of foresight may be civilization's greatest challenge, some writers believe it is beyond human capability. Analyst Roberto Vacca believes technological systems to be so technically complex as to defy human comprehension and control. Management scientist Rufus E. Miles concludes that delivery systems are too politically and socially complex to be managed. Systems engineer Jay Forrester contends that the forces at work are deterministic and thus impermeable to human guidance. Economist Robert Heilbroner argues that the limits to human character predispose the future to unceasing and irreversible decline. Political scientist Aaron Wildowski doubts both our capacity and our will to look ahead.

Yet, to do nothing to anticipate the unwanted consequences of decisions, to hope to muddle through, is capitulation to blind fate, an acquiescence to a belief that trends, no matter how threatening, are our destiny. "The consequent triumph of ignorance," predicted foreign policy advisor Zbigniew Brzezinski, "extracts its own tribute in the form of unstable and reactive policies." And in an optimistic vein, he counseled that existing postcrisis management practices should increasingly be supplanted by precrisis capabilities.

Still drawing on common human experience, we can find systematic practices of heading off situations we do not want. In the matter of personal health, we practice prevention: people attend to their hygiene, to nutrition, to weight control, and to exercise; they seek periodic checkups, inspect their anatomy for early detection of cancer, avoid excessive exposure to X-rays, use condoms, and wear overshoes and hats; they stop smoking and wear seat belts. As a social policy, we insist on immunization. All in the interest of health maintenance and disease prevention. For the individual, the excess of benefits over costs and inconvenience is worthwhile; for society as a whole, the savings are staggering.

To put the concept underlying the test ban and individual health maintenance another way, concern for the human condition simultaneously entails a concern for the future. That is to say, where vital interests are at stake, and crises and calamities are to be avoided, it is crucial to bring a vision of the way ahead within the decision horizon. In recent years, analyst Stuart Chase conceived of a special governmental unit to evaluate impacts of technological innovations before they could inadvertently undermine the culture. In 1970, Alvin Toffler called for a technology ombudsman in an anticipatory democracy. In 1965, the author of this book joined a colleague in the Congressional Research Service in offering the U.S. Congress an identical concept that became the analytical technique of technology assessment and a cornerstone of environmental impact analysis.

The central idea has always been to utilize faculties of anticipation so systematically as to define a doctrine, or in other terms, to practice vigilance in the form of an early warning system. In the name of military security we work to heighten awareness of potential threats, exercise sensitive intelligence functions, some aided by high technology, invest in contingency planning, and create reserves for emergencies. There seems to be no corresponding strategy for dealing with nonmilitary threats. In 1985, Senators Mathias and Gore proposed a Cultural Trends Assessment Act as an early warning device. Unfortunately, its prospects for early enactment seem dim.

Attention to signals about the future, however, raises even deeper questions about how we as a society and as individuals cope with the future's most salient feature: that it is unknown and largely unknowable. In what follows, we explore some positive and realistic strategies to deal especially with the futures we do not want.

Foresight as Fantasy

We can begin by asking, "What will tomorrow be like?" That question intrigues almost everyone, partly because it is an invitation to daydream about the exquisite futures we want. Speculating about the future, however, may also uncork nightmares, involving either tragic futures we do not want or dismay that our dreams will never be realized. Nonetheless, conjecture about the future is essential to excite ambition; it is also the process for coping with risk and thus a basic mechanism for survival. Attempts to peer into the future often stir disdain, however, from the analytically minded. Partly this results from the observation that those who engage professionally in forecasting—meteorologists, economists, and stock analysts—are not distinguished by stunning track records. Futurists do not enjoy universal credibility.

Inquiring about technological futures follows two paths. One involves forecasts of the next stages of technological evolution, derived from the study of inventions, the implications of recent scientific discoveries, and institutional commitments to particular hardware developments. Equally important is the reciprocal influence of the culture on technology. The second mode of inquiry must be tuned to the public attitudes and emerging social directions that nudge, push, shove, and piggyback technological initiatives, or generate eddies, backwaters, and backlash. In recent years, Americans were polled by the Bureau of Census on what they considered essential for a high quality of life (QOL). In order of preference, they listed health, good family relationships, peace of mind, respect from others, friendships, education, a satisfying job, religion, money, sex, and romantic love. Attaining these things clearly spurs personal drives.

These goals also dictate choices regarding technology, here recognized as a powerful means toward these golden ends. As examples, we can list immunization against infectious disease to maintain health; artificial organs to extend life; weapons systems to guard against surprise attack and contribute to national peace of mind; machines to ease backbreaking labor; running water and electrical appliances to simplify household tasks; the automobile to make possible suburban living in private dwellings; television, films, and recorded music for entertainment.

Given the significance of religion in the QOL list, has it benefited from technology? Certainly it has been impacted, first by the printing press, now by radio and television ministries, by the availability of furnaces in winter, air conditioning in summer. Given the stability of human needs and wants, we can say something about social futures as they stimulate and mold technological advance no matter how quixotic.

To attain the good life, however, requires thought beyond long-range goals, to strategies for achievement. Indeed, planning the journey is essential to convert dreams to reality. The point is that both ends and means are the things dreams are made of.

The same is true of the nightmares. Now, however, our strategies revolve around heading off the futures we do not want. Through fantasies of potential perils or even through rehearsals such as fire drills, we develop a repertoire of mental patterns for testing the significance of early warning signals. When observations are confirmed as threats, we respond.

Reactions, however, span a wide fight-or-flight range: from knee-jerk overreaction, panic, denial, aggression, evasive maneuver, or retreat, to problem-solving countermeasures toward prevention if the threat is detected in time, or toward mitigation and damage control. Curiously enough, many actual nightmares seem composed mainly of scenarios of dread and escape.

Some early warning signals trigger the most basic human instincts for self-preservation. Some draw on indoctrinations for safety inculcated by family and community, or on lessons from bitter personal experience. Deeply subconscious premonitions can surface as attention to subtle changes in the environment that arouse suspicion, vigilance, and a search for additional information on which to judge the degree of danger. Finally, the ringing of alarm bells can startle us into awareness of an emergency.

This mental process may also apply to an intermediate case: if actual steps toward dream fulfillment are carefully monitored to detect impediments, the course can be periodically corrected to achieve goals.

In both cases, after an alert, we go through three stages: situation analysis, evaluation, and decision. In the first step, we draw both on external warning signs and memory. We ask whether the perceived threat has clear consequences and how certainly cause is related to effect. Are the signals clear, familiar, free of noise? Have several different threats erupted simultaneously, and can they be separated and ranked as to potency? Once the situation has been clarified, what options need to be evaluated for crisis avoidance or containment? At what cost in resources? How soon can they be mustered? Can the consequences of no action or weak action be tolerated? Is the response weakened by lack of preparation, by distraction, confusion, complexity, inadequacy of resources to extinguish threat, or just plain exhaustion?

Lest this scenario of catastrophe avoidance sound pedantic or applicable only to military strategy, consider ordinary auto driving—the practiced, subconscious evaluations and conscious actions to avoid collisions. These involve driver training, familiarization with vehicle performance, and the role of maps in strange territory. Then there are tactical demands for high visibility, caution on curves, in darkness, or inclement weather. Radio messages provide data on traffic viscosity. Finally, but by no means least important, we employ defensive driving as a maneuver to fend off careless or drunken drivers.

Of all these essentials for auto safety, the most fundamental need is for a clear view ahead, and the continuous processing of visual cues on possible dangers. We would never drive with an opaque windshield, or simply by the rear view mirror. This is foresight in action.

Foresight, however, is more than looking ahead and collecting information. It involves a continuous fantasy as to what might happen, if—or what might happen, unless. Through fantasy, foresight is the exercise of discernment and then *judgment on what to do* in order either to reach the intended goals more effectively or to head off disaster. Although this discussion suggests the application of a well-ordered procedure, as though foresight were simply another dimension of logic, that is not entirely the case. Fantasy cannot be structured by pure reasoning; neither can it be switched on at will. The process involves imagination, daring to think the unthinkable, dream the impossible. It may be stimulated by myths, fables, science fiction. Or by deliberate exercises to expand consciousness, to stimulate creative and lateral thinking, and to unearth those deeply buried, random, intuitive elements that can be summoned up from the subconscious and connected together in new and productive ways. Meditation and mulling have dramatic rewards.

We cheer that creative approach to innovation and invention of hardware. Paradoxically, we overlook or even deprecate the role of fantasy in anticipating social, economic, and ecological effects of technological initiatives. Until we break from that shocking neglect and from rigid paradigms about what the future can be, the steering of technology to achieve long-run, socially satisfactory outcomes is almost certain to be frustrated.

As an example of conventional technological thinking, consider initial proposals for the American supersonic transport (SST). The machine was a jewel at the leading edge of aeronautics. But its advocates failed to recognize the human objections to sonic booms that could burst on communities many times a day, much less to the jet noise at takeoff (which later constrained operation of the British and French Concorde). They overlooked the effect that a plethora of contrails in the stratosphere might have on climate. Most serious, however, they failed to consider what the effect of an increase in world oil prices would be, in view of the fact that an economically viable fleet of SST's would consume roughly 25 percent of the nation's oil budget. The U.S. Senate saved the nation the cost or embarrassment of a technological white elephant by only a few votes.

The decline of American railroads, discussed previously, is another example of cramped thinking for which we are today paying a price. The failure to anticipate the need to dispose of radioactive waste from nuclear power plants and to decommission them at the end of their useful life simply underscores the syndrome.

Examples of foresight having been exercised are far harder to come by.

One such general practice involves the design of public water supply systems on the basis of fifty-year projections of urban growth. Another is the protection that has been offered to wilderness areas and endangered species. But this list is not impressive. And so in the quest for a mechanism to cope with technological progress, we must search for policy, not technical, countermeasures.

Technology Assessment: Choosing Can Be Learned

Everyone knows how to make decisions; we make dozens every day. Many are trained reflexes. Crucial choices, however, materialize very seldom: in picking an occupation, a residence, a mate. And when they do, we may not feel so confident about how to decide. Choosing is rarely taught in the schools, but it can be learned.

All choices are attended by anxiety. Some apprehension arises naturally from awareness of possibly adverse consequences, in relation both to the problem at hand and to the decider. If the repercussions are potentially harmful or irreversible, we prefer to ruminate over things so as to open the gates of intuition and enrich what otherwise might be a purely rational choice. But what is the methodology of rational choice?

Even in its simplest expression, a decision is not merely a confrontation with a dilemma, no matter how forcefully it compels action. It is that occasion which invites a choice among alternatives. In all likelihood, none are obviously best, and all carry a burden of new predicaments. So we drill into these options to identify the positive and negative implications of each. Although this process seems to be a cataloging of pros and cons, it is more useful to apply another technique, that of tracing the consequences of each. Then, after adopting some criteria for choice, we choose.

Always, there are uncertainties. The quality of decision making may thus rest on how we deal with uncertainty or, better, with risk. One of the most pernicious aspects of this process is the tendency under stress to discount the future, with the discount rate depending heavily on our emotional state at the instant of choice. Side effects are also obscure, because of failures in imagination, overemphasis on swift results, and organization on a project basis. We often neglect impacted parties who were geographically, socially, institutionally, and chronologically remote from the transaction.

In a completely rational atmosphere, these conditions should prompt a search for more information, at least to narrow the uncertainties. But there is a price—taking time. Management analyst Herbert A. Simon puts it this way: information is never gratis; it has a cost, an opportunity cost in terms of the other ways we could use that time. Under these pressures of a time-constrained search, the *sequence* with which options and impacts are scanned influences choice. Weighed against a daily agenda of other imperatives, in the hurly-burly of political offices, the most immediate and intimate effects are examined first; the broader and future consequences are attacked later and in a time bind, may not be examined at all.

Neither will nor resources may be present for crisis avoidance. Indeed, the more advanced in development a technology may be or the closer to implementation, and the more powerful the organization may be in protecting vested interests, the more reluctant it may be to examine impacts and alternatives. It is this imperative that is often diagnosed as "Technological Determinism."

It would be naive to suggest that all blunder or folly in decision making can be suppressed simply by method. Yet, there are strategies in choice that help make explicit the potential for adverse consequences in the long run. One such method has been labelled technology assessment. This process involves nine steps:

1. Defining the technology, first in terms of its purposes (ends) and its hardware content (means)
2. Defining the social, economic, political, and ecological context into which the hardware is introduced and the institutions which make it work, including assumptions about behavior of the system participants; in short, sketching the technological delivery system and its kinetic history
3. Establishing the relevant base of facts and investigating uncertainties
4. Forecasting what is foreseeable with sophistication, sensitivity, and a regard for the evolution of hardware, the dynamics of public attitudes, and the behavior of the interacting organizations that manage the technology
5. Inventing action alternatives, realizing that one of these is to do nothing
6. Identifying impacted parties, including future generations.
7. Identifying for each option the positive and negative impacts, and the tradeoffs, by asking, "What might happen, if, to whom, and when?"
8. Designing the policy or implementation plan that has the greatest promise of producing the desired objective with the least unwanted effects
9. Monitoring performance so as to continue postimplementation assessment

It is this methodological instruction that was imbedded in the unprecedented initiative of the U.S. Congress to create in 1972 a new staff arm of an Office of Technology Assessment. And it is this concept of operational acumen that is called for from the president's Office of Science and Technology Policy.

At least four of these nine steps require the exercise of foresight. It is here that we go beyond the purely rational. The typical reductionist approach of dividing the problem into logical elements must be supplemented by a holistic visualization of the complete system in operation. Multiple perspectives must be drawn upon so as to accommodate diversity within the culture, and especially to appreciate the point of view of the affected public, which most likely differs from that of the expert and of the political actor making decisions. The severe limitations of quantitative models— including the futility of optimization in an ambiguous real world—need to be recognized.

The product may be instantly illuminating. In the most elementary form of assessment, a score card can be constructed listing different types of impacts versus different stakeholders, with ratings of positive, null, or negative. Impacts can be listed in the chronological sequence of occurrence, so as to highlight the later ones that might be overlooked. In a nutshell, technology assessment should define who wins, who loses, how much, and when.

Such an aid to decision making does not automatically tell policy makers what to do. Rather, it helps them identify what to think about— that is, what questions to ask. In some important ways, it is a process of learning. Most important, the technique integrates the future into technological choice and extends the boundaries beyond those of the direct transaction so as to bring out the possible implications for innocent bystanders, who are usually outside of the bargaining process. In short, technology assessment makes it possible to visualize the tradeoffs.

I should add several important footnotes about this concept. The first is that a technology assessment must deal honestly with uncertainties, laying out what we know, what we don't know, then what we should know to reduce vagueness, doubt, and perplexity.

Second, technology assessment has a potential function in conflict management, both with regard to technological initiatives and with regard to technological regulations. All too often the resolution of differences is blocked by an emotionally charged atmosphere, an attempt to search for villains and fix blame, perhaps a siege mentality and an adversarial mood. With an impact analysis we may clarify how different parties feel and guess *why* they perceive their situation differently. By considering different options, we can separate out partiality and bias, even if we can't eliminate them, and rank remedial steps that may quench a firestorm. By group participation, in a problem-solving rather than confrontational style, opportunities are enhanced to discover and relieve previously hidden sources of conflict.

Third, a word needs to be said about who performs impact assessments and who should read them. No matter how diligently assessors strive for objectivity, that virtue so devoutly to be sought is impossible to attain. It should be very clear, however, that all studies prepared within organizations that have a stake in the outcome are likely to be biased. Having studies performed by independent analysts increases the credibility but even then problems exist. Each analyst brings to the study a package of personal attitudes that influence both substance and process. Perhaps the only countermeasure to that weakness is duplication of analysis by different groups, or at least the testing at various steps along the way with individuals who manifest different perspectives.

Fourth, in a democratic society, people who are affected by the outcome of a technological decision should be partners in the enterprise. To be sure, there cannot be referenda on every issue. In representative government, we must rely on elected officials to exercise the intellect and independent judgment that earned them support. But we must also recognize the influence of lobbying. Special interests have their say in a variety of forums. For a technology assessment to fulfill expectations, it should involve the attentive public both at the front end and at completion.

Finally, technology assessment must be approached with a certain modesty as to its effectiveness. Some are too massive, and the door-stop size puts off readers; some are too late to be useful, and then engender cynicism that the decision had already been made and the assessment was only window dressing. Some are too technical for public comprehension. Some are dishonest, masking the full truth. Some will be ignored if the findings, however elegantly researched, collide with the self-interests of the decider or the implementing authority. Some may also be ignored because many leaders still make policy decisions more on the basis of convictions, ideology, and instinct than on analysis of facts and future consequences.

In some industrial circles, there is a basic antipathy to technology assessment because managers worry about its leading to technology *arrestment*. Depending on the dominant mood of society at the time, and certainly in a politically volatile atmosphere, such paralysis is possible. Experience shows, however, that delays to impetuous choice, as with the Alaskan pipeline, usually lead to superior hardware design and benefits to *all* parties.

And of course, technology assessments arouse skepticism because the future is obscured. In that vein, critics of assessments such as political scientist Aaron Wildowsky claim that it would be preferable for government to maintain a strategy of resilience so as to absorb the costs of errant technology when it is detected and then effect a cure. This school of thought follows the administrative dictum of "disjointed incrementalism." In this strategy, decisions follow the line of least political resistance until a new event or perception forces course correction. Although that philosophy mirrors what often happens in politics, it is an extremely dangerous strategy in regard to technology. The hazards of nuclear war, chemical plant leaks, massive terrorism, and a host of other risks are simply intolerable.

There is, however, a middle ground. Technology assessment should not be considered a one-shot exercise leading to a single decision by a political actor having many interests to guard. Rather, it is a process of continuous information-gathering that includes periodic monitoring of all the effects of an initiative so as to improve the zig-zags associated with incrementalism. In addition, it identifies criticial resources to be protected and the hazards of irreversibility. Especially if all affected parties have access to the monitored data, social as well as technical, there is a chance that the full power of the democratic process can be energized, not simply that part stimulated or irritated by the loudest or most affluent special interests.

The Future as Common Property

Toward the end of each century, people seem to exhibit a deeper, more philosophical interest in the human condition. Publications taking stock of where we are and speculating on the way ahead increase sharply. Partly this phenomenon reflects the eternal hope of people for a better world and the notion that somehow the opening of a new century marks a turning point. At the very least, it is symbolic of a new beginning. As we approach the year 2000, history repeats itself. In the 1930s, according to futurist Michael Marien, books on new directions were published in the United States at the rate of three a year; in the 1960s there were eighteen per year. By 1980, not counting an enormous volume of science fiction, they amounted to well over a hundred, with a few, such as *Future Shock* and *Megatrends,* even making the best-seller list.

This wholesale reconnaissance of the future by prophets and philosophers, systems analysts and planners, is focused largely on *what* the future might be like or should be like. Conspicuous by its absence is consideration of *how* to think about the future. Economist Hazel Henderson has proposed that, in our concern for future generations, the resources of the planet be treated, not as an inheritance that we can use or abuse at will, but as a loan from future generations that should be handed back enhanced, as it were, with interest. Jacques Cousteau has proposed a Bill of Rights for Future Generations.

There is another approach to generate perspective. It is to consider the future as common property. That way, we can apply the long experience of history and the framework of law to inquire as to the relative merits of some proposed course of action that has inevitable and potent future consequences. In law, common property is that to which everyone has equal rights of ownership. This is in contrast to private property, whose title is usually deeded to a specific individual or institution. Representing this collective ownership is usually some governmental body that acts as agent for the public in regard to any transactions altering the ownership or in exercising prudent management. For U.S. citizens, for example, the seabed adjoining the coasts, and the oil or gas within, are considered common property held by either state or federal government and subject to leasing for commercial exploitation on behalf of the public. The government has thus traditionally assumed a fiduciary responsibility, a steward-ship, to conserve these assets. Legal restraints prevent individuals, even as parties to the collective ownership, from claiming jurisdiction over a portion representing their share, or from engaging in actions that are inimical to the general welfare. It is here that the notion of common property is enriched by its treatment as a public trust.

In principle, at least, there is protection against the tragedy of the commons that economist Garrett Hardin so well dramatized as the fate of common property wherein everyone claimed rights but failed to accept corresponding obligations of responsibility. In his allegory, the common pastureland of medieval villages was destroyed because none of the owners of sheep who were the owners in common of the pasture used any restraint to prevent overgrazing and ultimate destruction of the resource. There was no collective management. In the short run, everyone seemed to win; in the long run, no one did.

If this concept is applied to the future, several features become clear. For one thing, the future must be assumed to belong equally to everyone. This implies that everyone has equal rights with regard to access to the future. No individual can claim a specific share for individual exploitation, nor degrade the future so as to lessen its value for the other shareholders. The concept carries the obligation of collective responsibilities to conserve the assets, or at least to make a deliberate tradeoff between short-run use, say in an emergency, against the longer run. As a practical matter, some entity must be elected by the group as trustee to guarantee that these respon-sibilities are fulfilled. If this concept were adopted in legislative terms (imagine this as a constitutional amendment), then the government would be put into a position of having to evaluate the future impacts of its own initiatives in order to fulfill its trusteeship.

As abstract as this notion is, it confirms validity of the principles previously enunciated for moving toward a harmony of economy and ecology, albeit at a price. We must expect to live with perpetual tension between those taking private initiatives that may be inimical to the commonweal in the long run and the government as trustee of the future. When that tension lags, as it might if we continue to drift to a corporate state, we may then know that a major shift has occurred in our social arrangements. That, in itself, might be an early warning.

Taming the Wild Computer Chip

To fully uncloak the interaction of technology with politics is to lay bare the anatomy of power—not the energy that drives machines, not even the goading of society by what has been termed technological determinism, the deportment of machines appearing to be outside of human control. Rather, it is to recognize that *those who control technology control the future.*

That reality stings. Most people shudder at the notion of slavery, whether by the technology and its controllers according to Orwell's model or by uncongenial side effects triggered by the actions of strangers in remote districts at an earlier time. One such outcome is simply feeling isolated by a techno-culture that has left them thrashing alone in its wake.

Equally troublesome are the side effects of power. For as old-fashioned as power may be, it acquires fresh attributes from having been conferred on the interlocking owners and managers of newly minted technology in a manner that is seemingly inaccessible to the people who both benefit from and bear its risks. The cleavage between the information-rich and the information-poor has also increased. Apart from reinforcing a cultural polarity in our society between those infatuated with technology and those alienated by it, that gulf in knowledge and understanding serves to confirm the trickling away of control that engenders feelings of vulnerability and impotence.

In the early 1980s, as in the 1950s, society as a whole was enthusiastic about technology's exotic developments. Judging not by what people said but by how they acted, people loved the festival of commerce; they seemed quite unwilling to unplug what has been termed the Christmas Machine. TV ads for beer and autos chanted, "You can have it all!" "All" generally involved something tangible. It was almost as though to consume was a hallmark of patriotism, of being a good, worthy, and fulfilled person who is also invulnerable to the nuclear Sword of Damocles. Thus began the age of the personal computer.

By 1985, technology became more explicitly connected with the future because we were having to bite the bullet of choice. Society could no longer afford to "have it all," and the ambiguous love-hate relationship of the 1960s seemed about to return. Anxieties about potentially devastating threats to survival that had centered on bombs and mushroom clouds, chemical plants and noxious fluids, now shifted to economic confrontations involving Toyotas and jobs, deficits and defense spending. Along with the attention-getting headlines was a quiet awakening to the fact that the computer had sharply changed our lives, but in ways not clearly seen or understood. Notwithstanding the appeal of an advertising campaign by IBM with a clone of Charlie Chaplin, the more thoughtful were not so sure that computers were all that user friendly.

If increased utilization of the computer for management and control of industrial processes is a symbol of this bewildering high-tech era, it may also serve metaphorically to represent what is at stake regarding the human experience. Not only involved is computer literacy in using the machine or its robotic application to efficient industrial production. The more subtle questions have to do with social management, with computers as symbols of or surrogates to the uses of power. Thus the notion of taming the wild computer chip.

This metaphor has nothing to do with the hardware of technology, with circuit design, or even with computer software. Rather, it concerns the institutions associated with technological delivery and their behavior, along with the information networks that lace them together, the systems that spun the golden webs. Going beyond questions of what to think about, we need to ponder the much more baffling question, "*How* do we think about technology and power?"

In computer programming as well as use, steps are developed sequentially, each to induce a particular effect. We can wrestle with enormous quantities of information and with a large number of variables, some independent and arbitrarily defined and some dependent. By varying parameters one at a time, we can investigate their interactions and diagnose causality. Such is the reductionist mode of problem solving. It underpins scientific research and engineering development because it helps us answer "How do we do it?" That train of thought, however, may not be productive in solving the sociotechnical enigma of "Ought we to do it?" or, even before that, "What might happen, if we do it?"

Now we need brainstorming, creative inspiration, imagination, and the blending of facts with values. As compared with the verticality of the reductionist mode in connecting elements of the same family, these processes might be thought of as horizontal, what analyst Adams in *Conceptual Blockbusting* calls "lateral." In the mind's eye, they are broader; they involve making connections between disparate parameters, deciphering far more complex patterns. To understand and to synthesize goes beyond pure knowledge and its application. Aptitudes and attitudes are involved that are quite different from the intense specialization of experts.

Other distinctions arise because technical analysis, unlike synthesis, raises expectations of arriving at clear, concise, unambiguous, quantitative answers. And somehow, these can be graded right or wrong. Social phenomena simply do not fit those conditions. For one thing, the delivery system is not a mechanism wherein elements have relatively fixed properties. It is an organism in which the elements change, grow, and especially learn as they interact with each other. Achieving a comfortable fit between society and technology cannot be approached with the same methods and prospects of exactitude as are found in the development of the hardware or its industrial husbandry. Students of artificial computer intelligence expect some day to bridge that disparity, but they are as yet far from it.

So the first encounter with taming the wild computer chip requires deciding how to think about the problem. And thinking about thinking is very uncomfortable. It is just as uncomfortable as a thoughtful approach to choice. As Michael Montalbano wrote in this piece of whimsy:

Nay, lad! *Deciding's* not your ploy,
For that's a risky game.
It's *Making a decision*
That's your surest road to fame.

Decide means to take action
And actions rock the boat,
And if you act and don't succeed,
Small chance you'll stay afloat.

So get yourself a task force
Well skilled in all the arts,
And call them all together
And watch them flip their charts.

"The figures prove—" "The model says—"
"The forecast bears me out,"
"The complex simplex program
Shows I'm right without a doubt."

So diddle with a model
To glorify your name,
Then get yourself a task force
And learn to play the game.
                    (From *Decision Tables, 1974*, Science Research Associates, Inc.)

The next step requires a recognition that technology is a means rather than an end in itself. Where, indeed, do we stand with regard to purposes? As the maritime adage has it, "Without a destination, there is never a favorable wind." The crux of the matter lies in people caring about the future enough to include it in their tradeoffs. This is not so much a renewed quest for goals as it is a renewed search for—and consensus on—coherent directions, in an era of scarcity. We need a process of imaging the future, of setting forth those themes and convictions that are central to a pluralistic society. For it is such images that serve as the great blast furnaces of progress. In a sensitive blend of vision and realism, society might realize that, as Alfred North Whitehead succinctly taught, "It is the business of the future to be dangerous." What is as stake here would be to head off trends that make the future treacherous.

In 1958, President Eisenhower inaugurated a national goals study by distinguished citizens that led to an enormous shopping list of wants as well as needs. The Brookings Institution estimated its price. To no one's surprise, the cost far exceeded feasibility, perhaps accelerating the demise of the study without even an opportunity to salvage its valuable core. In 1970, President Nixon switched on a similar, albeit more modest, study. Under the chairmanship of Ambassador (later Senator) Moynihan, White House staff members and consultants turned out a sensitive and perceptive analysis of national goals, focusing also on the processes of governance and their changes in response to technology. The study unequivocally advocated the practice of technology assessment. Curiously enough, President Nixon first delayed release of the study and then swiftly disbanded the study team, so as to hold the findings at arm's length. With that disclaimer, any follow-through was aborted.

There is a lesson to be extracted from these two exercises that might well provide the strength for another try, that such a study should be shielded from the heavy influence of White House sponsorship. Otherwise, findings no matter how sound and finely honed may either be bruised from partisan squabbling or, as with the Nixon project, ignored because they were incompatible with institutional self-interest and mindset.

Because people are frustrated by not having access to the power structure or lacking information free of self-serving bias from which to generate informed judgment, the role of mass media is crucial. In a society peppered with advertising, the facts are all too frequently packaged with a huckster's techniques of persuasion. New aids to public understanding could well follow patterns of technology assessment and environmental impact analysis. But missing is an independent institutional host. Proposals to fill that need were offered separately by Nicholas Golovin and by the author as far back as 1970. The latter led Senator Warren G. Magnuson to introduce legislation for a Commission on the Social Management of Technology. It disappeared without a trace.

In taming the computer chip, therefore, perhaps we need to look again at the notion of a fourth arm of government, an information network. From the experience of the General Accounting Office and the Congressional Research Service, for example, we have learned how to shield advisory bodies from political intimidation without their suffering the intellectual isolation of scholarly enterprise. It is this key proposition that is elaborated in the final section of this chapter.

With motivation from the very nature of the issues, with preparation aided by new sources of information as to issues, options, and tradeoffs, more citizens might participate effectively in the political process. First, however, people must understand how vital and sensitive is this act of civic responsibility in *setting* the course for the future, not simply *staying* the course.

A Catalog of Tradeoffs

Society has faced a stream of critical choices throughout most of the twentieth century. Few have been fully resolved. Perhaps this is because history repeats itself: with people exposed to the same enigmas over and over again, it seems as if none is eliminated from the social agenda. Amidst technology-pulsed change, human nature remains constant, so that the past and its imperfections are ever with us. But there are other explanations. Perhaps whatever we term as progress undergoes cycles rather than steady advances, with valleys always following peaks of achievement. And perhaps we have temporarily crashed against limits: limits to our understanding, to human intelligence, to natural resources, or to our capacity to manage.

But the situation may also be because too many issues were attacked piecemeal, with provisional, opportunistic, short-term remedies to meet the pressures of narrow, vested interests. With our current portfolio of dilemmas, what do we do? Do we tackle issues one at a time, seeking, as with a well-known pharmaceutical, quick relief from the stress of choice? Or do we investigate possible universal malfunctions in the decision process by searching for commonalities, either in the source of predicaments or in their resolution?

The imperative of looking before we leap is of crucial import because technology itself forces more, and more difficult, choices. Options, risks, and uncertainties are all unprecedented. And it is also true that the expectations of technological optimists have run ahead of resources; there is neither enough wealth nor enough political maneuvering room to evade critical choices by denial or illusion.

In technological affairs, we can meet this challenge by trying to draw first on a rich experience with decision methods. Their elegance, however, must be qualified. We must guard against the seduction of pure rationality: optimization, reductionism, excessive reliance on numbers, illusory claims of objectivity. All of these rational methods undermine the process of choice if the human element and its diversity is neglected. Selection depends on value preferences. In engineering design, there are always exchanges between cost and safety, or between cost and convenience or durability. In that situation, consumers often demand a scorecard of tradeoffs, say in buying a car, to help them decide. With the grand issues, however, complete and objective information is seldom availale even to the policy maker, much less to the affected citizen. So people may spend far more time selecting their automobiles than considering policies for arms reduction.

Finally, criteria for choice vary with the cultural set. Unlike the Japanese, Americans are not inclined to sacrifice individualism for higher

Table 10.1 A Catalog of Tradeoffs

Issue	Options
Maintain current employment levels and growth in GNP	(*a*) Continue to invest government funds in development and procurement of new weapons to maintain a war economy
	(*b*) Nurture ideas and industrial firms that concentrate on making peace profitable
Protect national security	(*a*) Concentrate on the perceived military threat by continued buildup of nuclear arms, with a hair-trigger, launch-on-warning arrangement
	(*b*) Reduce global tension by fostering economic interdependence and seeking nonviolent exits to superpower conflict
Anticipate mismatch in future supply and demand of energy	(*a*) Develop renewable resources and stimulate conservation
	(*b*) Protect role of private sector and depend on free market to allocate resources, even if that continues North-South disparity
Reduce mismatch of Third World population and resources	(*a*) Continue arms sales to Third World countries to facilitate their predilection to defense against antagonists
	(*b*) Stimulate Third World economy by fostering, not appropriate technological hardware, but appropriate technological delivery system infrastructure
Attack the mismatch in supply and demand of nonrenewable materials	(*a*) Accellerate research on substitution and conservation
	(*b*) Protect laissez-faire by subsidy and stockpiling
Improve governmental performance of existing functions	(*a*) Decentralize functions and emphasize internal efficiency
	(*b*) Improve foresight, accountability, and internal coherence by reducing response to single-issue advocates
Improve equity in distribution of domestic resources	(*a*) Foster long-term economic stability and vitality by incentives to the private sector to increase productivity
	(*b*) Transfer wealth by social policy, calling on people for an equitable distribution of sacrifice
Reduce vulnerability to terrorism	(*a*) Mitigate social disparities alleged to breed terrorism
	(*b*) Contain threats by investing significantly more funds in intelligence for early warning and prevention
Guarantee availability of quality health care	(*a*) Foster responsibility of private practitioners of medicine
	(*b*) Mandate equal access for all but contain costs

Table 10.1   continued

Issue	Options
Protect public from ubiquitous toxic waste	(a) Intensify government control over hazards (b) Depend on legal and free-market process to provide economic incentives for prevention or to redress damages
Strengthen role of education in U.S. technological culture	(a) Enhance scientific literacy (b) Emphasize need for civic competence to comprehend and act on adverse effects of technology
Improve efficiency of food production	(a) Provide incentives or constraints (b) Leave to consumer taste and the market economy
Analyze emerging information capacities	(a) Maintain free flow while protecting privacy (b) Treat information as a property subject to controls
Examine interactions of technology and culture	(a) Leave unfettered development to influences of power, wealth and consumer preference (b) Monitor pernicious dislocations of society and foster nonmaterialistic goals

industrial productivity. Europeans are not as disposed as Americans are to invest such a large fraction of medical care in brief but strenuous extensions of life for the terminally ill.

With these general understandings, we can test for commonalities with the list of several grand issues contained in Table 10.1. The issues have been phrased in value-neutral terms except where the U.S. Constitution or custom have clearly defined a preferred standard. With each issue is listed a pair of options, expressed not so much in terms of explicit policy or programs as in terms of fundamentally different directions which would then reveal which tradeoffs are entailed as between one course of action or another. It should be obvious that issues are not mutually exclusive; and that for each issue, there exists a galaxy of policy options, each with its special tradeoffs.

This excerpt of modern predicaments reminds us that virtually all these critical choices are loaded with technological ingredients, implicitly manifesting a duality of impacts and thus *common* tradeoffs: as between free commercial enterprise and governmental control; between parochial, short-term self-interest and global comity contributing to longer-term (enlightened) self-interest; between voluntary and involuntary risk; between low risk, low return on capital versus high return, high risk; between present certainty and future surprise; between husbanding of natural resources and their immediate exploitation; between public and private techno-delivery roles; between different sectors of the population enjoying benefits or suffering exposure to adverse side effects. Many of these issues involve tradeoffs between conventional practices and value preferences against new possibilities opened up by breaking out of familiar paradigms.

To summarize, tradeoffs are involved among social priorities, between costs and risks, between various sectors of the population, between the long and the short run. *It is on these fundamental directions rather than on individual goals, policies, and programs that we must choose.* Here we must tolerate the stress of making fundamental exchanges that take into account the impacts on our progeny rather than saddling them with our debts and other consequences of our shortsightedness. If we do not approach this balance self-consciously, we ourselves ironically become self-inflicted victims of the same piecemeal approach, because short-sightedness leads to futures that we do not want even in our own lifetimes.

Principles for the Social Management of Technology

The notion of an Operating Manual for Spaceship Earth has been around for some time. Initially, this frivolous instruction was intended to raise consciousness about the ecological integrity of the planet and the potential of technology to disrupt the natural environment. In time came the recognition that people, like animals, were an endangered species.

At root of this concept was an ideology, a doctrine that we must be more attentive in creating our futures with technological initiatives because of the awesome power entailed. As arrogant as it may at first seem, the destructive potential of a power subject to human control is a harsh reality. So whatever values we subscribe to, the formulation of an operating manual assumes, first, that technology has great strength and that its exercise, inadvertently or otherwise, imposes unwanted and sometimes sinister risks. A second premise is the need for prudent choice. A third premise is that humankind can—indeed must—take responsibility to control its artificial creations. The metaphor of an operating manual suggests that a set of rules or principles can be formulated as a framework for wise decision making. A final premise, albeit less sharply defined, is that society cares enough about its progeny that it not only seeks to tune and tame technology for immediate purposes; it also accepts a fiduciary duty to future generations by balancing longer-term effects with the short-term.

Such generic principles or guidelines for the management of technology should be universal and relatively value-free. That is, each principle should have such wide applicability as to be relevant to all species of technological hardware and should be sufficiently free of bias toward any particular value-set that the public and policy makers can employ the principle when testing the desirability of a specific technology against *any* value standard they select.

What follows is a distillation from my earlier discussion and from a number of detailed case studies I conducted independently. These principles represent the universal characteristics of the interaction between technology and people and politics that need to be understood as the foundation for technology's social management.

1. Technology is more than technique; it is a social process. Its components include the hardware that distinguishes one technology from another, but also the software of instructions (laws) for its use and the squishyware of human institutions for delivery. Involved are public and private organizations and affected parties, communication networks, the broad cultural context, and social, economic, and political processes which mediate interactions among interests.

2. Technologies are best considered as means rather than ends, means which are continuously reinvested by society for various purposes.

3. The instantaneous mood and deep subterranean currents of culture may have more to do with technological choice than the elegance, novelty, or virtuosity of the hardware.

4. Every technology introduced for particular purposes induces side effects, social, economic, cultural, political, and ecological. Some are benign, even serendipitous; some are malignant; and some are both, affecting different populations, including innocent bystanders remote in location and time from the hardware installation. These side effects impose new types and dimensions of risk on life, capital, property, and the environment.

5. Technology acts as an organizing force around which are mobilized massive physical, human, and fiscal resources. Participants then tend to exploit technology to promote institutional size and power. The greater the monopoly of a given institution in the development of a technology, the greater its influence over the decision process.

6. Key technological choices involving the grand issues are made in the political arena by public policy rather than at the marketplace. That is, the modern state defines the political space in which key technological acts occur. So technology plays a political role in society as to distribution of benefits and selection of beneficiaries, tending to be discriminatory against the unrepresented, the economically disadvantaged, and the information-poor, and favoring the informed and the economically rich.

7. Government is involved in policy direction and implementation phases of every major technological system—stimulating initia-

tives, funding research and development, regulating for safety and equity, facilitating infrastructure, influencing the money market, and functioning as a primary customer of high technology itself. The role of technology and the role of government have grown together—indeed, each because of the other. Technology has become more political as politics has become more technological.

8. Because there are usually winners and losers associated with each initiative and because of a plurality of social norms, every technological enterprise generates conflict.

9. All technological choices require tradeoffs, as between benefits, costs, and risks among different interests, and between the short- and long-run effects. Indeed, risk is a social judgment and must be accommodated by compromises, usually at some economic cost.

10. Technology-intensive public policies differ from nontechnical policies in the crucial role of fact, the elevated risk of dangerous side effects, the plurality and complexity of options, the heavy public investments required, and the difficulty of policy or ecological reversal.

11. Implementation of most technological enterprises requires a close partnership between private and public sectors. While government and industry are often cast as protagonists, each sector needs the other. Public interests to harness science and technology require a vigorous industrial capacity. And the resulting economic system generates the tax base that government needs to function. Conversely, industry needs government to share risks and underwrite resources, especially for functions that do not follow tenets of a free market economy when competing internationally, or meeting disaggregated needs domestically. As trends toward this partnership increase, it becomes especially important for government-industry connections to be rendered visible and accountable.

12. Technology tends to nurture social as well as technical complexity because of the number and diversity of organizations involved, complicated and fuzzy linkages, unsystematic or sharp changes in relationships, disruptions in historical structures and process, and richness of information content.

13. Decisions regarding technology depend heavily on the quality of information available to all parties: optimally, it should be timely, complete, comprehensible, uncontaminated by self-interest, and packaged so as to reveal uncertainties and implications. The maxim "Knowledge is power" is truer than ever, especially with its technology-aided concentration. Impulses to control information grow, while access to its custodians shrinks.

14. Five types of information are required: (*a*) expert knowledge; (*b*) the context of conditions, constraints, and events external to

the technological core but affecting the behavior of all participants; (c) a map of the organizations and their linkages associated with a particular transaction; (d) a memory of past
performance of the system under study; and (e) a view of the
challenges and obstacles that lie ahead.

15. The art of technological choice requires an imaginative search
for options and the consequences of each, in order to minimize
surprise and unwanted side effects. Of critical importance are
vision and foresight.

16. Images of the future are essential to drive progress and foster
survival. Failure to look ahead could entail serious penalties—
economic cost, political instability, ecological disaster, or loss of
freedom.

17. The more advanced the investment in technology and the closer
the technology to implementation, the more inhibited are advocates in examining undesirable impacts and alternatives. Thus
originates a form of technological determinism.

18. Policy planning can help to reduce uncertainty and surprise, enhance understanding of causal relationships, dilate perspectives,
stimulate nomination of options, minimize arbitrary solutions,
improve allocation of resources, and foster accountability.

19. In policy planning three questions should be addressed: "Can
we do it?" "Ought we to do it?" and "Can we manage it?"

20. Decision making should incorporate multiple perspectives at
every step of analysis, to counteract shortness of vision, narrowness of perspective, institutional bias, groupthink, and personal, institutional, regional, and temporal provincialism.

21. The mass media are the most powerful transmitters of technological information to link all participants. Given the present
disjuncture between technological culture and scientific literacy,
unfettered investigative reporting is crucial, not just to elucidate
the wonders of science but also to alert the public to social
repercussions.

22. Those affected by technologies now have a legal right to know
what is planned and what the estimated consequences may be,
and then the right to intervene equitably with those interests
having more intimate access to the decision process.

23. When decisions under review are thought to be unpopular, slogans such as "more jobs," "national defense," "protection of
free enterprise," or "getting government off our backs" may be
employed as rationales.

24. Technological decisions should be implemented in a full understanding of the resources required and available. No technology
should be installed and then ignored: all need constant monitoring for malfunctioning, for maintenance, and for possible revi-
sion as a result of shifting policy goals and social priorities, a

changed value context, or simply an original decision that was inappropriate, foolish, or just plain dumb.

25. Under stress, decision makers may discount the future so that the possibility of decision error increases. Moreover, with implementation, most malfunctions stem from human error.

26. Virtually all major technological decisions involve the president, not only because of the salient role of government, but because the incumbent occupies a central position of power to set national priorities of public purpose and public purse. His office constantly reviews the parade of technological issues regarding their influence on the nation, the office, the base of political power, and the place the incumbent might have in history.

27. The primary countervailing force to excessive presidential ambition or inertia, and the primary forum of corrective action for inequities, is the Congress. In its choice of issues, however, Congress displays a randomness forced by short-term expediency and by the preferences of powerful committee chairs. Because executive concentration of power has no counterpart in the legislature, the process suffers from incongruity and incoherence.

28. Massive technological initiatives should be implemented slowly if possible, to permit review of past performance and future promise.

29. The validity of a decision is best judged on the basis of long-term consequences, both direct and indirect, and of its impact on the health of the decision system, in the system's capacity to absorb future shocks, to learn and change, and to preserve the fundamental creed of the society being served.

30. Every salient technology raises ethical questions. Thus, the most important principle in the social management of technology is the exercise of moral vision.

Citizens may consider this a check-off list similar to reminders employed by airline pilots to confirm that their machine is properly functioning before it is exposed to the risks of flight. People should have nothing less as they embark on technological initiatives that can so profoundly affect their lives.

Challenger *and* Chernobyl: Lessons for the Future

Early in 1986, two high technologies, space exploration and nuclear power, earned headlines as a result of tragedies—the explosion of the U.S. space shuttle *Challenger* and the nuclear reactor accident at Chernobyl in the Soviet Union. To be sure, *Challenger* and Chernobyl differed substantially in their functions—one a spacecraft to lift satellite payloads into orbit; the other a civilian nuclear power generator. Both disasters, however, attracted worldwide attention, partly because the events dramatized so starkly the down side of contemporary technological culture. In the aftershock, people everywhere asked what could be learned from these episodes to reduce the risk of similar failures in the future.

There are two sets of lessons, one generic to the social management of all technology, and one substantive and specific. As to the first group, we discover that the thirty principles just enunciated to characterize technological delivery systems prove directly useful in understanding both what happened with these accidents and why. The easy application of these principles is a consequence of a general phenomenon—severe accidents so violently agitate delivery systems that there is almost instant exposure of the institutions involved and how they behave under stress. In applying these principles to extract key descriptors of both situations, we find striking similarities. There are also sharp differences, stemming more from distinctions in the social and political systems of the two nations than from the scientific or technical ingredients.

An examination of the similarities reveals that both accidents involved highly complex technical hardware that had been conceived and designed by the best and the brightest of American and Soviet scientists and engineers. The accidents proved that even the best sometimes fails; there is no absolute immunity from risk. We also find that both involved highly complex institutional infrastructures, which had malfunctioned before the events, adding to the manifest danger. Both malfunctioned afterward. From both episodes we learned that technology is more than exotic hardware, that it performs as a social ensemble of interrelated administrative and industrial organizations, the media, and the general public.

After the accidents, both technologies generated adverse side effects. The reactor at Chernobyl threatened human health on an enormous scale. The incident simultaneously exposed the difficulties involved in treating several thousand radiation casualties—far fewer than would result from a nuclear detonation such as the one at Hiroshima. In the immediate aftermath, the world price of wheat rose while utility stocks in the United States declined. And everywhere in the West, anti-nuclear groups mounted renewed offensives. Repercussions from the explosion of *Challenger* threatened our national space capability and its momentum for both peaceful and military purposes. The accident undermined our confidence in NASA and its contractors and affected our competitive stature with other nations having launch capacity. Both technologies—spun by public policy and involving decisions at the very pinnacle of government—led to disaster. Suddenly we were confronted with disconcerting views of internal frailty.

Both accidents illuminated the perils of a high-tech world. With Chernobyl it was a case of low probability but catastrophic scope, subjecting unwitting bystanders—some well beyond the Soviet boundaries—to risk. With *Challenger* it was a case of the high risk associated with experimental technology. Although the number of casualties was limited, a similar universal shock was felt because the explosion of the capsule, with its civilian teacher-passenger aboard, was witnessed by many during live television broadcast of the launch. There is also a question whether the astronauts and teacher were fully aware of the warnings about O-ring deficiencies, or whether they, too, were innocent victims.

In both accidents, organizational complexity was revealed: the number and variety of interacting components, their communication linkages (or lack thereof), and the critical need for information to ensure proper functioning. Not just technical information, but also information about the architecture of decision processes present at design, implementation, and postcrisis damage control stages. With *Challenger,* the communication problem surfaced in the failure of launch managers either to receive or to act on advice regarding temperature sensitivity of O-ring seals. At Chernobyl, there was serious delay in communicating the occurrence of the accident to those who would be exposed to the dangers, either because of local bungling or a reflex action at all levels to cover up.

It was revealed in both postaccident investigations that foresight had been conspicuously absent, especially as to possibilities illuminated by the question, "What might happen if . . . ?" Both reflect an awesome penalty for failing to look ahead. In both accidents, the probable cause was human error. Responsible organizations demonstrated reduced vigilance, perhaps a decay in quality (a halflife characteristic of aging bureaucratic organizations). Attention seemed diverted from original functional objectives in order to maintain the institutional status quo, to meet intensely squeezed deadlines or quotas, or to cut costs.

The news media occupied a key role in focusing worldwide attention on both incidents, and, in turn, being focused upon. Writers at the *Washington Post* curiously accused the media of complicity in the *Challenger* disaster because of the pressure the press had previously put on the launch managers by publicizing past embarrassing delays. I strongly disagree. Decision makers are subject to a variety of pressures, including criticism from the news media, especially when members of the press are invited to observe an event deliberately with the hope of inducing favorable public reaction. In no way can the responsibility of the launch managers be absolved. On the contrary, it has been the media and citizen activists in the United States who publicized concern over possible weaknesses in civilian nuclear power plants. In the public outcry that followed the accident at Three Mile Island, safety requirements were sharpened. Chernobyl spawned another cycle of public cries for review. It was discovered that older

American reactors producing weapons-grade plutonium were not meeting safety standards for commercial power facilities, lacking as they were containment structures and systems of thorough inspections. The absence of an independent watchdog function by the Soviet press may well have contributed to overconfidence by Soviet nuclear power operators.

It is noteworthy that during the time the Soviets maintained a news blackout concerning Chernobyl, there appeared in the Western press a series of headlines, later proved wildly erroneous, on the number of immediate casualties and on the triggering of a meltdown. How such disinformation was injected into the wire and TV services and why there was an uncritical and impetuous rush to disseminate this news is not entirely clear. The incident, and its implications, were so deeply tragic they needed no exaggeration to capture attention.

Both accidents point up the principle that no high-tech equipment can be installed and then ignored. Indeed, with high risks, the need seems confirmed for continuous surveillance of performance, plus monitoring conducted by independent—and impartial—groups.

The immediate response of NASA and Soviet nuclear authorities to the disasters was to downplay the impact of the accidents and to deny that there had been early warnings. Yet, the two bearers of bad tidings about *Challenger*, the Thiokol engineers who had warned of weaknesses in the seals, were quickly assigned to different jobs. The presidential commission that investigated the disaster was highly critical of NASA and its contractors for such examples of gross irresponsibility. It is probable, too, that on-site managers at Chernobyl had delayed warning of dangers, first out of confusion and then in fear of punishment.

The Soviets are not the only ones trying to keep incidents of exposure to radiation under wraps. Decades ago, the United States conducted experiments in which the same radionuclides that were accidently emitted at Chernobyl were deliberately released into the atmosphere, an unconscionable act revealed only recently through appeal to the freedom-of-information laws. And the United States denied for at least ten days having exposed native residents of Pacific Islands to harmful radiation during an early test of an H-bomb, radiation so intense that, forty years later, the islands are still uninhabitable.

From this account, the value of general principles to describe technological systems and decision processes seems confirmed. The point, of course, is that all actors on the technological stage might find this mapping tool useful in making decisions that would head off calamity.

What major changes will be instituted as a result of these accidents? In both cases, as in the aftermath of all technological failures, the hardware is certain to be made safer. The successors to *Challenger* will have superior booster seals, more thorough proof testing, and better assembly monitoring. With nuclear reactors, attention will be focused on more universal requirements for containment structures, on damage control, on enhanced safety of design, and on perpetual surveillance required over entombment of such radiation products as plutonium with a 24,000-year halflife.

With nuclear power, also, the benefits of public information and the presence of public interest organizations should lead to renewed vigilance. Nevertheless, because government sources of information have been found too often engaging in distortions, half-truths, and cover-ups, the public may insist more strenuously on independent assessments of safety and may expect the press to perform more energetically and courageously in that old-fashioned role of investigative reporting. Whatever the costs associated with excessive zeal, they are less than the benefits. Indeed, that critical role of public information and understanding underscores one of the primary themes of this book—how to make technology more productive of socially satisfactory outcomes. This advice may carry a special poignancy for the Soviet Union, given its tradition of secrecy, intimidation of outspoken citizens, and bureaucratic compartmentalization. In a technological age, the Soviets must recognize the vital connections between technology and culture if threats to human society are to be mitigated.

The accidents revealed another problem. The lack of quality in military/space/nuclear hardware has become a public scandal—one to which the United States seems particularly vulnerable. Some shortcomings may be explained by problems with contractors who are more interested in profit than performance. Some stem from the public-private partnership that undercuts quality: the award of contracts based on political favoritism instead of merit, and the phenomenon of military officers, anticipating employment with their contractors after retirement, failing to monitor contracts conscientiously. Some of the problem may exist entirely in government: the loss of élan as a consequence of sleazy ethics at the top and the constant harping on employee inefficiency; the difficulty of attracting management talent to government unless the candidates are committed to public service and willingly accept the lower salaries. Some of the problem may lie in our legal and cultural failure to protect, even honor, whistle blowers.

The most salient lesson of the two accidents is that all technologies carry risks, some extremely high and deserving of careful evaluation of the tradeoffs of benefits with risk. Both reveal that, no matter how fancy the hardware, there remains a critical human role. Not only is there the presence of ignorance, error, folly, blunder, and mischief, but other factors, such as hubris, avarice, and fear seem to enter, too. All of which underscores the need to ask of every high technology, civilian or military, not only "can we do it?" and "ought we do it?" but also "can we manage it?"

Finally, we sense the role of moral vision, the concern for human life that made the losses of *Challenger* and Chernobyl such a widespread source of grief. Notwithstanding general anxiety of the novel and the strange, people sense a fundamental need in a technological age to introduce stronger safeguards, beyond those routinely serenaded by commercial or government public relations. Both accidents also exposed serious ethical shortcomings in the management, some perhaps even catering to the events. High performance of high technology depends on more than technical virtuosity.

As tragic as these disasters were, both have the potential to educate the entire world community to the need for examining what is at stake with powerful and life-threatening technological initiatives and the requirement for public disclosure and participation in the decision process.

History will record and report the extent to which all peoples and governments recognize this problem, most particularly with the threats to survival from nuclear arsenals.

Education and Homework for the Twenty-first Century

The year 1986 may go down in history as a major turning point in American perceptions of technology. It may also mark a major shift in relationships. Technology will force us to choose, to make some of the most fundamental tradeoffs since modern technology entered our lives, because we can't afford both guns and butter.

That fanciful utopia was based on expectations generated by a postwar experience that we could have everything we wished of material goods and services because technology was the growth machine. Simultaneously, we could enjoy the bewitching intangibles of life: improved health care, peace of mind, leisure, nature conservancy, universal higher education, and self-fulfillment—or self-indulgence—through freedom to practice a range of lifestyles. All of these were to be nourished by the economic surpluses that technology guaranteed. That the future isn't what it used to be is a shock.

This anguish of the 1980s is very different from that identified by futurists such as Alvin Toffler. Those warnings concerned pulses of technological change that rudely shoved the social structure more swiftly than it could comfortably move or accommodate. But Americans have always pragmatically adjusted to change, even while maintaining continuity in basic social structure and values. Transformation has been a major constant in our legacy.

No. The problem is that the psychology of technological abundance on which we built our hopes and dreams in the forties and fifties is coming unstuck. It was based on wrongheaded premises, assumptions that society was then unwilling to examine because of the narcotic effects of the technological age. After all, when the economy enjoyed exuberant growth at the same time that innovative civilian technologies were blossoming, people readily ascribed to technology a property of endless beneficence. They considered it an economic instrument that could be tuned according to classical principles of industrial management to function almost automatically. We could ride out any of the economic ruts in the road.

What we didn't recognize until the late seventies was the grim arithmetic that to sustain the daydream, we were borrowing from the future. In the first half of the eighties, economic signals became widely troubling. Evidence mounted that the control knobs which the high priests of economics had defined with such confidence seemed disconnected from the economic machine. Vital indices underwent wild gyrations and thwarted attempts to return, through monetary policy, to the "normalcy" of the fifties. When one parameter was brought under control, another went haywire. In jittery reaction, the concerns of both the public and the establishment oscillated sharply. First inflation captured the headlines, then unemployment; growth in the gross national product was sluggish; stock prices rode a roller coaster. Then by 1984, it was the imbalance of payments and the deficits. Desperation in a quest for a miracle cure led to the Gramm-Rudman-Hollings Act to coerce budget behavior. Meanwhile, few believed that the monster of inflation was permanently tamed.

But even with these unnerving signals of a pathology, the public was disposed to follow economic faith healers, to deny the realities and shut off leaders who dared to call attention to the storm signals. People wanted to postpone diagnosis, especially if remedies were suspected to entail hard choices that would sting every special interest group, contribute to gloom of the average citizen, and confront society with political chaos in deciding whether the shortfall in management of the economy meant pain for everyone or only for a naked minority. The election of 1984 epitomized that attitude.

Nothing, however, could blink away the reality that technology is not connected simply to the economy. It is entwined with the culture, with society as a whole, and with its political institutions. Cast in this light, dilemmas involving technology should not be expected to yield to the one-dimensional prescriptions of economics, nor to the relatively simple theorems in industrial management of measuring performance simply on the basis of efficiency. What is at stake in this rude awakening are not just choices among different economic goals. They involve the most deep-seated values; they involve choosing between continued feverish attempts at instant self-gratification and an old philosophy based on shared values within the nation and around the planet, a renewed sense of community, and a willingness to sacrifice. Collectively making these decisions, through constitutional structures and processes, is the social management of technology.

In the 1960s and 1970s, prodded by the radical movement, the nation was obliged to focus on other salient values, on human rights, on health, on environmental conservancy. By the early 1980s, however, enthusiasm for environmental affairs had waned, partly because of the vast amount of new legislation in place but also because pocketbook issues became too compelling. It is doubtful, for example, whether the package of legislation that was adopted in the Ninety-second Congress could have been adopted in the Ninety-seventh or Ninety-eighth. Also, there still remained the belief that we could have everything, including environmental protection. And the burden of environmental conservancy, health and safety measures was put on a third party, usually the government, in a belief that, like technology, its capacities were infinite.

The counterculture revolution of the sixties left another legacy, however, that continues to penetrate individual lives. In trying to decipher the numbing complexities associated with a technological world, many young people turned inward. The narcissism of "me, now," is today not so much a rejection of traditional values as a hopping onto the materialistic train as the vehicle for personal gratification. Energies go toward seeking fast-track jobs rather than trying to change the establishment or dropping out. And, unlike the counterculture, which disdained technology, the new psychology embellished it.

Indeed, the new cult was high-tech. Manufacturers obliged with high-tech movies, high-tech toys, personal computers, miniature television sets to prevent loneliness anywhere, cellular phones, VCR's that facilitate private showings of X-rated films, cameras that talk, cars that talk, digital record players, cash machines. Judging by the marketplace, people in the eighties did want more—of everything. There was continuation of an unstated confidence, like whistling in the dark to neutralize intuitive menace, that the economy would automatically grind out an endless variety of novelties and satisfactions.

Yet, in the midst of this seduction by technology, there was apprehension. According to many polls, people felt alienated by the substitution of machines for interpersonal relationships. They felt vulnerable to the growing number of threats to survival, from nuclear arms, chemical leaks, climate modification, terrorism, genetic manipulation. And they felt impotent, unable to understand the complexities of the technological world around them or to find a guidebook as to how to make their views count politically. Confidence shrank in institutions, both in private enterprises that produce the toys and in the government that is expected to protect the public from excesses and dangers.

This contradiction between technological bliss and fear was borne out in another way. While people were optimistic about their own personal future, they were increasingly pessimistic about that of society as a whole. Paradoxically, that anomaly rang no alarms; people seemed far less concerned with the fate of the world than with their private lives.

To be sure, society throbs with two types of vibrations. The more obvious pulses are triggered by day-to-day events refracted in newspaper headlines. Many of these spring from technological surprise—new scientific discoveries, new industrial applications and marketing, or new confrontations with mortal dangers. Accompanying these surface waves are subterranean currents of societal behavior. Some operate like constant streams, values that have not changed in millenia, but others represent sharp fluctuations in cultural norms. When the surface and subterranean currents are out of kilter, we can expect turbulence.

The initial shock is now slowly being manifest by a recognition of economic limits, of the fallacy of measuring the quality of life and the quality of the culture with purely economic indicators, and of the shallowness of concentrating so heavily on personal economic goals. Following that encounter with reality comes an awareness that we have been mesmerized by technology; suddenly we see the paradoxes: more communications but no more sense of community; more knowledge but no more understanding; more comforts but also more risks; more arms but no more security; more demands for institutional virtuosity but no improvement in effective response to surprise; more choices but no more time to choose; more education but less appreciation of the social contract. Then we ask, "What is our situation? Where are we now? Where are we headed?" And awakened from the dreams of technological paradise, "Where should we be headed?"

If by now there are doubts as to the past, those doubts should kindle interest in the future. This is a future with more technology, not less. To understand that prospect means to change the way we look at technology: less a matter of hardware, more a social network.

The debates about technology that lie ahead are likely to create an era of intense social conflict; it could tear us apart in spirit and undermine our institutions. Since we have behaved like children in wanting it all, we might initially expect some immature behavior, some temper tantrums, when the realization of limits sinks in. That period of stress is inevitable. Indeed, it should not be avoided. The time has come for hard choices, and choice at any level is always accompanied by stress, especially when the stakes are high or when our most cherished beliefs are threatened. But such epochs of instability also present opportunities for change, more so than when society is stuck in the ruts of an obsolete mindset. Moreover, America has always faced challenge with courage, change with resiliency, technological complexity with confidence in its mastery, cultural diversity with a sense

Table 10.2 Research in Science Policy Conducted by the Congressional Office of Technology Assessment from 1978 to 1985

I. Energy, Materials, and International Security
   Potential U.S. Natural Gas Availability, 1985
   U.S. Vulnerability to an Oil Import Curtailment, Sept. 1984
   Nuclear Power in an Age of Uncertainty, Feb. 1984
   Industrial Energy Use, June 1983
   Increased Automobile Fuel Efficiency and Synthetic Fuels, Sept. 1982
   Energy Efficiency of Buildings in Cities, Mar. 1982
   Solar Power Satellite Systems and Issues, Aug. 1981
   World Petroleum Availability, Oct. 1980
   Energy from Biological Processes, July 1980
   The Future of Liquified Natural Gas Imports, Mar. 1980
   Residential Energy Conservation, July 1979
   A Technology Assessment of Coal Slurry Pipelines, Mar. 1978
   Nuclear Proliferation and Safeguards, June 1977

II. Industry, Technology, and Employment
   Technologies to Reduce U.S. Materials Import Vulnerability, 1985
   Wood Use: U.S. Competitiveness and Technology, Aug. 1983
   Technologies and Management Strategies for Hazardous Waste Control, Mar. 1983
   Technology and Steel Industry Competitiveness, June 1980
   An Assessment of Alternative Economic Stockpiling Policies, Aug. 1976

III. International Security and Commerce
   International Cooperation and Competition in Civilian Space Activities, 1985
   Technology Transfer to the Middle East, Sept. 1984
   Arms Control in Space, May 1984
   Directed Energy Missile Defense in Space, Apr. 1984
   International Competitiveness in Electronics, Nov. 1983
   MX Missile Basing, Sept. 1981
   U.S. Industrial Competitiveness, July 1981
   Effects of Nuclear War, May 1979

IV. Health and Life Sciences
   Human Gene Therapy, 1985
   Technology and Aging in America, 1985
   Preventing Illness and Injury in the Workplace, 1985
   Federal Policies and Medical Devices, Oct. 1984
   Medical Technology and Costs of the Medicare Program, July 1984
   Commercial Biotechnology, Jan. 1984
   Scientific Validity of Polygraph Testing, Nov. 1983
   Strategies for Medical Technology Assessment, Sept. 1982
   Assessment Technologies for Determining Cancer Risks in the Environment, June 1981
   Impact of Applied Genetics, Apr. 1981
   Implications of Cost Effectiveness Analysis of Medical Technology, Aug. 1980
   CT Scanners, Aug. 1978

V. Communication and Information Technologies
   Information Technology R&D: Cultural Trends and Issues, 1985
   Effects of Information Technology on Financial Services Systems, Sept. 1984
   Computerized Manufacturing Automation, Apr. 1984
   Computer-Based National Information Systems, Sept. 1981

Table 10.2   continued

VI. Oceans and Environment
Protecting the Nation's Groundwater from Contamination, Oct. 1984
Acid Rain and Transported Air Pollutants, June 1984
Wetlands: Their Use and Regulation, Mar. 1984
An Assessment of Maritime Trade and Technology, Oct. 1983
Managing Commercial High-Level Radioactive Waste, June 1981
Ocean Margin Drilling, May 1981
Coastal Effects of Offshore Energy Systems, Nov. 1978

VII. Science, Transportation, and Innovation
Feasibility of the Strategic Defense Initiative, 1985
Civilian Space Stations and U.S. Future in Space, Nov. 1984
Airport System Development, Aug. 1984
Technology, Innovation, and Regional Economic Development, July 1984
Salyut: Soviet Steps toward a Permanent Human Presence in Space, Dec. 1983
Review of FAA 1982 National Airspace System Plan, Aug. 1982
Global Models, World Futures, and Public Policy, Apr. 1982
Airport and Air Traffic Control Systems, Jan. 1982
Impact of Advanced Group Rapid Transit Technology, Jan. 1980
An Evaluation of Railroad Safety, May 1978

of shared goals and beliefs. Perhaps now, we are ready to get off the technological merry-go-round; indeed, we may choose to.

Our agenda of critical choices was suggested in the earlier nominations of tradeoffs (Table 10.1). Further substance can be found in a catalog of studies completed from 1978 to 1985 by the OTA, the Office of Technology Assessment (Table 10.2), that reflect what the U.S. Congress had on its mind. (All of these studies are available to the public, incidentally.)

Before tackling these hard choices ahead, however, people will have to do their homework. That preparation involves two different exercises. In the first, we must reassess our *attitudes* toward technology. In the second, we must strengthen our *aptitudes*.

In regard to social attitudes, will we break out of the psychological straitjacket in thinking of technology only as hardware driving economic growth and parochial material abundance? Will we recognize that technology is a social network, not value-free, with the potential to make the entire, wired planet a fit place for human sustenance?

The second choice in regard to attitudes concerns the future. Recognizing that since every technology carries side effects which hibernate, many exceedingly dangerous, will society choose to look before it leaps? Will we decide to honor our progeny by considering the future impacts of today's decisions, and choose to make sacrifices rather than imperil future generations? Put another way, will we include the future in our calculations, save for it, and take responsibility for it?

A third choice in attitude concerns whether citizens will take responsibility for the future management of technology and not abdicate it to the technically elite, the power structure, or a third-party surrogate. Will people choose to recognize that technology critically depends on knowledge and that possession of knowledge confers power, even inaccessible power, on the possessor? Will they choose to invest the necessary energy to make power accessible, or will they, like the counterculture leaders, continue to choose to opt out?

A fourth choice in attitude concerns facing up to the economic limits of contemporary society and being willing to choose among technological risks. To engage this most immediate and pressing dilemma, it is necessary to adopt a point of view that everyone on the planet carries a portfolio of risks. No technological endeavor is risk-free, and minimizing risks always entails costs. Since we cannot afford to mitigate risks across the board, we are going to have to choose among them. For example, will the American people face up to their choices on defense expenditures? Uncritical investments have been made in almost every weapon system, rather than a choice being made among them, on the argument that all are essential to protecting the nation against a powerful, wily, expansionist Soviet adversary. Could it be that favoring this protection against military risk increases other risks of continued deficits that undermine both the domestic and international economy? Have we forgotten that the state of the economy is as much a measure of U.S. strength as its military forces?

Apart from attitudes, we must deal with aptitudes. In conjunction with the mass media, education is the principal means for enriching the capacity of the citizenry to deal with technology. To be sure, we have discovered that years in school have not guaranteed preservation of cultural virtues, a higher social wisdom, or a more prescient insight into political manipulation. Nor are people conspicuously better prepared for citizenship. The basic notion of education of philosopher John Dewey also goes untended: that the true purpose of knowledge lies in making choices among alternatives, based on estimates of future consequences.

So we may ask, What new curricula and mechanisms are necesssary to educate us for the future? What are the fundamentals for civic competence? In an important sense, all education is moral education because learning conditions conduct. People can learn that all choices involve tradeoffs, that group decision making entails multiple perspectives and nonviolent techniques of conflict management. Then they can learn the significance of deferred indulgence and the role of sacrifice, rather than merely seek education of short-term self-interest.

What reforms are needed? To begin with, a new agenda: graduates in higher education should be distinguished by breadth rather than by specialization, as suggested by the Association of American Colleges, schooled in a problem-centered rather than discipline-centered philosophy. They should be versatile, capable of continuous self-discovery and self-expression, better able to discover and distinguish truth, eager to participate in governance, able to make decisions, and willing to assume self-discipline and personal responsibility for their fate. This is not simply vocational training for career achievement. New academic offerings, such as "Creating the Future," are needed to dilate perspective. History should be taught in terms of lessons for the way ahead and deal with the processes of social and technical innovation. There should be offerings in engineering for nonengineers to teach technological literacy as well as scientific literacy. And there should be enhancement of decision skills that are otherwise randomly self-taught.

Many scholars have argued for these reforms. Given the reality that young faculty are still discouraged from innovation, from making music with colleagues in other departments, higher education has moved little from its proud fourteenth-century traditions. It is a melancholy fact that reform may happen only when students realize that they are failing to get the education they pay dearly for, and rebel.

The Art of Technological Choice: What We Should Do

In a democratic society, the social management of technology fundamentally depends on a large number of people making thoughtful, realistic choices—*with the aid of information*. Throughout this book, that has been the main theme. Because of the potency of technology's side effects, we must strengthen our decision-making process; we need to inquire more seriously about estimated future consequences to be traded off against more certain, immediate benefits. The "we" means everyone, not only the scientific, business, and political elite, and vested interests grappling for influence. Strengthening our decision processes anticipates efforts to match technological virtuosity with political wisdom. A more serious inquiry can arise from better information and preparation by the public so as to engage the political process more effectively. Estimating future consequences represents both a concern for the future and a sharper image of what technology is, how it affects our lives, and "what might happen if" regarding alternatives for action. Finally, the reference to tradeoffs underscores the virtue in decision making of baldly identifying what is at stake if we neglect the future.

Assuming that readers have developed a richer perspective on how technology interacts with people and politics, they could well conclude that such understandings are necessary but not sufficient. There is a second ingredient, the need to improve the quality of information and access to it. Such fundamentals in the art of technological choice should enhance a strategy of coping with a wide range of situations, not simply issue by issue or technology by technology. With that objective, readers might well have compounded their own prescriptions as to what we should do.

Not surprisingly, after so many years engaged in a search for ways to reap the benefits of technology more sensitively, the author has a number of his own propositions to nominate. The previous chapters have presented proposals concerned with redefining national purpose and with engaging more effectively in a new world economy. Those which follow are nested in a single theme: to make available better information to citizens, information of all kinds that would facilitate their exercise of democratic choice in a technological world.

1. People in the electorate recognize that they have responsibilities as well as rights. These embrace homework to strengthen their competence for the social management of technology. In a faster-paced world, shoved by technology-induced change, with heightened interdependencies, complexity, risks, and stress, fulfilling social responsibility will take more personal time, greater self-confidence and heightened commitment. Because of unrealistic and somewhat reckless demands, we have already pushed our institutions to the limits of their capabilities. The unfinished business now is for individual citizens (*a*) to become better informed not so much on the scientific ingredients of technological choice as on the social, economic, ecological, and political impacts; (*b*) to weigh these effects, especially in terms of tradeoffs with long- versus short-range implications and in terms of a noblesse oblige to endow progeny with a social and environmental ambience at least as healthy as the one we inherited; and (*c*) to share their insights on particular issues or decision processes with elected officials. In this way, everyone affected by the output of technological intiatives might have a better say at the input.

2. Every institution in our society should heighten its consciousness of the future and should fortify the role of foresight in its functions. This does not mean idle dreaming. Nor should uncertainty about the way ahead or seeming uncontrollability stir denial. Every church, university, business, professional and public interest organization, and unit of government has the capacity to identify its provincial but longer-run aspirations; its premises for society as a whole concerning trends, obstacles, and options; and the grand issues facing society which affect its fate and require resolution by consensus. Apart from the creative ideas that might be generated by such foresight, people may begin to overcome feelings of impotence and develop a greater hope of some control over their destiny. Methods on how to undertake futures studies can draw on available literature and on the past exercises by businesses, universities, churches, local and state governments, and even entire nations. In

addition, organizations engaged in futures studies could communicate with each other to develop insight as to common values, sources of deep-seated conflict, and opportunities for a shared cultural stance.

3. Every public library should have computer terminals wired into a national communication network established by the federal government. Libraries would then be able to store and retrieve a wide range of information related to the policy process, at state and local as well as the national level. The technical feasibility of such services has been well demonstrated. Owners of personal computers, for example, can already subscribe through their telephone lines to an enormous number of data banks. In Great Britain, TV subscribers can select from their home the contents of a daily newspaper, details of a domestic crisis, stock quotations, weather reports, and airline schedules.

4. The Library of Congress as the national library could function as the hub of such a network, to standardize communication techniques, to insert data on "who knows what," and as a source of information identical to that provided members of Congress on the status and content of pending federal legislation (including such OTA reports as previously listed) and on trend data that reflect what we know best about the future. The integrity of the system could follow patterns of the Congressional Research Service and its oversight, with additional monitoring by an advisory council with long, overlapping terms, appointed by the Supreme Court with advice and consent of the House of Representatives.

5. Schools of public administration in every university should undertake interpretive critiques of the grand issues in terms of near- and far-term consequences and tradeoffs. Abstracts setting forth options and tradeoffs should be prepared for the nonscholar and should be accessible to the public by computer. No institutional consensus or position would be expected. No central research organization would be involved, and the diversity of studies should be a strength in providing multiple perspectives and in subjecting them to the usual tests of scholarship. Faculty members should be expected to undertake these studies pro bono publico, with the products contributing to academic advancement and professional recognition of the authors. Private foundations should underwrite the transaction costs within universities.

6. Congress should mandate that all legislative proposals be accompanied by a brief policy analysis of alternatives and a conjecture as to future impacts of each. In short, for every major bill that entails technology, the public should be provided with an impact assessment that, along with issue studies from universities, would facilitate understanding of tradeoffs and thus permit a more informed public participation.

7. Cable networks and satellite transmission facilities should be required by the Federal Communications Commissin to dedicate channels for the interactive communications as a public service commitment in return for privileges afforded by government licensing. In 1972, the Federal Communications Commission saw these opportunities with the opening up of cable networks and set targets for twenty major cities to incorporate public service channels with their entertainment offerings. That concept, however, was never fully implemented.

8. Educational institutions at every level should reexamine their role in a changing society to sharpen both the appetites and the aptitudes of students to engage in the social contract of democracy. Most schools prepare students to use personal computers to enhance their earning capacity. That training might be equally employed, using the proposed network capabilities, to facilitate social responsibility.

9. Professional organizations of scientists and engineers, and national academies, should increase their efforts to help the public understand science and the consequences of new discoveries or initiatives. In a sense, this is an extension of their responsibilities as stewards of public knowledge and as frequent recipients of tax-funded subsidies. Their contributions to the network would help the nonspecialist grasp the technical foundations of modern life as well as provide information not inadvertently contaminated by private and public interests with a stake in the issue under study. By their tapping other contributions in the circuit from nontechnical participants, these same organizations might appreciate the intellectual, social, and ethical considerations—and the human wisdom beyond their special expertise—that must enter the policy process.

10. Public interest organizations such as Public Citizen and Common Cause, the League of Women Voters and People for the American Way, and a host of those more specialized, should play the role of advocate for better information systems.

This catalog might well seem to be founded on excessive idealism. If that is true, so be it. Such philosophical enzymes seem today in mighty short supply. Moreover, we can certainly depend on public process to add a bath of pragmatism, but pragmatism introduced prematurely could drown reform completely.

None of these propositions may be completely original. Certainly the notion of wiring the nation is not new. The literature on policy analysis, public administration, and futures studies is bursting with suggestions, so many and so varied that, without a catalog, it is difficult even to name their parentage. What may be distinctive, however, is this combination of instruments which, when first advanced by the author at a congressional hearing in 1970, was characterized by Representative Emilio Q. Daddario as a fourth branch of government. If that be the case, it is unlike the other three. In operating as a neutral information network, itself exempt from the decisions rendered with its aid, this fourth branch has only the purpose of helping the other three function in the twenty-first century.

To some, this concept may seem like a technological fix for a thoroughly complex social process. Perhaps it is worth recalling an apocryphal conversation between Henry Thoreau and Ralph Waldo Emerson. With headlines shouting completion of a transcontinental telegraph line, Emerson supposedly said, "Isn't that technology wonderful? Now Maine can talk to California." To which Thoreau replied, "But what if Maine had nothing to say?" I hope I have made the case here that there are abundant messages to transmit. What we need is the will to construct the network.

While thoughtfully and systematically applying new information techniques to the practice of democracy, we need to be aware of technology's capacity to produce side effects. Thus, as part of the process of strengthening information resources, their delivery systems should be independently evaluated to assure prudent social management. In short, it means practicing what has, here, been preached.

These proposals have one common objective. It is to help people regain their self-confidence—and hope—by translating their concerns into productive political action, by joining advocacy groups to foster accountability of the power structure, and by ensuring that government accepts a gentle partnership as steward of the future for our natural legacy and that of our children. The public would then have more of a say in those technological choices that so profoundly affect their lives: on the goals to which science and technology are directed; on the equity of benefits, costs, and risks; on the selection of winners and losers; on closer, more open relationships between government and industry; on ways to harmonize economy with ecology, with the grace of human satisfactions, and with military preparedness. In that process, we will rediscover that ethical dilemmas cannot be solved by scientific facts, information processing, and intellect alone, but only by reference to cultural norms, Constitutional principles, and attention to the spirit. Then, with better understanding, critical judgment can be engaged to ponder value- as well as technically-based alternatives for resolving the grand issues of the misty way ahead.

Realistically, engaging more people in the policy process runs the risk of slowing it down. But fewer decisions could well mean better decisions. By engaging *all* stakeholders at the front end of the process, and not just the powerful interests that maintain their own intelligence networks, the public interest could be better served. A civilian communications network should prove a strong antidote to the increasing use of technology in politics as a one-way instrument of persuasion and subtle coercion.

If we have lost touch with each other as interest groups wrestle for their piece of the action; if we have let natural tendencies for immediate economic gratification discount costs to future generations; if we have lost confidence in our institutions, our leadership, and that leadership's accountability to the public; and if we exclude ourselves from the decision process because the issues are seemingly too technically complex, we may reinforce a self-fulfilling prophecy of democracy's doom. For without a passionate concern about the future, we may unwittingly disregard threats to survival, to be both alive and free. There are simply too many dangers—from a continued buildup of nuclear weapons, an unstable world economy, the inept and self-serving performance of our health, legal, insurance, and banking systems, chemicals in the environment, and the role of TV in politics—all of which pose risks, not from their science and engineering content, but from their paucity of social management.

If technology as a social process is the source of some of our maladies, here, then is an opportunity to turn it to constructive purpose.

As the nation proceeds into its third century, it might be quite a revelation to rediscover the special blessings of this land and its people. Whatever our pluralism, we still hold common ideals—freedom, social justice, compassion, a sense of global community, a respect for individual dignity, self-expression, and the opportunity for fulfillment. In the face of challenge, we have constantly been buoyed up by our vitality. We are steady under stress. We accept swift change. It would be fascinating to provide opportunities for modern communications technology to tap the native, grass-roots ingenuity, not just for invention of new hardware but for problem solving.

By transforming our information age to an age of understanding, we may well ripen from unseasoned and immature stages of dealing with technology, from asking, "Can we do it?" and "Ought we to do it?" to "Can we manage it?" and "Can we afford it?" With more citizens appreciating the vital connections between technology and politics, their involvement enlivened by informed discussion, with a deliberate and sensitive integration of the future with shorter-run considerations in responding to imperatives of choosing in a high-tech world, we can, in the twenty-first century, build a curriculum of democracy.

Recommended Readings

Many of the references that follow develop themes germane to more than one chapter of this book. They are listed, however, only once.

Chapter 1: Technology and Culture

Boulding, Kenneth E. *The Meaning of the Twentieth Century.* Harper & Row, 1964.

Burke, John G., and Eakin, Marshall C. *Technology and Change.* Boyd and Fraser, 1979.

Illich, Ivan. *Tools for Conviviality.* Harper & Row, 1973.

Noble, David F. *Forces of Production: A Social History of Industrial Automation.* Knopf, 1984.

Pacey, Arnold. *The Culture of Technology.* MIT Press, 1983.

Wenk, Edward, Jr. *Margins for Survival: Overcoming Political Limits in Steering Technology.* Pergamon, 1979.

Teich, Albert H., ed. *Technology and the Future.* St. Martin's, 1986.

Chapter 2: Technology and Social Systems

Easton, David. *A Systems Analysis of Political Life.* Wiley, 1965.

Haberer, Joseph, ed. *Science and Technology Policy.* Heath, 1977.

McDougall, Walter A. *The Heaven and the Earth: A Political History of the Space Age.* Basic Books, 1985.

Sahal, Devendra. *Patterns of Technological Innovations.* Addison-Wesley, 1981.

Vickers, Geoffrey. *Value Systems and Social Process.* Tavistock, 1968.

Chapter 3: A Sampling of Issues

Kuehn, Thomas J., and Porter, Alan L., eds. *Science, Technology, and National Policy.* Cornell Univ. Press, 1981.

Miller, Jon. *The American People and Science Policy: The Role of Public Attitudes in the Policy Process.* Pergamon, 1983.

Chapter 4: Technology and Risk

Hohenemser, Christoph, and Kasperson, Jeanne X., eds. *Risk in the Technological Society.* Westview, 1982.

Lowrance, William O. *Of Acceptable Risk: Science and Determination of Safety.* William Kaufman, 1976.

Tuchman, Barbara. *The March of Folly.* Knopf, 1984.

Chapter 5: Technology and Politics

Brzezinski, Zbigniew. *Between Two Ages: America's Role in the Technetronic Era.* Viking, 1970.

Deutsch, Karl W. *The Nerves of Government.* Free Press, 1966.

LaPorte, Todd, ed. *Organized Social Complexity.* Princeton Univ. Press, 1975.

Linder, Steffan B. *The Harried Leisure Class.* Columbia Univ. Press, 1970.

Seidman, Harold. *Politics, Position, and Power.* Oxford Univ. Press, 1983.

Wenk, Edward, Jr. *The Politics of the Oceans.* Univ. of Washington Press, 1972.

Chapter 6: Technology and Industry

Galbraith, John Kenneth. *The New Industrial State.* Mentor, 1978.

Johnson, Chalmers. *MITI and the Japanese Miracle.* Stanford Univ. Press, 1982.

Peters, Thomas J., and Waterman, Robert H., Jr. *In Search of Excellence.* Harper & Row, 1982.

Reich, Robert. *The Next American Frontier.* Penguin, 1982.

Yates, Brock. *The Decline and Fall of the American Automobile Industry.* Random House, 1984.

Chapter 7: Technology and Science

Dickson, David. *The New Politics of Science.* Pantheon, 1984.

National Science Foundation. *National Patterns of Science and Technology Resources.* (NSF 84-311). GPO, 1984.

National Science Foundation. *Science Indicators.* GPO, 1983.

Price, Don K. *The Scientific Estate.* Harvard Univ. Press, 1965.

Chapter 8: How Decisions Are Made

Council on Environmental Quality. *The Global 2000 Report to the President.* Penguin, 1979.

Janis, Irving L., and Mann, Leon. *Decision Making.* Free Press, 1977.

Roszak, Theodore. *The Cult of Information.* Pantheon, 1986.

Chapter 9: Technology and Citizens

Ackroyd, Carol, et al. *The Technology of Political Control.* Pluto Press, 1980.

Akey, Denise S., ed. *Encyclopedia of Associations.* Gale Research Co., 1984.

Cleveland, Harlan. *The Knowledge Executive.* Dutton, 1985.

Diamond, Edwin, and Bates, Stephen. *The Spot: The Rise of Political Advertising on Television.* MIT Press, 1984.

Ford, Daniel. *The Pentagon's Strategic Command and Control System.* Simon and Schuster, 1985.

Henderson, Hazel. *Creating Alternative Futures.* Berkeley Publishing, 1978.

Isaacs, Norman E. *Untended Gates: The Mismanaged Press.* Columbia Univ. Press, 1986.

Linstone, Harold A. *The Multiple Perspective Concept.* Elsevier, 1984.

Naisbitt, John. *Megatrends.* Warner, 1982.

Steiner, George. *In Bluebeard's Castle: Some Notes toward the Redefinition of Culture.* Yale Univ. Press, 1973.

Turkle, Sherry. *The Second Self: Computers and the Human Spirit.* Simon & Schuster, 1984.

U.S. Department of the Census. *Social Indicators.* GPO, 1980.

Yankelovich, Daniel. *New Rules.* Random House, 1981.

Chapter 10: Technology and the Future

Brown, Lester R., et al. *State of the World 1986: A Worldwatch Institute Report on Progress Toward a Sustainable Society.* Norton, 1986.

Coates, Joseph F. *Issues Management.* Lomond, 1986.

Diebold, John. *Making the Future Work.* Simon & Schuster, 1984.

Finsterbusch, Kurt. *Understanding Social Impacts.* Sage, 1980.

Porter, Alan R., et al. *A Guidebook for Technology Assessment and Impact Analysis.* Elsevier, 1980.

Will, George F. *Statecraft as Soulcraft.* Simon & Schuster, 1983.

World Future Society. *The Future: A Guide to Information Sources.* Second edition. World Future Society, 1979.

Index

Advisory functions, 33, 64–70; biases in, 79. *See also* Science advisor
Allison, Graham, 174, 175
American Association of Engineering Societies, 183
American Society of Mechanical Engineers, 183
Anticipation, doctrine of, 190, 193–94. *See also* Foresight
Arms control, 120. *See also* National security
Asbestos hazards, 46
Atomic Energy Commission, 33, 63

Behavior: of industrial leaders, 96, 97, 98–102; of institutions, 30; of political leaders, 85–86. *See also* Congress, U.S.
Bhopal, India, accident in, 2, 46
Bok, Derek, 184
Broder, David S., 182
Brooks, Harvey, 25, 130
Brooks, Overton, 136
Brzezinski, Zbigniew, 67, 189
Budget: approval process of, 90–93; deficits in, 115; for science and technology, 91
Bush, Vannevar, 65, 68, 135–36
Business Executives for National Security (BENS), 118

Capital formation, 21, 94, 115
Carson, Rachel, 9, 103
Carter, Jimmy, 61, 63, 67, 165
Center for Defense Information, 116
Challenger, accident involving, 29, 54, 183, 211–16
Chase, Stuart, 190
Chernobyl, USSR, accident in, 2, 54, 183, 211–16
Choices, critical, 2, 149, 182, 205–6, 219; art of deciding what we should do, 222–28; commonalities among, 204,

206; difficulties with, 13, 93
Churchill, Winston, 179
Citizen participation, 2, 158–59, 177–79, 210, 222, 227–28; modes of, 11; preparation for, 203, 223–24. *See also* Social indicators
Coast Guard, U.S., 50, 55, 56, 57
Collision avoidance, 4–5, 192, 195. *See also* Risk
Commission on Industrial Competitiveness, 67, 138; proposals of, 109
Common Cause, 226
Communication networks, 26, 152, 220; for citizens, 225, 226, 227; and community, 19
Complexity in social process, 8, 18, 31, 80, 150, 189; as fostering the short run, 87; as a problem in choice, 209; as a source of risk, 47, 212–13
Computers, 96, 156
Conceptual Blockbusting (Adams), 201
Conflict, 12, 147, 148, 172, 173, 209; management of, 19, 196. *See also* Mediation
Congress, U.S., 26, 33, 70–73, 89, 136, 164, 215, 217; committees of, 68, 72, 107, 136; functions of, 70, 211; reforms in, 71. *See also* Legislation
Congressional Budget Office, 71
Congressional Research Service, 72
Constitution, U.S., 28, 59, 88, 176, 206; and patent clause, 135
Consumerism, 101, 200
Coolidge, Calvin, 98
Coordination, interagency, 88–90
Corporate state, 102, 167, 199. *See also* Industry, partnership of, with government
Council on Environmental Quality, 47
Counterculture, 2, 10, 173, 217
Cousteau, Jacques-Yves, 198
Cousteau Society, The, 145

Edward Wenk, Jr., has had a distinguished career as engineer, science policy analyst, and educator. In 1959 he was appointed the first science and technology advisor to Congress, and he later served on the science policy staffs of Presidents Kennedy, Johnson, and Nixon. Among his previous books are *The Politics of the Oceans* and *Margins for Survival: Overcoming Political Limits in Steering Technology*. He is emeritus professor of engineering, public affairs, and social management of technology at the University of Washington in Seattle. Currently he is engaged in teaching and advising on technology-related policy, risk assessment, futures studies, and public and industrial administration.

Tradeoffs

Designed by Chris L. Smith
Composed by Brushwood Graphics in Sabon text and display
Printed by The Maple Press Company on 50-lb. Sebago Eggshell Cream Offset paper
Bound by The Maple Press Company in Holliston's Kingston Natural and stamped in silver